EQUATOR

A

WIND

FROM

THE

NORTH

HENRY THE NAVIGATOR

Detail from the painting by Nuño Gonçalves.
By courtesy of the Museum of Ancient Art, Lisbon.

A
Wind
from the North

THE LIFE OF HENRY THE NAVIGATOR

BY ERNLE BRADFORD

HARCOURT, BRACE AND

COMPANY · NEW YORK

"What is Alexander crowned with trophies at the head
of his army, compared with Henry contemplating
the ocean from his window on the rock of Sagres?"

W. J. MICKLE, 1775

Enthusiasm fathered this book. I am not a Portuguese scholar or a
historian of any distinction, so it may seem an impertinence to
have attempted a biography of Portugal's great national hero. My
interest in Prince Henry came about by accident. Some years ago,
I was sailing in a small yacht from Gibraltar to the West Indies
and by chance called in at the port of Safi on the Moroccan coast.
There was one building that immediately impressed me—and
which still remains in my memory—the old Portuguese fortress on
the heights surmounting the town. It was the first I had ever seen,
but I know now that there are many such fortresses on lonely coves
and headlands throughout the world, or overlooking flourishing
cities and big modern ports. They are the monuments to the Portuguese sailors and pioneers who opened the sea lanes of the world,
and blazed the trail that was afterward followed by all the other
maritime nations. It was on this same voyage that I sailed to the
Canaries, and then took my departure for the New World from the
Cape Verde Islands. I found again that I was following in the
footsteps of the Portuguese, men who in boats little bigger (and
much more primitive) than my forty-foot yacht had preceded me
by at least five centuries.

A few years later I sailed in a small yacht to Lisbon and down
the coast of Portugal to Cape St. Vincent and Sagres. The shadow

of the Navigator lies heavy across that stretch of sea. I felt that he had been unfairly neglected in the English-speaking countries. Since then I have sailed to Madeira and the Azores—on each occasion in a boat of about twenty tons, a little smaller perhaps than the caravels of Prince Henry's time, but equipped with modern charts, efficient instruments, and a navigational knowledge, all of which stemmed from Prince Henry and his pioneers. A practical acquaintance with sailing, seamanship, and navigation, in the areas in which the Portuguese made their first voyages, gave me an added appreciation of the problems they had to face. In a crossing by yacht from the Azores to New York, I also—by sheer chance—followed a route very similar to that which Diogo de Teive must have taken when he sailed from Flores to the Newfoundland Banks.

I have anglicized the names of many of the principal characters in this biography—thus, Prince Henry for the Infante Dom Henrique and Prince Peter for the Infante Dom Pedro. In other respects I have followed the Portuguese spellings, except in the case of certain geographical place names where I have preferred those better known to English-speaking mariners—such as Cape Blanco for Cabo Branco and so on.

None of the dialogue is invented, although in many cases I have paraphrased or modernized the diction slightly. The biographer of Prince Henry is fortunate in having so reliable a contemporary chronicler as Azurara to draw on for his source material. Other principal authorities I have indicated at the end of this book, but I must not omit to mention the debt that any historian of the period must owe to the researches of R. H. Major in the nineteenth century. I am indebted for his kindness and help to Sr. A. B. F. Mendes, director of the Casa de Portugal, London, also to the authorities of the British Museum, the National Maritime Museum, Greenwich, the Royal Academy of Arts, Burlington House, and the Museum of Ancient Art, Lisbon. The researches of Sr. Quirino da Fonseca on the ships of Prince Henry's time are invaluable to any biographer of the Prince.

Prince Henry has had his detractors as well as admirers, and any who feel that I may have taken too favorable a view of him and his achievements are recommended to read J. P. Oliveira Martins's classic *The Golden Age of Prince Henry the Navigator* for an adverse view of the Prince.

It is five hundred years since Prince Henry died, and a gulf not only of time, but also of psychology, separates him from us. In endeavoring to trace his character and to comprehend his outlook, I have inevitably had to draw on writings concerning the medieval Christian church. In this connection I would like to acknowledge my debt to R. H. Tawney's *Religion and the Rise of Capitalism*, and in particular to the section entitled "The Mediaeval Background."

E. B.

Brixham, Devon.
1960

A
WIND
FROM
THE
NORTH

1

Bright with pennants and devices, the ships lifted over the horizon. They came onward in a half-moon shape, and their music sounded across the water, as gay and confident as the summer sky. Soon the leading vessels were nearing the mouth of the Tagus.

Another fleet waited to meet them. It bore the arms and emblem of the King of Portugal, and was commanded by Prince Peter, the King's second son. The fleet that proudly advanced its sails toward the shining city of Lisbon was under the command of Peter's younger brother, Henry, whose twenty-first birthday had been celebrated only a few months before. Thousands of people from Lisbon thronged the banks of the great river to watch the two fleets meet. They did not know on what venture the King and his sons were engaged. They only knew that the preparations for this day had occupied every shipbuilder, sailmaker, victualer, and chandler in Portugal for the past year and more. The lighter craft came first, wafting over the bar at the mouth of the river. They were small boats of fifty tons and less, spreading their new sails to the lazy on-shore wind. Behind them sauntered the tubby shapes of the first-class ships, their square sails puffing and lifting as they met the swell at the river mouth. Behind these again came the lean greyhounds: the oared galleys, whose design had changed little since the Phoenicians and the Romans had made the Tagus their anchoring place.

The names of the ships had a poetry of their own. In the front echelon of light sailing boats were *carracas* and *fustas*, *balenares, pinazas,* and *carabelas*. Then there were the *barcas*, their broad-beamed hulls flickering with the arms of soldiers. The oared vessels, moving like insects over a pond, were galleys and *galeotas, tardantes,* and *saetias*. In these two types of ship the traditional Mediterranean was united with the new commercial world of the north; the first represented by the galley, and the latter by the high-pooped trading bark. But the gull-winged *carabelas*, which crossed the bar first, were the forerunners of a new type of ship, one that would dredge an undiscovered world and a thousand new coastlines out of the uncharted rollers of the Atlantic.

As the fleets of the two princes met, the music from their garlanded poops blended with the time-keeping gongs aboard the galleys, and the brassy note of trumpets from the barks. The onlookers cheered, as a hundred and one small rowing boats put off to accompany the fleet to its anchorage. Church bells sounded, dim in the blue distance, and the midsummer heat shook over the hills beyond the city. Catching the slants of wind that dropped down the river mouth, and with the thrust of the tide giving them way against the current of the river, the ships moved slowly upstream. They dropped anchor under the golden walls of Belém on the outskirts of Lisbon. The oars of the galleys were secured, the sails of the barks and pinnaces were furled, and the graceful lateen-rigged *carabelas* idled over their reflections in the quiet water.

It was July, 1415. The building of so many ships—over twenty oared galleys, twenty-six barks, and many dozen lighter craft—had occupied the whole seaboard of Portugal for over three years. The destination of the fleet had occupied the councils of Europe for almost as long.

"Is it peace or war?" had come their inquiries, and to most of them King John of Portugal had returned a fair answer. But, even now, no one except the King, his sons, and a few ministers of state, knew against whom they were preparing to sail.

The secret had been well kept. The people of Lisbon, who had worked for and contributed to this armada, were as curious as any. But while they cheered the brave ensigns and the panoply of the anchored squadrons, they had another, and even greater, preoccupation. The plague had broken out in the city, and in Porto too—whence Prince Henry's ships had sailed—the pestilence was raging. "How reluctant," says the chronicler, "were the souls of the brave men who were dying of the pest to leave their bodies! It was not only that natural regret which seizes upon every soul when it leaves the flesh, it was above all regret that they must leave the world without seeing the conclusion of this great enterprise."

Members of the court were waiting to greet the two young princes as they disembarked.

This was a moment of triumph for Prince Henry, for to him had been entrusted the whole ordering and commissioning of the Porto fleet. Whereas his brother Peter had been under the eye of his father at Lisbon, he—the younger of the two—had been allowed to organize the major part of the expedition on his own. It was evidence enough of King John's trust in his twenty-one-year-old son.

Thickset, of medium height, with broad shoulders and powerful arms (like a seaman or a shipwright more than a prince), Henry already had the air of an older and graver man. In contrast to his brother Peter's mercurial curiosity, there was about him a withdrawn and thoughtful air. Something of his mother's English ancestry was revealed in his eyes and in his manner: something of the phlegmatic nature that belongs to the country of gray skies and rain-swept sea. He was his father's favorite son. His mother, for her part, may well have seen in him traces of her own father, John of Gaunt, Duke of Lancaster. For there was in Prince Henry an iron determination, evident even as a youth, and something of the same imaginative chivalry that had made John of Gaunt the protector of the reformer Wycliffe, and the patron of the poet Chaucer.

Of the three princes who had now reached manhood, Edward, the eldest, was quiet and sensitive; Peter was of an inquiring and volatile frame of mind; Henry alone had something about him that set him apart from other men. Born under the watery sign of Pisces, he would either succeed in a measure beyond most men's dreams, or fail disastrously. Even his motto and device, which were portrayed on the livery of the serving men who surrounded him, revealed something of his character—*Talent de bien faire, "talent"* meaning not so much the power as the desire to do well. *Talent de bien faire*—it represented an aspiration and a dream, which would inspire him all his life. Even Peter's device contained something of his nature—the one simple word *Désir*. It was a restless desire that would never leave him at peace. So the young princes stood there in the brazen sunlight of July, with their great enterprise ahead of them and with all their lives to make.

The messenger who spurred through the hot streets of Lisbon brought the first somber warning into their dreams. ("We must live as we must, and not as we would.")

"Your mother, Queen Philippa, is ill."

At that time, and in that month, there was no doubt that it was the plague.

The Queen had recently joined her husband at Odivelas. The

royal family had left the hot stricken city for the cleaner air
of their summer palace, some seven miles to the north, where
the wind came off the Atlantic rinsed by thousands of miles of
ocean. Queen Philippa was now in her fifty-seventh year, pious
and devout, and with a deep practical strain. If her husband
had passed on to his children the fire and sagacity that had made
him ruler of Portugal, it was from Queen Philippa that they
had inherited their chivalrous idealism. As the daughter of
John of Gaunt, she was proud of the expedition upon which her
husband and her three eldest sons would soon be engaged. As
a woman she feared for them. But she had hidden her natural
feelings and reproved her ladies in waiting, who had burst into
tears on hearing that not only her sons but also her husband
were going into battle.

She made only one request.

"My Lord," she said to King John, "I ask you a favor before
you leave. Knight your sons before me, with the swords that
I shall give them. I know there are people who say that arms
which are given by women weaken the hearts of noble knights.
But as for me, I believe—in view of the blood from which I am
descended—that this will never be the case."

Now the moment that should have crowned the young
princes' lives—setting off to war in company with their father,
and with the swords given them by their mother—was darkened.
As they waited in the great palace, they heard from the physicians that there was no longer any hope of saving the Queen.
Like the innumerable poor of Lisbon, she was doomed. But
Philippa of Lancaster, knowing that she was dying, sent to the
jewelers and demanded that the swords be completed quickly
and delivered to her. Before she died, she was determined to
make her sons the promised gift. The long blades of tempered
steel, with their hilts of gold set with seed pearls, were brought
to her chamber. She sent for her sons.

Prince Edward, who had looked after his mother with great tenderness during her illness, was the most moved. In him there was more of the Latin temperament, and he was unable to hide his emotions. It was to him, as her eldest son, that the Queen turned first.

"God has chosen you to be the heir to this kingdom," she said. "I know your virtue and your kindness, so I give you this sword of justice. With it you will govern both great and small, when at your father's death this land shall be yours. I commend the people of Portugal to you. I pray you to defend them with steadfastness of soul. Do not suffer any to do wrong, and see always that right and justice are served. And when I say justice, my son, I mean justice with mercy—for justice without mercy is no more than cruelty. Take this sword, then, with my blessing—"

Prince Edward kissed the Queen's hand reverently.

"—and with the blessing of those from whom I am descended."

Prince Peter then knelt to receive his sword and his mother's injunction that whereas she had commended the people of Portugal to his brother, on him should rest the duty of protecting the women of the land. With solemn faces the two princes stood back, while she summoned the youngest. Courageous and proud in her last hours, the Queen smiled at Prince Henry.

"I give you this third sword," she said. "It is strong as you are. To you I commend all the lords, knights, squires, and those of noble blood. It is true that all of them are servants of the King, nevertheless they will require that special protection which is now your charge. You will do this, I know, not only through the inclination of your heart, but because it is now your duty. I give you this sword with my blessing. I desire that with it you shall be knighted."

Henry took the sword upon his knees and was silent for a moment. Then he raised his eyes to his mother.

"Lady, you may be sure that so long as my life endures I will cherish the memory of your commands."

He kissed the sword and thanked her, saying that he would guard it always, for its value to him was beyond any price.

The Queen now summoned her husband. His grief was so great that, unable to bear the sight of her suffering, he had been roaming the woods around the palace. To King John the Queen gave her most sacred relic, a fragment of the True Cross. She asked him to divide it into four pieces, keeping one for himself and giving the others to her three eldest sons.

The King, whose bravery on the battlefield was famous throughout Europe, could not bear to face the advance of the one unconquerable enemy. He rushed from her chamber, mounted his horse, and rode blindly into the sheltering woods of Alhos Vedros. The three princes remained with her.

Queen Philippa's courage did not desert her. Rallying herself against the exhaustion which came as a final symptom of the disease, she gave them her last commands.

"Remain always as you have been, my sons—loving and united."

Some memory of her childhood, of the distant land of the gray goose feathers, came back to her. Perhaps she had heard many years ago from old men in her father's house of the driving hail that had destroyed the flower of France on the battlefield of Crécy.

"In my country," she said, "they tell a story about the arrow. Take one arrow by itself, and it is nothing—you can break it in your hands. But if you take many of them together, it is beyond your strength to break them."

The darkness gathered in the room. The princes prayed in silence, as the Queen commended herself to God. The priests,

the physicians, and the ladies in waiting moved quietly about
their tasks. Above the tense quiet that surrounded the deathbed, the wind began to sound; low at first, and hot off the summer plains of Portugal. Soon the noise of it disturbed even the
princes at their devotions. Queen Philippa also heard the great
wind that began to drum against the walls of her room.

"What is that wind?"

"It is a wind from the north."

The Queen was silent. Then "A wind from the north," she
said, "a good wind for your voyage. How strange that I, who
looked forward to the day of your departure, thinking I would
see you knighted—how strange that I shall never see this."

"You will see us leave," Edward protested. "You will re-
cover, and you will see us leave."

"I shall not see you from this world. But still, my death must
not prevent your departure. You will sail by the feast of St.
James."

The princes looked at one another. The feast of St. James
was only a week away. The Queen lifted her head. Her face was
transfigured with joy.

"Praise be to you, Holy Virgin," she said, "since it has
pleased you to come from Heaven to visit me."

The wind began to boom around the turrets and crenelated
stones of the palace. The carpets rose and flickered over the
stone floors. In the long corridors the tapestries billowed like
sails.

2

Genius is elusive. We know little about the ancestry of many of the world's great men. But in the case of Prince Henry of Portugal, distinction of breeding, intellect, and a healthy stock on both sides of his family might lead one to expect exceptional qualities.

His father, King John, was the illegitimate son of King Pedro I (last of the Burgundian dynasty in Portugal) by Teresa Lourenço, a lady of the court. As well as being illegitimate, John was also King Pedro's youngest son, so that his accession to the throne never seemed likely. As was expected, John's eldest half-brother, Ferdinand, succeeded Pedro I on his death. Ferdinand married his mistress, Leonora Telles de Meneses, who has been recorded in history as "an infamous and adulterous Queen." She was also a woman of great subtlety and cunning, who suspected and feared all the rival claimants to the throne. Having arranged for Ferdinand's other legitimate brothers to be banished from the court (whence they took refuge in Castile), she was left with only John, grand master of the House of Aviz, as the sole potential claimant to the throne. He was the one whom she mistrusted more than any other. But

Dom John had learned a foxlike astuteness and capacity for survival. He did nothing that could enable Leonora to procure his banishment or his death.

When King Ferdinand died, Queen Leonora was left in the position of regent. Her only daughter, Beatrice, who was married to the King of Castile, was on the point of being proclaimed queen of Portugal. The accession of Beatrice would have brought the Portuguese under the sway of the kingdom of Castile, with which they had long been at daggers drawn. The astute Dom John saw that the time of waiting was nearly over. Queen Leonora was unpopular not only because of her daughter's Castilian marriage, but also because she herself was conducting a liaison with a Castilian nobleman, Fernando Andeiro, the Count of Ourem. The Portuguese saw the Castilian influence invading their country, not only through the Queen's daughter Beatrice, but also through the Queen's lover.

Within two months Dom John assassinated the Count of Ourem and forced Leonora to leave Lisbon. The forces of Castile immediately intervened to protect their own interests and those of their King and Queen Beatrice. Nothing could have served better to unite the people of Portugal behind Dom John. On August 14, 1385, on the battlefield of Aljubarrota, he and his Portuguese army under the command of the great general Nuño Alvares Pereira defeated the Castilians. It is significant that helping the Portuguese in their hour of need was an English mercenary force, consisting mainly of archers. The bowmen of England had established their mastery at Crécy, and would dominate Continental warfare from Agincourt onward. It was they who were largely responsible for giving Dom John, master of Aviz, the victory that secured for him the crown of Portugal.

Frequent treaties with England had marked the rise of Portugal from what had once been a Moorish state to a

European power. This friendship between two struggling maritime nations was further consolidated in 1387 by King John's marriage to Philippa of Lancaster, the twenty-nine-year-old daughter of John of Gaunt. John of Gaunt, who was fishing in the troubled waters of the Castilian succession, had hoped perhaps that King John would marry his eldest daughter, Catherine, heir presumptive to the throne of Castile. But John of Aviz showed his usual astuteness by marrying Philippa. He had no wish to embroil himself in further and future complications. He had only just gained one throne, and he was a realist who perceived that one step at a time is enough for most mortals. He was pleased to have the friendship of the powerful House of Lancaster, but he had no desire to further John of Gaunt's designs on the kingdom of Castile.

This then was the course of events that led to the marriage of the illegitimate son of Pedro I of Portugal with an English princess of the House of Lancaster. From this marriage stemmed the dynasty of Aviz, those brilliant monarchs and princes under whom Portugal rose from a small obscure power to the greatest maritime nation in the world. King John's sons —and above all Prince Henry—contributed so much to Portugal's development that it has truly been said: ". . . In her triumphal maritime progress Portugal discovered the whole world; she shattered the medieval bonds that fettered the knowledge of mankind. . . ."

The Queen who lay dying in the palace at Odivelas on July 18, 1415, was no ordinary woman. She had inherited much of the virtue and strength of her grandmother Philippa of Hainaut, wife of King Edward III of England. (It was that Philippa whose piety and generosity had made her loved by all her people, and whose kindness is recalled by the famous occasion when her prayers saved the citizens of Calais from Edward III's vengeance.)

Philippa, the wife of King John, inherited this kindness and piety. During the twenty-eight happy years of her marriage to King John, she made the court of Portugal one of the most respected in Europe. It is true to say that she found it an epitome of the medieval courts of Europe—where drinking, wenching, gallantry, and the chase filled in the long day's idle hours. She left it a court of distinction, respected by the greater powers, and a center toward which men of learning and ability were glad to make their way.

Writing of this court, her son Prince Edward later remarked, "If it be said that few were virtuous I say that many became so; for neither do I hear, nor do I know, of any nobleman who is other than loyal, notwithstanding that more than a hundred have been ordered in marriage by my father the King, and my mother the Queen."

Queen Philippa possessed the puritanical temperament that is a peculiar product of her native island. It is one that has often been mocked, but which, when united with a Latin vitality and *joie de vivre*, may sometimes produce remarkable characters. She possessed "that unconscious mixture of pride and convention which, though much below the level of religious duty, is nevertheless the opposite of hypocrisy. It was a feeling that kept Philippa above all attempts at subterfuge. There are no more despotic characters than those possessing such a temperament. The Queen came to rule the King with a rod of iron . . . and when Philippa fixed him with her cold blue eyes the King felt bound to do whatever she wished him to. Fortunately she was as sensible as she was good. Under her tutelage the King became another man."

Prior to his marriage, King John had been far from averse to the natural pleasures of a young man of rank and fashion. His English wife's puritanism may have changed him greatly, but not before he had already fathered an illegitimate son, the

Count of Barcellos, founder of the future House of Bragança. The Count of Barcellos would ultimately play an important and unhappy part in the lives of King John's legitimate sons. Like King John himself, he was to prove that the illegitimate sons of princes are often the greatest menace to the throne. There is little that they will not stoop to, determined to efface their mother's shame and to surpass their legitimate half-brothers.

But all this was far in the future. The three young princes and their distraught father, who mourned for Queen Philippa, were preoccupied also by the fate of their expedition. On hearing of the Queen's death, many of the nobles, let alone the superstitious peasants and fisherfolk of the country, had declared that this was a further omen that the expedition should be postponed—if not canceled altogether. The plague, they said, was one sure sign that the hand of God was against them. On a practical basis it was also asked how the King could sail off to war, taking thousands of men from the thinly populated land, at a time when Lisbon and Porto were being decimated.

The King, in his grief, and Prince Edward, through his gentle nature, may have hesitated. But there was one son who was determined that nothing should prevent the fleet from sailing. Upon Prince Henry had fallen much of the burden of preparation, and it was he who had been the driving force behind the whole idea since his eighteenth birthday, three years before. The expedition could not be called off at such a critical moment. The venture had the blessing of the Church. More than that, it had the blessing of his dead mother.

It was Queen Philippa's last words and actions that determined the King. As he pointed out, when he overruled the advisers who maintained that there should be a period of public mourning, it was in accordance with his wife's wishes that the fleet should sail. The wind was in the north. The

Queen had heard it as she lay dying, the favorable wind that would drive the ships south to Africa. For it was to Africa that they were going.

The Portuguese invasion fleet was bound for the great Moorish garrison and trading post of Ceuta, on the African mainland opposite Gibraltar. The reasons for the expedition were medieval, but the planning and the execution of it belonged to the Renaissance. Indeed, they foreshadowed, in many respects, methods and techniques that would be used centuries later in another invasion of North Africa.

The establishment of a European military base in Africa was to prove the first check to the Moors' power and prestige in their own continent. More than that, it would ultimately provide the springboard of ambition from which the ships and men of Portugal would be launched onto the trade-wind routes of the world. The attack on Ceuta was a turning point not only in European, but in world, history.

The daughter of John of Gaunt, whose indomitable will ensured that the expedition left as planned, played a small but not insignificant part in a great drama. One day, the sons of men who had fought at Ceuta would round the southernmost cape of Africa and trade directly with India and the Far East. One day a Genoese, married to a Portuguese captain's daughter and trained in navigation by Portuguese seafarers, would come breasting out of the Atlantic to discover the New World. The linchpin of all this achievement was the attack and capture of Ceuta.

3

Ceuta lies on a peninsula, which juts out like an arm into the Mediterranean. At the end of the arm is the clenched fist of Mount Hacko, rising nearly seven hundred feet above the sea. Mount Hacko, the ancient Abyla, the second of the Pillars of Hercules, is the complement to the Rock of Gibraltar, which looms over the strait only 14 miles away. Gibraltar was also occupied by the Moors at this time, but of the two strongholds, Ceuta was the more important.

From the bold headland where Mount Hacko stoops into the straits, one looks across at Europe, and it was from here that the Arabs had always launched their attacks on the Spanish peninsula. Even now, when their power in Spain was so diminished that only the kingdom of Granada remained to them, Ceuta was of vital importance. "It is a great city, rich and goodly. . . ." It provided an excellent harbor and refuge for the oared galleys and lateen-rigged sailing boats of the corsairs that preyed upon Mediterranean shipping. From Ceuta they commanded the rich traffic of the straits. From Ceuta they sent out raiding parties to the Balearic Islands, to Sardinia, and to the southern coast of Sicily. Slaves sweated over the long looms of the galleys' oars, and Christian slaves were one of Ceuta's profitable imports.

The city derived its name from the Arabic Sebta, which in its turn derived from the ancient Roman colony *Septem Fratres* (The Seven Brothers), and, like Rome itself, was built upon seven hills. Even before the Romans came, its importance had been seen by those great navigators of the ancient world, the Phoenicians, who had established a trading post on this rocky outcrop of the Dark Continent. The craggy shoulders of Gibraltar and Mount Hacko constituted the western limit of the ancient world. Beyond them began the surge and swallow of the great ocean, "the untraversed sea beyond the Pillars," where—as Euripides wrote—"lies the end of voyaging, and the Ruler of the Ocean no longer permits mariners to travel on the purple sea."

To Ceuta came the caravans from the interior of Africa and from the Atlantic seaboard of Morocco. Its importance as a trading post with the unknown and unexplored continent had long been obvious. The city was not only a haven for pirates, but an industrial and commercial center as well, famous among other things for its magnificent brassware. It was the first place in the West where a paper manufactory was established. To Ceuta came the carpets and ceramics of the East, ivory and gold from Africa, and slaves from every quarter. To attack such an important center of the Mohammedan world was a daring enterprise for a small European country that had only recently established its own security.

Twenty-six years had passed since King John's decisive victory at Aljubarrota, when, in 1411, a peace treaty was signed between Portugal and Castile. King John's sons, Edward, Peter, and Henry, were then twenty, nineteen, and seventeen. It was time in that day and age for young men of their rank to receive the honor of knighthood. But spurs might be won only upon the battlefield or in the lists of the tournament. The conception of life was medieval still, and if the lifework of Prince Henry was to constitute the first dawning of the Renaissance, the fact remains that it was a medieval idea of chivalry that first led to the attack on Ceuta.

Now that the peace treaty was concluded with Castile, there was no available battlefield on which the young princes might win their spurs. To remedy this, King John suggested that he should hold a series of tournaments—to take place every day throughout a year—to which all the European nations would be invited to send their champions. Amid such a gathering of European nobility, the princes might honorably win their spurs and be knighted in front of their peers.

But the blood that the young men had inherited from their fiery father and from the House of Lancaster revolted against such a means of winning their knighthood. Tournaments might be a suitable field for the minor nobility or the sons of merchants, but not for the Portuguese royal house and the grandsons of John of Gaunt.

It was at this point that João Affonso, the King's treasurer, introduced the name of the Moorish city, and to him must go the credit for perceiving Ceuta's economic and strategic importance.

"Why not a campaign against Ceuta?" he said.

The young men enthusiastically proposed the idea to the King, who countered it with many logical objections. Among them were the financial expense of such an expedition and the fact that while the Portuguese fleet and army were away, the kingdom would be defenseless if Castile should see fit to break the peace treaty. The princes digested their father's arguments and returned to the subject a few days later. Having heard them out, King John sent privately for Prince Henry.

It is a mark of distinction that the King should have sent

for the youngest of his sons. Even at seventeen Henry must have shown evidence of a nature stronger and more dedicated than his brothers'. If he said less than the volatile Peter, and was less sensitive than the heir, Prince Edward, he had a quiet certainty inherited from his mother.

"Everything we do in this world," said the young Prince, "must be based on three factors: the past, the present, and the future. In the past, my father, you had nothing but this city of Lisbon on your side. Nearly all the strongholds of Portugal were barred against you. Yet, all the same, with the help of God, you triumphed. You are stronger now, and there is no reason to think that God's help is withdrawn from you. To judge, then, from the past, I maintain that if you did not then fear Castile, there is less reason why you should do so now. As for the present, reason again tells me that you should not shrink from war against the infidels out of fear of Castile. The Castilians are Christians like ourselves, whereas the others are our natural enemies. As for the future, I cannot see how the capture of Ceuta can in any way be construed as a threat against Castile. In fact, the Castilians will only see it as further evidence of the strength of our nation. It will deter, rather than encourage them. They will also see that our taking Ceuta will one day facilitate the conquest of Granada—something that can only please them."

The expense of the expedition, he pointed out, would cost little more than the series of tournaments would have done. The King's other objections were those that any thoughtful ruler would have put forward, and could easily be dismissed. But Henry had gone straight to the root of the matter, in perceiving that the thing that really troubled his father was the possible threat from Castile while his back was turned. There was little time in those days for a protracted adolescence, and young men of the nobility became involved in adult affairs soon after the sixteenth birthday. Even so, this discernment shown by a seventeen-year-old was remarkable.

The King seemed to hear his own voice echoed in his son's words. When Prince Henry had finished, his father embraced him.

"There is no need for further argument," he said. "With the help of God I will begin this enterprise and continue it to the end. And since you and I have been together in making this decision, you must be the one to carry the news to your brothers."

It was in this way that Prince Henry was instrumental in deciding his father, and being involved in the expedition against Ceuta from the beginning. "It is quite true that all the King's sons greatly wanted to see the project adopted and accomplished, but none of them desired it so strongly as Prince Henry. . . ." He had never yet seen the shores of Africa. He knew no more of Ceuta than did his father. Yet it was as if his destiny already urged him south toward the unknown land.

But if the initial reason that prompted the attack on Ceuta stemmed from a medieval idea of "knighthood with honor," the way in which the expedition was prepared anticipated Machiavelli. "[It is necessary to find out] the situation and plan of this city, the height and thickness of its walls, and the nature of its towers and turrets, so as to know what artillery will be required. Also the anchorages that exist there, and what are the prevailing winds for ships at anchor, and whether the beaches are open and sufficiently undefended to allow us to disembark without great risk, or whether the sea is deep enough for us to be able to fight directly from our ships." Such might well have been the preamble to the initial requirements of D day. It was the directive issued by King John of Portugal in 1412.

To obtain this information would not be easy. The Moslem

world was unremittingly hostile to Christian Europe. From
the Moroccan shores of the Atlantic to the coastline of Turkey,
their barrier was drawn—a barrier that shut off Europe from
communication with the Far East, allowing from India and
the distant Spice Islands only such merchandise as was ap-
proved by the Moslem rulers. Clearly, no Portuguese ship could
sail openly into the harbor of Ceuta, land spies, and take
soundings of the anchorage. Even in those days, however, there
was a tacit agreement that ships carrying ambassadors from
one power to another might be permitted to take in water and
provisions at ports along their route. On what pretext could
King John send an embassy to some Mediterranean power east
of Ceuta?

At this time the widowed queen of Martino I of Sicily was
looking for a husband. She had already sent ambassadors to
King John, suggesting that he might consider his eldest son,
Edward, as a suitable bridegroom for her. But King John,
who had years before circumvented John of Gaunt's attempts
to involve him in the dispute over the Castilian succession, was
not to be taken in by the lure of Sicilian entanglements. Sicily,
though—. An idea came to him. He ordered his two finest
galleys to be equipped for an embassy, and appointed Affonso
Furtado in command, with the Prior of St. John as his co-
ambassador.

"I have thought of a clever stratagem," he said to his sons.
"You know that the Queen of Sicily has already asked me
whether I would consider Prince Edward as her husband?
Now, I am going to reply. I am going to ask her if she would
accept Prince Peter instead. There's no danger of it! I know
very well she will not consider anyone less than my heir. I
shall send the two galleys with my ambassadors. Everyone
will know the history of this negotiation, so the reason for
their voyage will be well publicized. The Queen, of course,

will turn down their proposals. But that doesn't matter—the point is that the galleys will have occasion to pass Ceuta, both coming and going. The ambassadors will land there, and we shall be able to find out all we want to know about the city, its defenses, and its anchorages."

The two ships left Lisbon and turned east out of the surge of the Atlantic into the tideless Mediterranean. On a fine summer day they dropped anchor beneath the walls of Ceuta and announced to the authorities that they wished to rest and provision before continuing their embassy to Sicily. They were given permission.

While the Prior concentrated on the defenses and dispositions of the city, Captain Furtado and his sailors surveyed the bay, noting where the rocks were fewest, and where soldiers might most easily be landed. When night fell, they hoisted out a boat and made a survey of the area: from Ceuta Bay on the west, round Almina Point, and so to the other bay on the east. The men rowed silently, the leadsman in the bows, Captain Furtado taking note of shoals and off-lying rocks.

The whole operation went off without a hitch. It was a masterpiece of co-ordination, and when the Captain and the Prior compared and cross-checked their notes, they found that they had between them all the information necessary for a seaborne attack on the great Moorish citadel. The galleys weighed anchor and turned east.

Under oar and sail, they made their way across the summer sea to Palermo and the waiting Queen. Their embassy was as fruitless as King John had known it would be. The Queen had no intention of marrying any of his sons except the heir to the throne.

On their return to Lisbon the ambassadors were received in open court and the King and his councilors heard the Queen's rejection of Prince Peter. That news, he was well aware, would quickly find its way out into the streets of Lisbon, and so to the waterfront, and so via traders and merchants back to Granada, Castile, and Ceuta itself. Any doubts as to the authenticity of the King of Portugal's recent embassy would soon be set at rest.

Afterward, the King sent privately for Captain Furtado and the Prior of St. John. So confident were they of the accuracy of their findings, and so certain that the city could be taken from the sea, that they had arranged to play a joke on the King. When he eagerly asked the Captain for his views, the latter embarked on a rambling tale of how, as a youth, he had been told by an old Arab that the city of Ceuta would one day fall to a king of Portugal, and that this would be the beginning of the end of the Moorish power in Africa. (Curiously enough, the Mallorcan mystic Ramon Lull in the thirteenth century had indeed prophesied that the Portuguese would one day capture Ceuta and circumnavigate Africa. It may be that Captain Furtado was retelling some version of this story current at the time.) In any case, the King was in no mood for old wives' tales. He had evolved a brilliant stratagem for spying out Ceuta, and here was Captain Furtado rambling on like an old woman by the fireside. He shrugged his shoulders and turned impatiently to the Prior.

"What news have you, my Lord Prior? Something a little more definite, I hope?"

"Sire, I have seen much. But I can tell you nothing until you have had brought to me four things: two sacks of sand, a roll of ribbon, a half-bushel of beans, and a basin."

King John scowled. "Don't you think we have had enough stupidity with the Captain here and his prophecies? If this is a jest, then the time for it is over. Tell me what you have seen."

"It is not my habit to jest with your Lordship. I only repeat that I can say nothing until I have the things I have asked for."

The King turned angrily to his sons. "Look at the answers I get from men whom I thought reliable! I ask them about their mission, and one babbles about astrology, and the other talks as if he were a magician demanding the tools of his trade!"

But there was something in the Prior's manner that convinced the princes that the old man was not merely joking. The sand, the beans, and the ribbon were sent for, and the Prior went away with them into another room. Still mystified, the King waited impatiently. After a long time the door was opened.

"Now, my Lord, you may see the result of our observations."

With the simple materials at his disposal the Prior had constructed a relief map of the Strait of Gibraltar, showing the anchorages of Ceuta, and its fortifications and defenses. There across the strait they could see where Algeciras lay, its bright bay, the Rock of Gibraltar, and the foothills of southern Spain. And there to the south lay the target—Ceuta, with the thickness of the walls on the seaward side indicated by lines of tape. There was Mount Hacko, and Almina Point; and then the city itself, with its buildings marked by beans, and the lines of its streets etched in the sand.

This is the first time in history that we hear of the use of such a model in the planning of war. King John's subtlety in devising a means for his spies to enter Ceuta had been paralleled by the inventiveness of the Prior of the Hospital of St. John.

The King and his sons gathered round. Prince Henry stared intently at the contour map as if he would engrave every feature of it on his memory.

"You see," said the Prior, "the main anchorage lies to the west, the Bay of Ceuta itself. There is a good beach free of rocks at this point, just at the eastern end of the city. On the other side of the peninsula to the east, round Desnaricado Point—where there is a fort—you see this second bay? Captain Furtado investigated that also. It is suitable for landing small boats and men."

The Portuguese would be able to make a two-pronged attack from either side of the city, cutting it off from the fortress on Mount Hacko. The neck of the peninsula, where the two bays swirled in toward each other, was only about half a mile wide. If the landings were made simultaneously, their troops should be able to join forces quickly.

The King was smiling now. He paid a willing tribute to the skill of his two "ambassadors," as the Prior went on to show him how the fertile land lay in a crescent at the back of the city—gardens and fields of sugar cane, lime and orange groves round the foot of Mount Musa, and crystal-clear springs forming the oasis. They could see where the caravan routes converged from east and west on the coast. They knew already that Ceuta was one of the finest fishing ports in the Mediterranean, and this alone was an inducement to a nation whose prosperity was largely dependent on the sea. There, at the meeting place of the Atlantic and Mediterranean, the sea was rich in fish. The tunny fishery of Ceuta was famous. (It was the Arabs who had first discovered how to catch these great fish, in nets laid out from the shore at the season when they close the coast to spawn—a method still practiced in the once Arab-dominated countries of Sicily and Spain.) Coral abounded off the headland, and the coral jewelry of Ceuta was one of its exports.

The King and his sons saw at once what the capture of Ceuta could mean to their country. As the Prior answered their questions, they were already planning the attack and dreaming of the spoils. Prince Henry remained silent with his arms folded across his chest, and absorbed the details of the relief map. This new method of accurately depicting the unknown shore and coastline fascinated him. If it is true that "to see the general in the particular is the very foundation of genius," Prince Henry gave evidence of this ability all his life. The known shape of a headland, the accurately measured latitude of a bay—these were particulars from which he could deduce a Grand Design that was beyond the comprehension of other observers.

The means whereby their objective was kept secret could also have served as a model for any campaign in the succeeding centuries. The Queen, of course, had to be told, and her assent obtained for her sons' and her husband's participation in the venture. This in itself was not difficult. The daughter of the House of Lancaster made only the one request, that she should personally hand their swords to her sons before they embarked.

There was one other man who had to be let into the secret, and that was the Constable of Portugal, Nuño Alvares Pereira, the general under whose command the Portuguese forces had won their victory at Aljubarrota. Here again the King made use of a clever ruse. Had he sent for the Constable in audience at the palace, his councilors and courtiers would soon have guessed that something was in the wind—for, unless a war was contemplated, why should the King send for the head of his armed forces? Nuño Pereira was living in well-earned retirement on his estates, so the King and the three princes set out on a hunting expedition in Alentejo near Pereira's home. What could be more natural than that one day the Constable should come out to meet them? The King and his military adviser met, and during a stroll under the shadowing cork trees of Montemor the project was broached. Pereira saw at once what the capture of Ceuta and the establishment of a Portuguese base in North Africa could mean to his country. He was enthusiastic.

Now, as the orders went out to the mint, to the shipwrights, to the armorers, the ropemakers and sailmakers, the victualers and ships' chandlers, there began the most difficult operation of all—to conceal the destination of the expedition. That Portugal was preparing for war could no longer be disguised from anyone. Already foreign merchants and ships' captains, who in those days often acted as agents for their countries, were passing on the news. There were Moors in Lisbon too, engaged in trade between Portugal and Granada. France and Italy, Granada, Castile, Aragon, Sicily, and even England and Holland were quickly told, "The Portuguese are preparing for war."

"Who at that time could speak of anything but arms and munitions of war? For the King had written to all the lords, nobility, and men of property, telling them that he was preparing a fleet and that his sons Prince Peter and Prince Henry would be in command of it. . . ." He ordered them to put themselves at the disposal of the princes. He told them how much they were expected to contribute, and what forces they were expected to raise. He did not tell them where they were going. But once the news was out that the country was on a war footing, the endless questioning began. Where was the expedition bound for? Was it for the Holy Land, or against Granada, or Castile?

For three years the country was occupied in the preparations. Everywhere men were busy. The rhythmic clash of hammers told where armorers forged casques and breastplates, and the ceaseless tapping where they riveted greaves and doublets. The swordsmiths, overworked at their delicate craft, were tempering steel blades and fashioning the tangs of swords, which goldsmiths, jewelers, and engravers would turn into instruments of beauty.

The chandlers' and victualers' stores were noisy with the cries of coopers casking biscuits, and boxing sun-dried fish. Along the banks of the Tagus and on the shores of the fishing ports, the long silver lines of fish lay out to dry under the bright sun. In Lisbon the hum of activity was so great that in the quiet villages along the river the ceaseless clamor was heard even above the noise of daily life.

The banks of the Douro and the Tagus were lined with craft refitting, taking aboard stores, rerigging, or newly launched and waiting for their masts and gear. Round the ships swarmed calkers, shipwrights, riggers, and sailmakers. The thump of the calking hammers was steady on the air, like the ceaseless dynamo of cicadas in midsummer. In the dusty ropewalks, under the eyes of the master ropemakers, the men spun the wheels. The long threads gathered, and twisted, and turned, forming the yarns of rope for standing and running rigging. In the Royal Ordnance, amid the smoke and smell of gunpowder, they were testing cannon and culverin. In the Royal Mint the hammers thudded, turning silver and gold into coin to pay the vast army of workmen, as well as the soldiers and sailors whom the princes were recruiting.

The slaughterers' yards ran dark with blood as hundreds of cows and bullocks were dispatched. At their doors were piled great heaps of snow-white salt and tubs of brine for preserving the meat when it was put in cask. As the carcasses emerged from the slaughterhouses, one group of men seized them and began skinning them—the hides were needed for shoe leather, for leather doublets, and a hundred and one other things. The flayed carcasses then passed to the salters, and finally to the coopers who were waiting for them with barrels and casks.

At night the glare of Lisbon's furnaces could be seen for miles around, casting eerie shadows over the hills behind the city. Molten iron spouted into casts of clay to form hollow bombards, or ran off into small sand castings where pike heads, ships' fittings, and horse trappings were being formed. The red wine from the grapes of the Douro poured vivid into scoured barrels, while the greenish-yellow olive oil mounted high in vats. Tailors and weavers were as busy as the other tradesmen. It was a time when men went to war in silk and scarlet and rich embroidery. The colors and emblems of the nobility were emblazoned on the jerkins of their followers, and the standards of the great houses were worked with delicate needlework and silk threads. Carpenters were constructing chests for clothing, weapons, and victuals. They were making the mounts for cannon, and boxing the ammunition for the artillery. There was not a single trade that, in one way or another, was not involved in the preparations for war. The excitement mounted in the air like the tension of an impending thunderstorm.

Men who have lived through other wars know the strange exhilaration that seizes the heart when on every side is heard the rising hum of their country arming for battle. Even Prince Edward, deep in papers of state (his father had taken this opportunity to pass some of the burden of government over to his heir), heard it. Prince Peter, inspecting the shipyards of Lisbon at his father's side, felt the strange glamour of war. North in Porto, shouldering his burden alone, Prince Henry learned for the first time something of the splendors and miseries of high command.

Before long the ambassadors began to arrive. They came from Castile first; then from Aragon; and then from the Moors of Granada. To the first two countries King John gave every assurance of his friendship and good will. He had no intention of attacking them, he said, and they might be sure that he would always respect his pledges to them. With the Moors he was less inclined to waste fair words. Beyond assuring them that he had no intentions on Granada, he left them with the uncomfortable feeling that he might well be lying. Accordingly, they tried to secure the Queen's good graces by offering gifts to her young daughter Isabel. The suggestion that her interest might be secured behind her husband's back was enough to incense Queen Philippa. She was English, and in the words of the chronicler Azurara, "England is one of those nations that hate all infidels." So the ambassadors from Granada went back with their report. They said they had been told officially that nothing was contemplated against their kingdom, but that in private they suspected the Portuguese preparations boded them no good. Granada began to garrison her coastline.

Attracted by the news of an impending war, knights, men-at-arms, and mercenaries from many countries began to flock to Portugal. It was an era when the professional soldier, like the later *condottieri* of Italy, would fight under any standard, provided that it was made worth his while. Many of them could have taken as their motto the cry of the Spanish Foreign Legion, *"Viva la Muerte!"*—"Long Live Death!"—for it was only on the battlefield, or in the smoke of burning cities, that such men could earn a living. Among them, we learn, were "a puissant Baron from Germany and three great lords from France." Also, among the ships that sailed in the armada were four provided "by a rich citizen of London." His name was Mundy, and the ships were manned by English archers, the dreaded longbowmen.

It was while inquiry, supposition, and conjecture as to the fleet's destination were at their height, that King John evolved a further stratagem. In order to silence the curious, and allay the suspicions of other nations, he would openly declare an enemy. The direction in which he made his feint was Holland.

Dispatching ambassadors to the court of Count William of Holland, King John instructed them to complain in public audience of piracy carried out against Portuguese merchants by Dutch ships. In public the ambassadors declared war on Holland, and in public Count William accepted the challenge. In private, however, he alone among the European monarchs was let into the secret. There was an exchange of gifts and good wishes between the two rulers, and the Portuguese ambassadors returned to Lisbon. A sigh of relief seemed to echo through the courts of Europe, and the news was quickly passed by the Moors of Granada to their brothers in North Africa.

At the age of fifty-eight King John was at the peak of his career. Neither the victory of Aljubarrota, nor even the great reforms of law and custom that distinguished his reign, show him at a higher level of ability. It was at this moment that personal tragedy struck him in the sickness and death of his wife. Had it not been for her last words, it is possible, even at that late hour, that he would have countermanded the expedition. But the Queen herself had said—had prophesied—that the fleet would sail by the feast of St. James. Besides, in action he might forget his sorrow.

"Will the fleet need long preparation?" he asked Prince Henry.

"You may embark now, Sire. Give the order to sail when you will. The only thing that needs be done is weigh anchor and set sail."

"We shall leave then on Wednesday. And since there should be no sadness, nor tears, when feats of arms are contemplated, I order you, your brothers, and your knights, to dress as you were before your mother's death. Later, if God is willing, we shall find time to mourn."

When Prince Henry announced that the fleet would sail, there were many among the people of Lisbon who murmured that it was the young Prince who was driving his father into a dangerous enterprise at a time when, by all custom and convention, he should be mourning the Queen. If this was the first time, it was not to be the last that an implacable quality in Henry's nature made him disliked by the ordinary people. "The King," they said, "has always held this son of his to be more of a man than his brothers, both in feats of arms and combats. But slaying wild boars in the forests of Beira is one thing, and meeting an armed foe face to face is another. Let us only pray that all this does not come to a bad end."

The reaction in the fleet was quite different. Soldiers and sailors who have been keyed up for action are always loath to postpone it. So it was with pleasure, as well perhaps as some astonishment, that they saw the princes come down to the quayside in colorful clothes. It was with excitement that they heard the trumpets sound, and saw the boats of the captains make their way for a conference on the princes' galley.

"In the morning the fleet was like a forest which had lost all its leaves and fruit. Then, suddenly, it was changed into a glowing orchard, brilliant with green leaves and many-colored flowers; for the thousands of flags and standards were of every color and shape. And in this floating orchard one might have imagined that strange birds had suddenly begun to sing, for from every ship there sounded musical instruments and the music did not cease all that day. . . ."

4

❀

Three days later the fleet set sail. Queen Philippa's prophecy
had come true. It was July 25, the feast of St. James.

The wind was still in the north, and as the ships lifted over
the bar at the river mouth, their new canvas began to crackle
and fill. Square sails lifted in proud curves, lateen sails leaned
like wings, ropes shook, and tackles sighed and squealed. The
sunlight flared on armored men, on sailors sweating over Spanish windlasses as they boused in shrouds and standing rigging,
and on the gay liveries and dress of the nobility and their
attendants. The people of Lisbon gathered to watch them go.
It was so fine, so noble a sight, that they stood all afternoon
on the hills, along the riverbanks, and on the foreshore. It
seemed as if they could not gaze long enough at these ships
that symbolized their country's power and pageantry.

As night fell, the last of the hulls were dropping below the
horizon, and the watchers on the shore turned homeward.
When they looked back, they could just see a faint twinkle
along the dark rim where sky met sea—the lights of the fleet
like starshine on the water.

Driven by the Portuguese trade winds, fifty thousand men

were southward bound; twenty thousand of them men-at-arms, the remainder oarsmen and sailors.

The combined fleet was one of the largest that had ever been assembled; sixty-three transports, twenty-seven triremes, thirty-two biremes, and one hundred and twenty other vessels.

The Mediterranean oared galley was still in predominance. Within twenty years its place would be taken by more efficient ships, sailing ships that would be as at home in coastal waters as on the broad planes of the Atlantic. These galleys had been brought to a high degree of perfection by the Venetians and Genoese, who chartered them all over Europe as trading vessels. With two or three banks of oars—biremes and triremes— they differed from their classical prototypes by having longer oars or sweeps. This increase in the weight of the oars meant that more than one man was employed to each—in some cases as many as seven. A framework stood out on either side of the galley's hull, in which were set the tholes against which the oars were rowed. The introduction of this framework to the medieval galley meant that the oars were arranged horizontally one above the other, instead of obliquely as in the ancient galleys. The bulk of the Portuguese fleet was of this type— vessels well suited to the long calms of the summer Mediterranean, but unwieldly in high seas or strong currents. Some of them carried no sails at all, but many stepped a mainmast from which they set a single square or lateen sail.

The fleet came slowly down the coast at two or three knots toward Cape St. Vincent. The sun was setting on the evening of July 27 when the bulk of the armada rounded the headland. *Sacrum Promontorium*, the Sacred Headland, the Romans had called it. It was from here, so they had said, that if you looked westward at the close of day, you could hear the sun sinking with a hiss into the terrible wastes of the Sea of Darkness. Beyond this promontory the unknown began.

If the great headland had been held sacred in classical days, it was equally so, though for different reasons, in the Middle Ages. The cape now took its name from an early Christian saint, Vincent, Deacon of Saragossa in the reign of the Emperor Diocletian, who had been canonized for his fortitude under torture and martyrdom—a fortitude which, so legend had it, had converted his jailers. The martyr of Saragossa baptized them just before he died. During the Moslem invasion of Spain the relics of Saint Vincent had been placed in a ship and sailed through the Strait of Gibraltar to remove them to a place of safety. Accompanied by the Saint's sacred ravens, the ship had been wrecked on the cape that forever after was to bear his name. Wind-washed and sea-whitened, this southwesternmost point of Europe is still awe-inspiring. In those days, hallowed by dim memories of its classical fame, it was doubly respected for its connection with the legend of Saint Vincent. Whenever ships passed this grim outrider of the Continent—where a wave forever breaks in a white curl at the bow—they lowered their sails and dipped their colors, and men knelt on the decks to pray.

As Prince Henry's galley passed the grim rock, he too fell on his knees in prayer. Perhaps it was then that he dedicated himself to this ocean and to this wind-swept rock. He may have noticed, as the swell lifted under the galley's stern, a narrow headland that juts into the sea three-quarters of a mile farther south. Sagres, its name corrupted from the ancient *Sacrum Promontorium*, is part of the main headland, and yet separate. Whereas Cape St. Vincent is 175 feet above sea level, the point of Sagres is only 120 feet. Even more remote from the world of men than the famous cape, Sagres is no more than a bare bone of rock. St. Vincent points southwest, but Sagres fronts into the Atlantic like the stem of a ship headed due south.

As the fleet passed under canvas and oars, Henry heard

the boom of the sea as it made up against the desolate rocks. When the wind is strong, the sound of the breaking waves can be heard for miles around. On Sagres a great tunneled blowhole, which links the headland with the Atlantic, spurts its salt foam over the bleak flatlands of the cape whenever there is an onshore gale. This may well have been the place that the poet Camoëns had in mind when he wrote *"Onde a terra se acaba e o mar começa"*—"Where the land has an end and the sea begins." There is nothing beyond Sagres but the long swell of the ocean and the curve of the horizon.

The fleet came to anchor 15 miles east of Sagres, in the small port of Lagos. Clear of dangers, and open only to southerly winds, the Bay of Lagos is the best and almost only natural anchorage on this inhospitable coast. The town lies on the western side of its bay, and it was here that the fleet took aboard its final stores, water, and supplies. It was here too that the destination of the expedition was announced to the soldiers, sailors, and to the world at large. The speed of news was the speed of the fastest horse or the fastest ship, and it seemed safe to proclaim the fleet's destination in its last port of call.

The preacher royal, Father John of Xira, proclaimed the object of the expedition. He read the men the crusading bull granted by the Pope, which gave absolution to all those who might die in the battle against the infidel. He urged them to forget any ideas they might have that this great purpose should have been postponed because of the death of the Queen. This, he reminded them, was a sacred mission.

Leaving Lagos on July 30, the fleet coasted down to Faro, where the off-lying banks and shoals run out to the hundred-fathom line and then drop steeply away into the Atlantic. The wind died, the current drove against them, and for a whole week they lay becalmed. A breeze would drift off the land, and the sailing ships would trim their sails to it, only to find that it had died almost as soon as the creaking yards had been eased round. The oarsmen strained at the oars, then rested as the sailing vessels checked their way and hung motionless again.

Now the King, the three princes, and their half-brother the Count of Barcellos learned the indifference of the sea. King John was familiar with war on land, but he was a poor sailor and out of his element in a ship. Like the Constable, Nuño Pereira, like his knights and his soldiers, he was a landsman. Portugal was still primarily a peasant country. Although her coastal fishermen were fine sailors, it would be many years before Portugal would recognize that her destiny lay on the ocean.

We know little of Prince Henry's early life, so we cannot tell how much experience he had of ships and the sea at the age of twenty-one. Most probably he had been sailing on the Tagus, and he would have been familiar since boyhood with the boats of the coastal fishermen and the merchantmen of Lisbon. It is doubtful whether he had ever been on a longer sea voyage than his recent excursion from Porto to Lisbon. In any case, this first experience of the contradictory ways of wind and weather was to serve him in good stead all his life. In later years, whenever his captains reported back to him with unsatisfactory news, he was always prepared to accept their excuse that the elements had been against them. Patience is a virtue learned at sea, and the quiet Prince absorbed this lesson early and thoroughly.

The plague was in the ships, and men were sickening and dying. The new pitch blistered and bubbled in the seams. The unfamiliar diet of salted food increased thirsts that could hardly be slaked with rationed water.

One morning the news was brought to Prince Henry that Fernando Alvares Cabral, the comptroller of his household, was delirious with a fever. The physician aboard the galley informed the Prince that Cabral was probably suffering from the plague. The sick man had the delusion that they were attacked by the Moors, and cried out that Prince Henry's life was in danger.

Henry's compassion was immediately aroused.

"Is there anything I can do for him?"

"As Cabral's medical adviser, I would suggest that you see him, and calm him by the evidence of your presence and safety. As *your* medical adviser, my Prince, I say—do not go near him!"

But Henry immediately went to the sick man, spoke to him, and comforted him. His devotion to those who served him was a quality that later became legendary.

During these long fretful days of calm, another incident occurred which bore witness to Prince Henry's bravery and presence of mind. His brother Edward, who was sleeping on deck, suddenly heard that most terrifying of all cries at sea— "Fire!" A lantern had burst into flames, and the burning oil was threatening to spread over the galley's wooden decks. Prince Edward's immediate reaction was to run below and wake his brother, who was sleeping in a stern cabin. Henry came straight out of a deep sleep, and ran up on deck. While the sailors were making ineffectual attempts to put out the fire, he seized the flaming lantern and threw it over the side. While the men sluiced water over the scorched deck, Prince Edward and other knights gathered round. Henry looked at his burned hands. Would he ever be able to fight and wield a sword? But the physician, who had twice been witness to the Prince's courage, advised him to plunge them into honey. The simple remedy proved effective.

After a week of calm the Atlantic wind came back again, and the fleet began to gather way. To the slop of water against their wooden planking, the sigh of rigging, and the monotonous creak and splash of the oars, they came down to the Strait of Gibraltar. At nightfall, they loomed out of the ocean and began to pass the city of Tarifa. Tarifa was in the kingdom of Castile, but the governor happened to be Portuguese. Perhaps he had advance word of the King's intentions. At any rate, he reassured the advisers who came running to him with the news that an unknown fleet was anchored in Algeciras Bay.

"They are Portuguese," he said.

"If all the trees of Portugal had been turned into planks, and all the Portuguese had become carpenters," said a skeptic, "they could never in the course of their lives have built such a multitude of ships."

"They are Portuguese," he said.

In the morning there was a thick summer haze over the sea. Nothing was visible, but through the white mist came the sounds of a great fleet. In Algeciras the people strained their eyes seaward. Across the bay in Gibraltar the Moorish garrison looked to its defenses. The cloud was heavy over the Rock, and the walls streamed with the sweat of summer dewfall. As the sun rose, the mist began to lift, and now the Castilians in Algeciras and the Moors in Gibraltar saw anchored in their bay the largest fleet ever known.

In the afternoon of August 10 the King summoned his council, and the decision was reached to attack Ceuta on the following Monday. If they sailed that same night, they would be able to get into formation during daylight on the eleventh, and they would be ready to make their assault on the morning of Monday, the twelfth. The reasoning was logical, the planning exact, but once again those unknown factors of wind and weather upset their calculations.

The currents in the Strait of Gibraltar are strong, setting mainly easterly from the Atlantic into the Mediterranean. The reason for this steady surface current is that the Mediterranean receives from its rivers and rainfall only about a third of the amount that it loses through evaporation. This almost tideless sea is largely replenished, therefore, by the constant inflow from the Atlantic. In late summer and early autumn the current is usually at its strongest, and it was this fact, coupled with a dense fog, that upset the Portuguese plans.

That night, as the ships moved out into the strait, the fog came down thick and heavy. It was a summer fog of the kind that often adds to the difficulty of navigating these narrow waters. The Portuguese pilots must almost certainly have known about the prevailing current in the strait, but perhaps they were ignorant that fog in summer often precedes a strong east wind (known locally as the Levanter). They could hardly have picked a worse moment to try to take a slow-moving fleet, dependent largely on the wind, across the strait. Perhaps the pilots advised against choosing this moment for the assault, but the advice of mariners was little heeded those days in the councils of the great. In any case, the fact that their presence in Algeciras Bay was known to the Moors in Gibraltar meant that by now, no doubt, a fast skiff or galley was on its way to Ceuta, to warn of the advance of a Christian fleet. The alarm would soon be out on both sides of the strait. Speed was essential.

So the fleet wallowed out into the thick clammy night, and their sails drooped. Soon the east-going current, as it whirled past Europa Point at the tip of Gibraltar, began to take the ships with it. The slow, heavy merchantmen, carrying the soldiers, drifted down the coast at half a knot or so. The lighter vessels drew away from them, some of them fetching up, finally, as far east as Malaga, 60 miles away. Only a few of the oared galleys, unaffected by the calm, managed to cross the strait. These were ready in position by Monday morning, but by now the main body of the fleet was dispersed over many miles of sea. Some were drifting off Malaga, others were striving to beat the current and cross to Ceuta, others again were being carried by a west-going ebb, away from Ceuta toward the Atlantic. It was on the Tuesday, while the King and the bulk of the fleet were once more making up for Ceuta Bay, that the Levanter began to blow. Wind against tide made a confused sea. The awkward square-sailed barks could make no further easting, the galleys were blown off course, and soon the main body of the fleet was driven back. They sought shelter in the deep arm of Algeciras Bay, which they had left just four days previously. It was this moment of confusion—this apparent disaster when the Portuguese attack seemed destined to fail—that contributed to their ultimate success.

Sala-ben-Sala, the governor of Ceuta, had been on the alert from the moment when the first galleys and small craft had appeared off his walls. He had seen the approach of the larger sailing vessels, some from the direction of Malaga, and some from Gibraltar. It seemed clear to him that his city was to be the target. But the confusion that had followed, the second dispersal of the fleet, and finally the disappearance of the bulk of it back to Algeciras, reassured him. It now looked as if the attack was to be made on his fellow governor in the citadel of Gibraltar.

It was true that some of the ships and galleys were still anchored off his walls, but there were few of them. He contented himself with ordering sporadic fire to be made on them from the cannon and arbalests. A few skirmishes took place, parties trying to land from rowing boats, and minor clashes on the shore. But there seemed to be no real threat to Ceuta. The Berber tribesmen who had been summoned to the garrison's defense were dismissed. The ruler of Fez, and other neighboring chieftains who had sent help, were told that reinforcements were no longer needed. The fact was that the prosperous merchants of Ceuta disliked the presence of these wild tribesmen in their rich and orderly city almost as much as they feared the threat of sea-borne invasion. They had watched the ragged approach of the first invasion force, and had seen it dispersed up and down the coast by the currents. They had watched the second attempt broken up by the onset of the Levanter. They felt quite confident that the Portuguese would not try again.

5

There was near mutiny in some of the Portuguese ships, and Prince Henry found himself called upon to deal with an instance of it. Two of his squires rashly suggested to him that the King did not mean to take Ceuta at all. Taking his silence for assent and blind to his rising anger, they went so far as to say that King John was only looking for some way of saving his face, and that he cared little if he lost a few men in the process. Henry was not a man to suffer lightly the halfhearted, or the doubting Thomas, let alone men who dared suggest that his father was a coward.

"You force me to tell you," he said, "something I would have preferred to keep secret. Tomorrow you will see me walking down the gangplank—the first man to land in Ceuta! As for you, I will have two men transferred from another ship to take your places."

As Prince Edward later wrote, ". . . The most victorious King, my father, may God rest his soul, finding himself between Gibraltar and Algeciras, with me, my beloved brothers Prince Peter and Prince Henry, the Count of Barcellos, and the Constable, was told by some, who were not in favour of our intentions, that for many reasons we should not return to Ceuta, because of the danger of crossing the Straits in a storm. Furthermore, many signs and omens from Heaven made them believe this: the death of the most virtuous Queen, my beloved mother, the storm which had not allowed us to stay in harbour, and the plague which we now had amongst us in the ships. . . ."

But if there were some among the nobility who were still reluctant or doubtful, the sailors and men-at-arms in Henry's galley had been convinced of success by another omen. While they were crossing the strait, a fish "rose out of the sea, and lifting itself in the air came and fell on the deck of the galley; and they ate of it that day. . . ." Flying fish are common in the Strait of Gibraltar—*angeletti*, "little angels," the sailors call them. In a low freeboard vessel, it is quite common for flying fish to skin aboard, particularly at night when they are attracted by the ship's light. But a flying fish would make no more than a mouthful for one man. However, when the sea has been disturbed, as in this case after a strong wind, it is not unusual to find the great tunny leaping out of the waves. It was probably a tunny that jumped the low guardrail of Prince Henry's galley and provided both a meal and a good omen.

Nine days later than originally planned, the Portuguese fleet regrouped for the attack on Ceuta. Sala-ben-Sala saw the fleet lift its sails over the horizon on the night of the twentieth. There could no longer be any doubt that his own city was the objective. It would take some time to recall the Berber tribesmen who had dispersed on his orders. He was also troubled by the reports of prophets and astrologers. A holy man had dreamed of a cloud of bees swarming in the city, and of a lion, bearing a gold crown on his head, which entered the strait in company with a swarm of sparrows and destroyed the bees. This had been interpreted as meaning that the lion was the King of Portugal, the sparrows his Christian troops, and the bees the Moors of Ceuta. An old prophecy had also been recalled, which said that a lion, with three cubs, would come out of the Spanish peninsula and would overthrow the city, and that this would be the beginning of the end of Moorish power in Africa.

The plan of the attack remained unchanged. Prince Henry, in command of forty or fifty ships, was to anchor off Almina on the eastern side of the headland, King John with the main body of the fleet coming in to Ceuta Bay on the west. At daybreak, on a signal from the King, Prince Henry was to lead his men ashore. It was hoped that the Moorish defenders would flock to the western walls of the city when they saw the bulk of the fleet anchored there. In this way Prince Henry's forces would be left practically unopposed to establish their beachhead and take the city in the rear.

Throughout the long summer night, as ship after ship came to anchor, Sala-ben-Sala ordered every window and embrasure to glow with lights to impress the enemy with his preparedness. Groups of men-at-arms appeared on the walls, shouting defiance at the assembled ships. The lights of the city lay mirrored in the calm water of the bay. The fleet winked back with the answering gleam of oil lamps and the flicker of torches. The groan of horns, the sonorous boom of time-keeping gongs aboard the oared galleys, and the shrill scream of whetstones as soldiers sharpened their swords, echoed across the water.

Silently Prince Henry's force crept round Almina Point. They passed the bulk of Mount Hacko, looming up against the night sky, rounded Desnaricado Point, and came to anchor in the small bay.

Dawn came with a flicker over the warm sea. The night mist peeled away from the mountains, and the scent of the land drew out across the damp decks. The ships came alive like birds waking at the first light. They began to stir and rustle.

Shouting the names of friends, and whistling to attract their attention, the men began to prepare themselves for battle. Some were sharpening their weapons, others polishing their armor, and others checking rivet points on their leather doublets. Here a knight was being helped by his squire into his shining casque. There a group of men-at-arms aimed mock blows at each other. Others, recalling their sins, were making their confessions to the priests, "laying bare to God the great repentance which was in their hearts." One man was trying the balance of a battle-ax, swinging it about his head to see if anything hindered him in his movements. The archers strung their bows, checked them to see that the damp air had not affected them, and fingered the goose feathers of their arrows. So the sun came up on the morning of the battle, and the landings began.

To Prince Henry's profound annoyance, the first man ashore was Ruy Gonçalves, a nobleman in the entourage of the Count of Barcellos. King John had promised Henry the honor of being the first man to set foot on infidel territory, and Henry had been waiting for his father's signal. But at the sight of armed men landing on the beach, he could no longer restrain himself. He ordered the trumpeters to sound the charge, and leapt into a boat, followed by Prince Edward.

Suddenly the still morning was savaged by noise as the enemy came streaming down the beach to repel the invaders. Soon the clash of metal upon metal was joined by the sharp hiss of arrows and the groans of wounded. To the rattle of sand and stones, boat after boat came lifting over the waves to ground on the African shore.

As King John had foreseen, the bulk of the Moorish fighting men was on the western walls of the city. Against the armor, the swords, and the lances of Prince Henry's men, these Moors were practically defenseless, opposing them with desperate

showers of stones—but little more. Even so, they gave way
slowly, some distinguishing themselves by a courage and
violence that the contemporary Portuguese chronicler recorded
with respect. ". . . and among all these Moors there was one,
very tall and of a most threatening complexion, all naked, who
used no other weapons than stones, but each of the stones that
he threw seemed to be hurled by a catapult or cannon, such was
the strength of his arm. And when the Moors were thrust back
against the gate of the city, he turned toward the Christians,
stooped, and threw a stone which struck Vasco Martins d'Albergaria and carried away the visor of his casque. The aspect
of this Moor was such as to inspire terror, since all his body
was black as a crow, and he had very long white teeth, and his
lips, which were fleshy, were turned back. But Vasco Martins,
despite the violence of the blow, did not lose countenance and
did not fail to pay back the Moor, who had barely time to turn
round when the lance of the Portuguese pierced him through."

As soon as their champion fell, the spirit went out of the
other defenders. They rushed back to the city, leaving the
invaders to follow them. The Portuguese, with Prince Henry
leading and Prince Edward close behind, were now at the
Almina gate of the city. Before the defenders could close the
vast, studded doors against them, they poured into the city.
Now the armored men were like a shining river sluicing
through the dusty streets of the old town.

Henry and Peter sighted a small mound that dominated that
part of Ceuta. Followed by the Count of Barcellos and a handful of soldiers, they hacked their way out of the dangerous
narrow alleys toward this vantage point. Gasping for breath
and drenched with sweat, they took the hillock at a run. The
stench, and the flies that rose up in a dark cloud, told them that
it was the city's main refuse dump. They paused at the top
to get their breath and survey the battle. It was here, on this

malodorous mound of refuse and ordure, that Henry's squires planted his standard. It shook and quivered in the light breeze that drew seaward out of the city—the standard of Prince Henry of Portugal, the first Christian flag to fly over North Africa.

King John, meanwhile, had sent word for the attack to begin, only to learn that his orders had been anticipated. Two of his sons were already in the city. He heard the sound of trumpets and the clash of arms within the walls. The noblemen around him said mournfully, "We shall arrive too late. There will be no glorious deeds of arms left for us."

The King ordered the main body of the troops to begin their attack. Gangplanks were lowered, and all the small boats were called away. Soon the waters of the bay were scissored by the wakes of the main invasion force making for the beach beneath the city's walls.

The King was wounded in the leg in the first stage of the assault. Reluctantly, he was forced to halt by the main gate of the city, and to watch the other knights and men-at-arms stream past him. Some were bound to the attack, and some were already burdening themselves with loot from the houses. Smoke and dust lifted in clouds over the tawny walls. The cries, the shouts, and the clamor of the trumpets were so great that it was said the sound of the battle was heard across the strait in Gibraltar.

Attacked on both sides, and with an increasing flood of Portuguese now pouring through the breached gate from the main invasion fleet, Sala-ben-Sala abandoned the city. He and a few other chiefs, together with their wives and valuables, escaped through the gate to the mainland. As they looked back, they could see the enemy ships busily disgorging soldiers in a pincer movement on either side of the headland. The sandy bays were dappled with boats and bright with sunlight on armor.

In the hot alleys of the old town the battle swayed back and forth. Prince Henry was lost in the confusion of the struggle. It was no longer a co-ordinated affair, but a series of individual skirmishes; parties of troops looting one house; others pursuing the defenders back to the citadel; and others again being driven in flight by more determined groups of the enemy. His brothers and his squires saw him disappear into the thick of the battle and despaired for him. His father, encamped at the main gate, was brought word that his favorite son was dead.

"Such is the end that soldiers must expect" was his laconic reply.

But Henry was at the outer door of the castle itself. He had cleared the enemy from the streets behind him, and had barricaded them into the one strong point that remained in the city. He was finally discovered by Garcia Moniz, who had been his tutor when he was a child. Most of Henry's followers had drifted away, some to loot and others intent on food and drink (they had had nothing to eat since early morning). He alone had been blind to everything but the task of victory.

Garcia Moniz discovered him thus, bloody and disheveled, sword in hand and his dark eyes exultant. He ran forward and clasped the young man to him.

"You wish to attempt things that are beyond the powers of man!" he said. The words were prophetic.

That evening the last strong point of Ceuta, the citadal, fell to the Portuguese. The last of the defenders fled to the mountains and inland villages, the treasure of Sala-ben-Sala was captured, and the flag of Prince Edward flaunted upon the tower of Fez. The golden city of Ceuta was taken.

The streets seethed with soldiers, and flames flickered over dark faces bent on plunder. They staggered under rich carpets and jewelry, Oriental vases and tapestries, wine and oil, and delicate silks. Order and discipline had long since gone. They were now drawing their pay in the manner of the time.

King John was overjoyed to find his son—despite his Spartan acceptance of the first ill news. He listened to tales of Henry's deeds, of how he had led the attack, and how for many hours he had always been in the forefront of battle. He learned that it was Prince Henry who had been first at the gate of the castle.

"I will knight you first before your brothers," he said fondly.

"God brought us into the world one after the other. I beg you, let the honor of knighthood go in the same succession."

On the first Sunday after the battle, in the cleansed and consecrated mosque, the victors prepared to celebrate Mass. *Te Deum Laudamus,* they sang, as two hundred trumpets sounded over the captured city. Above the heads of the King and his sons, two old church bells swung and boomed. Prince Henry had remembered that these bells, captured years before from the village of Sines in the Portuguese province of Algarve, were kept in Ceuta. He had made a search for them, and now, restored to their ancient use, they joined in the thanksgiving.

When Mass was over, the princes retired to their apartments and put on their armor before returning to the church for the ceremony of knighthood. ". . . and this was a noble sight indeed, for all three of the princes had tall well-built bodies, and their armour was gleaming and richly adorned. From their belts hung the swords which their mother had blessed. Before them went the trumpets and the drums. I do not believe that there was a single man there who did not take pleasure in beholding them."

One after the other, the young princes knelt to receive from King John the accolade of knighthood. This was their moment of triumph. Distinguished in their first battle, conquerors of the great city of Ceuta, they were knighted in a mosque consecrated to the Christian faith, under the recaptured bells of Sines. A medieval dream of knighthood with honor had led them to this North African shore, and to this brilliant moment. Throughout their lives they would remember it. It was the golden hour of youth, when all dreams seem capable of fulfillment.

6

The capture of Ceuta was the first great European success
against the Mohammedans in their own territory. Ceuta was
also the first European base to be established on the continent
of Africa. From it would spring that gradual occupation and
colonization of the continent, the problems arising from which
constitute one of the major issues of our own day.

The fleet, which "to the sound of divers instruments of
music" returned in triumph to Portugal, was celebrating no
more than a brilliant success in the long war between cross and
crescent. The news of the victory (which swiftly circulated
through the courts of Europe) meant little more to those
who heard it than a confirmation of the military prowess of
King John. It induced respect among the Castilians and the
Moors of Granada. It confirmed, for all who had previously
doubted, that the kingdom of Portugal was now a power to be
reckoned with, and that the dynasty founded by the master of
the House of Aviz was secure. The real achievement of Ceuta
was invisible to those whose eyes were fixed on the contemporary scene.

Only one man, perhaps, had any conception of what Ceuta

could mean to Portugal, and it is very doubtful whether even Prince Henry realized that this was to be the beginning of the discovery of Africa. His aims at this period of his life were simple. He saw Ceuta as the springboard for a Portuguese Moroccan empire, which might turn the flank of the Moham-medans as well as provide the necessary wealth to make his country a great power.

As the fleet turned northward past Cape Spartel and ran out into the Atlantic, Henry may have visualized all that foreign shore under Portuguese control, with garrisons and trading posts, safe harbors for ships, and markets whence the gold and spices of Africa might be transshipped to Portugal. If Ceuta, why not Gibraltar? With both of the Pillars of Hercules in Portuguese hands, the navigation of the strait would become a Portuguese monopoly. Beyond that again lay the dream of the capture of Tangier. This would give them both the major seaports of the Moroccan coastline, and enable them to expand into the interior. It was not until many years later, when his dream of a Portuguese Moroccan empire had been shattered, that he concentrated all his powers and ability on exploring the coastline of Africa.

When they sailed from Ceuta, the Portuguese left a garrison of three thousand men behind them. The garrison was under the command of Count Dom Pedro de Menezes, a nobleman who was to hold the governorship for over twenty years. During this time he had many opportunities for displaying his skill in repulsing numerous attacks, for the Moors did not despair of recovering their Golden City. Ceuta, after all, was only an island in the middle of a hostile empire, and an island can easily be blockaded. It was this fact, which had escaped the notice of the King and his advisers when they were contemplat-ing the venture, that rendered the capture of Ceuta a some-what hollow victory. The city was rich and prosperous only because it was an outlet for the Moroccan trade. But since that trade was in the hands of enemies, it very quickly began to dry up. The caravans came no longer, the metalworkers, the jewelers, the weavers, and the potters had all fled. Throughout Prince Henry's life Ceuta remained a valuable acquisition in terms of prestige, but an expensive one in other respects. The Barbary Coast, that famed haunt of the Moslem pirates, had lost one of its most important ports—that was all. The Portuguese had not gained, as they had hoped to do, a thriving city that would increase their prosperity. To begin with, it was enough for King John, for Nuño Pereira, and for the nobility and the courts of Europe, that the kingdom of Portugal had gained a great victory over the infidel. Only Prince Henry saw that Ceuta was no more than Dead Sea fruit unless Tangier and the coastline between the two cities were added to the Portuguese crown.

In recognition of his part in the landings, and in the taking of the city, his father made Prince Henry Duke of Viseu and Lord of Covilham. His brother Prince Peter was made Duke of Coimbra. For Prince Edward, heir to the throne, there could be no additional honors, but it was a curious lack of foresight on the part of the King that he passed over the claims of his bastard son, the Count of Barcellos, who had also fought bravely in the campaign. This omission increased a natural bitterness and sense of rivalry, which would have unhappy repercussions in the future. Prince Henry, in addition to these other marks of favor, was made governor of Ceuta. It was a post that he discharged faithfully to the end of his life. Although it did not necessitate his presence in the city, it gave him a permanent interest in Africa.

The sight of Africa combined with his first long sea voyage was to effect a revolution in Prince Henry. The attack on Ceuta had been planned so that he and his brothers might win their spurs of knighthood on a foreign battlefield. It was a religious crusading spirit that had given Henry his certainty and purpose when even the King contemplated calling off the expedition. This medieval, militant conception of Christianity remained an integral part of Prince Henry's character all his life.

No man of Henry's temperament could sail into the Atlantic and see the illimitable ocean spreading away to south and west without wondering what secrets it contained. There it lay, mile upon mile of unknown ocean, the long level planes of water dovetailing into one another under the swell. The sun went down beyond the western rim, and there was no hiss of expiring fires, as the ancients had maintained. Flying fish rose in silver flights in front of the galley's bows, and in the silence he could hear the flicker of their wings. He saw no sea monsters.

The capture of Ceuta had strengthened his self-confidence. All his life he had heard tales of the Moors, the terror of Christendom, the heathen who had once occupied his own country, Portugal, and all of Spain. Yet Ceuta had fallen easily enough, with only a handful of Portuguese dead to weigh in the balance against the capture of so great a city, and the slaughter of many of the infidel. Perhaps even the power of the Moors was something of a legend? If Ceuta, why not Gibraltar, and then Tangier, and then all Morocco? As the galley turned north and headed toward the coast of Algarve, the southernmost province of Portugal, he could see the bulk of Cape Spartel dropping away astern. Cape Spartel was the western limit of Morocco, yet beyond it, as he could see, the coastline still existed. It trended away to the southwest, tawny under the midday sun, a land of desert, but nevertheless a land.

It may have been during those days aboard the galley that he heard for the first time the old sailors' saying: *"Quem passar o Cabo de Nam, ou tornara ou nam,"* "He who would pass

Cape Not, either will return or not." Beyond it few ships had ever gone, and not far to the south lay Cape Bojador, where the unknown began, the boiling sea and the Ocean of Darkness. At that point it seemed as if the waters ran downward in a curve, so that, it was said, no ship could ever sail back. The winds drew always from astern, so that even if the curved ocean was a myth, the fact remained that a square-sailed vessel had little chance of beating her way north again. Cape Not lay almost opposite Lançarote, the northernmost of the Canary Islands, and—whatever else might be unknown—the Canaries had been familiar to mariners for many centuries. One established fact weighs heavily against a vast bulk of legend, and it was the facts that Henry acquired on the expedition to Ceuta that gave him the foundation on which to build a whole system of acquired knowledge. If he had been no more than a dreamer, he might have been content to evolve poetry or fantasy out of the unknown ocean. But instead, he dedicated himself to finding out more about that coastline, which with every stroke of the galley's oars faded into the distance.

He went back to Ceuta three years later, in 1418. The Governor had reported that the city was heavily beseiged by Moors from Granada and Fez, and that he required help. Once again, King John put Prince Henry in command of the fleet that was sent to Ceuta's relief. This time there were no calms or foul weather to delay the ships, and they reached the city in three days. At the sight of the Portuguese sails lifting over the horizon, the Moors lost heart. Prince Henry, who was this time accompanied by his young brother John, now aged eighteen, had the satisfaction of raising the seige and reinforcing the garrison. But it was a satisfaction that was mingled with disappointment, for the Moors withdrew at once. Henry found himself in command of a fleet and a body of trained soldiers, and no enemy to engage.

The idea of attacking Gibraltar immediately suggested itself and, had he been king, there is no doubt that this would
have been his next move. But his father was growing old and
consequently less ambitious. He had foreseen that—finding
nothing to do at Ceuta—Prince Henry would turn to Gibraltar.
Orders were sent for the Portuguese fleet to return home immediately. King John no longer required additional proofs
of his country's ability in war, and he still feared Castile. He
knew that the capture of Gibraltar would seem a provocative
act to the King of Castile—who no doubt preferred an in-
active Moorish garrison on the Rock to an active army under
the command of Prince Henry, the son of his old enemy.

This second expedition was a stimulant to Henry's interest
in Africa. He had spent three months in Ceuta after the city
had been relieved, and it was probably during this time that
he first made acquaintance with some of the desert Arabs.
There were captives from the army of Fez, and there were still
some traders who had dealings with the city that had once provided their principal market. These men had information of
value: tales to tell of the direction in which caravan routes ran
inland after leaving the coastline; gossip, fact and fiction, inextricably interwoven about the interior of the continent.
Henry now learned the feel of Africa—the blinding sun at
noon, the hot dusty streets, the shuttered houses, the bite of
the sand when the wind comes off the desert, and the extraordinary clarity of the nights. Then, when the desert suddenly
shudders to an icy coldness—within an hour of sundown—the
stars seem big as brilliants.

On his return, Prince Henry's fame was such that the kings
of Europe vied with each other to secure his services. It was
now widely known that he had been the driving force behind
the original capture of the city, and the alacrity with which he
had just come to its relief was taken as further evidence of his

ability. At twenty-four he was governor of Ceuta, and—by merit alone—one of the first dukes in Portugal.

The ambassadors of the various powers resident at Lisbon confirmed all that rumor said. This prince, they reported, possessed his father's military prowess and astuteness. More than that, he was a man who seemed impervious to the weaknesses of the flesh. In an age of license, he was chaste. In an age when noblemen habitually befuddled themselves, he drank little or nothing. In an age when the letter of the Church was obeyed, but not its spirit, he was ascetic. Mindful of all the Christian observances, he spent many hours of the week in solitary prayer. Such a strange, if somewhat disturbing, paragon of virtue could hardly fail to impress. The Pope, Martin V, invited him to take command of the Greek armies of Emperor Manuel II Palaeologus in the war against the Turks. Sigismund, Emperor of Germany, offered him the command of his army in the field. Even the King of Castile, his father's former enemy, asked for help in ridding Granada of the Moors.

Henry V of England, whose ideal was a Christian hero and leader like King Arthur, offered him command of the English armies in a war against the infidel. Henry V (whose last wish was that he might live to rebuild the walls of Jerusalem) saw perhaps in his Portuguese cousin the qualities that he respected more than any other. If one were searching for a parallel character in British history to Henry of Portugal, Henry V is perhaps as close as one could come. He too was courageous and resourceful, a skilled leader in war, and a far-sighted diplomatist. He too delighted in sport and was a man of culture and learning. The difference between the cousins lay in the quality of intensity that Henry of Portugal possessed in an uncommon degree. But the youthful vices of Henry V (probably exaggerated by Shakespeare) make him more comprehensible to us. Like Nelson's passion for Emma Hamilton, they serve to make him a weaker, but nevertheless more lovable, figure. Henry of Portugal had few such fallible human characteristics. He moves across the stage of history a remote and somewhat perplexing figure—because of his lack of vices. If, as John Addington Symonds remarked, ". . . the best known figures of history are not necessarily the most important," the reason is that their fame often stems from their weaknesses. Every schoolboy has heard of Henry VIII, because of his private life and not because of his political brilliance.

Henry of Portugal, who set in motion a train of events of more far-reaching consequence than either Henry V or Henry VIII of England, has been commonly ignored outside his own country. As Marshal Lyautey said of him, "He combined the disinterestedness of the scientist with the austerity of the saint." Such men are admired but not loved. Human beings tend to make their heroes out of men in whom they can see reflected not only their own potentialities but also their weaknesses. In his own lifetime, though, his talents were so conspicuous that no one could ignore them. This was the reason why two kings, an emperor, and even a pope tried to secure his services. Henry was flattered, no doubt, but he was not to be distracted from the vast plans that obsessed him. As a prince of Portugal his duty lay first with his own country, and he had seen already the goal of his ambitions in the long shores of Africa.

Disappointed at his father's rejection of his plan for attacking Gibraltar, he retired more and more from the court. His eldest brother, Prince Edward, was being groomed for the throne. Prince Peter—still cherishing his enigmatic motto *Désir*—had set out on a series of travels that would take him all over Europe and most of the Near East. His two younger brothers, and his sister Isabel, remained as companions to the King. There was little to detain him in the court. As duke of Viseu in the southern province of Algarve, and governor of Ceuta, it was natural that Henry should establish himself somewhere in the south of Portugal. From there he could be ready, if need be, to sail again to the relief of Ceuta, and from there he could find out more about the African coastline. If his father's respect for political considerations did not allow him to attack Gibraltar, then he must seek another way. The Moors must be outflanked, not from the land but from the sea.

The key to power, Henry sensed, lay in the unknown Atlantic, and in order to win it he must study his opponent. Ships in those days were small and chancy craft, unsuitable as headquarters from which to plan campaigns, or conduct affairs of state. Henry sought a place that would be as like a ship as possible, where he could be alone with his grand design, and yet where he could have easy access to all sources of information. He found this place in the bluff, spray-swept rock of Sagres. It was there that, shortly after his second return from Ceuta, he began to build the *Vila do Infante*—the City of the Prince.

7

In Sagres the surge and thunder of the sea are never absent. Standing on this scoured promontory, where the Atlantic meets the southwestern point of Europe, man is dwarfed by the ocean. There is no room here for anything other than contemplation and speculation. To a man of Prince Henry's day, speculation may have been uppermost; to a man of his character, contemplation was never absent. Sagres was a happy accord between an ambition, a temperament, and a world.

It is difficult today to understand the magnitude of the task he had set himself. It may be that within a few years we shall see men landing on the moon or exploring other planets. They will meet hazards as yet unknown, but they will know a great deal more about the geography and the probabilities of those areas than was known in the fifteenth century about the Atlantic. In the early fifteenth century, the long sleep of the Middle Ages was only just ending and the Renaissance had not begun. Throughout his life Prince Henry was a divided personality—a Janus with one face looking into the medieval past and one into the new age of scientific thought. To him, more than to any other individual, we owe the direction that the world was to take in the succeeding five hundred years. He was born into an age of myth and superstition, where no certainty existed except in what was promulgated by the Church. When he died, the mists were peeling away off the sea, half of the Atlantic and the west coast of Africa had been explored, and all the central and eastern Atlantic islands had been charted. At the time of his death in 1460 the main fruits of the Age of Discovery were yet to come—the discovery of the sea route round the Cape of Good Hope to India, of the West Indies and America. But it was Prince Henry alone who had initiated and set in motion this chain of events.

We have seen some of the reasons that prompted him to devote himself to the exploration of the Moroccan coast of Africa, but it was only his position and office that enabled him to devote money and ships and time to the enterprise. The fact that his father had made Prince Henry grand master of the Order of Christ enabled him in the first place to have money to equip his expeditions. The Order of Christ, the supreme pontifical order, had been founded by Diniz of Portugal in conjunction with Pope John XXII in 1318 on the abolition of the Templars. Today the papal branch survives as a distinct order from the Portuguese order, but in the time of Prince Henry nominations to it could be made either by the King of Portugal or by the Pope. Such was the expense of equipping ships and expeditions, however, that when Henry died he was deeply in debt. The funds of the order enabled him to begin his task, that was all. Because it was in his office of grand master that he sent out his ships, one of the chief objectives was the conversion of the heathen and the establishment of the Christian faith. It was for this reason too that the galleys and caravels dispatched by Prince Henry bore the red Cross of Christ on their sails.

The riddle of the unknown Atlantic had perplexed and fascinated men for centuries. There were several reasons why, before Prince Henry, no one had attempted to do anything about it. The first was the superstitious and legendary awe in which the ocean was held. The second was that no one attempted navigation except for profit, and what profit could there be in the unknown? The trade routes of Europe were established—the northern route from Holland and England to Portugal and Spain, and the Mediterranean routes. Merchant ships sail only where there is trade, and there was no trade in the Sea of Obscurity.

The Sea of Obscurity, or the Ocean of Darkness, it was called. There dwelt monsters, and the sun stood so high overhead that the water boiled. The men who lived on the outermost edge of the African shore were known to be burned black by the sun, so how could man go farther without being roasted alive? There were magnetic rocks that made a compass spin like a wheel, rocks that would draw the iron fastenings from a ship's side. The pitch would boil in the seams, the calking would be lost, and the ships would sink. If you escaped these hazards, worse was to come. As you neared the outermost limits of the earth, you would be caught in the steady flow of water that poured night and day over the edge. It was not an old wives' tale—sailors themselves would tell you that you could see the edge of the world running away downhill. It dropped down in a great shimmering curve, and if you went too far south, the hill would grow steeper and you could never sail back. Then the eternally rushing water would catch you and sweep you away, into the darkness.

Yet men had not always been so superstitious or so ignorant. Centuries earlier, the Phoenicians, the Greeks, and the Carthaginians had known as much, or more, than the early fifteenth-century navigators. The coasts of Asia Minor, Europe, and North Africa had all been explored by these early sailors. Greek astronomers and cartographers had plotted the general configuration and position of most of Europe and some, if not all, of its off-lying islands. Most astonishing of all, the fact that Africa could be circumnavigated had been known to the Greek historian Herodotus in the fifth century B.C.

"Libya [Africa] shows itself to be surrounded by water, except so much of it as borders upon Asia. Neco, King of Egypt, was the first whom we know of, to prove this . . . he sent certain Phoenicians in ships, with orders to sail back through the Pillars of Hercules into the northern sea [the Mediterranean] and so return to Egypt. The Phoenicians accordingly, setting out from the Red Sea, navigated the Southern Sea [Indian Ocean]; when autumn came, they went ashore, and sowed the land, by whatever part of Libya they happened to be sailing and waited for harvest; than having reaped the corn, they put to sea again. When two years had thus passed, in the third, having doubled the Pillars of Hercules, they arrived in Egypt, and related what to me does not seem credible, but may to others, that as they sailed round Libya, they had the sun on their right hand."

This voyage was undertaken by the Phoenicians, those master mariners of the ancient world, about 600 B.C. The fact that even the "Father of History" disbelieved their report may have been the reason for the discovery's being buried in obscurity. Prince Henry may possibly have heard this story from the scholars and savants whom he later collected at Sagres. If so, it must have reinforced his determination not to rest until the extent of Africa was known. Curiously enough, the fact that made the report suspect to Herodotus proves that the Phoenicians really did circumnavigate Africa. When rounding the Cape of Good Hope, in the latitude of about 35 degrees south of the equator, it would indeed have seemed to sailors used to the northern latitude of the Mediterranean that the sun at midday was "on their right hand."

In these early years of Prince Henry's life we know that he was concerned only with the western Atlantic coast of Morocco. The time had not yet come when men could say of him that he thought in continents and not in islands. He had some knowledge of the burning, barren coast that stretched beyond Tangier. He had met Arabs in Ceuta, and later he was to employ some of them among his cartographers, navigators, and astronomers. The Arabs knew that there were islands in the Atlantic; they knew at any rate about the Canaries. So did Prince Henry, for the Castilians, the French, and many others had made voyages to the Canaries. Only thirteen years before the capture of Ceuta, a Norman baron, Jean de Béthencourt, had colonized part of the islands and built churches there. The Canaries had even been known to the ancients as the Fortunate Islands. Standing at the outermost limits of the known world, they had been poeticized as the Elysian Fields, the Isles of the Blest—the land, in fact, "where it was always afternoon."

At this period of history, Arabic knowledge of geography and astronomy was superior to that of Europe. As traders and merchants they were in contact with Arabia and India by sea, and with the interior of Africa by overland routes. As early as the twelfth century the Xerife Idrisi had written a book of geography for King Roger II of Sicily, which was far in advance of any European knowledge at that time. Idrisi knew, for instance, that beyond the dreary wastes of the Sahara there was a fertile land beginning at the Senegal River. Called Bilad Ghana, "Land of Wealth," it appears on a map made for King Roger about 1150. Even so, the Arabs' knowledge was confined to the Mediterranean and North Africa and, to some extent, the east coast of Africa. Little was known about the Atlantic coast, and most people accepted the statement of the traveler Ibn Said that the world ended in the Sea of Obscurity near Cape Bojador. But whereas Cape Not—the limit

of the world, according to the Portuguese fisherman's saying
—lies on the same latitude as the Canary Islands, Cape Bojador is 100 miles farther south. No doubt Prince Henry thought
that the perils of Cape Bojador were also grossly exaggerated.

Azurara gives us a picture of Prince Henry's early life at
Sagres. ". . . After the taking of Ceuta, the Prince had ships
always at sea to do battle against the Infidel." It was these
ships with the cross on their sails that now began to harry the
Arab traders, just as the latter had, for centuries, harried the
Christian merchantmen. Soon the Portuguese ships would do
more than that, for Azurara tells us that "he desired to know
what lands there were beyond the Canary Isles and a cape
called Bojador. For at that time there was no knowledge, either
in writing or in the memory of any man, of what might lie
beyond this cape."

Azurara states the reasons for Prince Henry's embarking
upon his career of discovery. It is particularly interesting
that he gives first the scientific reason that "no sailor or merchant would undertake it, for it is very sure that such men do
not dream of navigating other than to places where they already know they can make a profit." Later historians have
sometimes tended to denigrate Prince Henry by saying either
that his aims were those of a militant medieval knight, or that
he was guided solely by the desire of material gain. There
seems no justification for either of these views. The fact that
a contemporary like Azurara puts the scientific aspect first is
evidence enough that he was impressed by this—at that time
unusual—motive. As the second reason he gives the commercial one, that Henry wanted to know whether there were any
Christians to the south of Morocco with whom the Portuguese
might trade, and what harbors there might be. Thirdly he gives
the strategic reason, that Henry wanted to know the strength
of his enemy and how far south Moorish power extended.

Fourthly comes the political reason, the desire to know whether he might find a Christian ally against the Mohammedans. Only fifthly does he cite the religious motive: "to increase the Holy Faith . . . that lost souls might be saved." Lastly—and curiously enough Azurara devotes considerable space to it—comes the fact that, astrologically, the disposition of the planets at Henry's birth was such that he "was bound to engage in great and noble conquests and, above all, to attempt the discovery of things hidden from other men, and secret." Henry was a "man of a star," and it is evidence of the curious awe that surrounded him that his contemporaries should have felt this prince was not as other men.

A thing that strikes one at once about this early assessment of Henry's motives in setting out on the exploration of Africa is the double reference to the possibility of finding a "Christian ally" somewhere to the south and beyond the kingdom of the Moors. What reason had anyone for thinking that a Christian country might lie hidden behind the iron curtain of Mohammedan power? The answer lies in that enigmatic, and still problematical, figure, Prester John.

Prester John was a legend, a dream of hope that had fascinated Europeans since the twelfth century. He was supposed to be a powerful Christian monarch living in either Africa or Asia—reports varied—and eternally at war with the heathen and the infidel. In 1144 a Syrian bishop had told Bishop Otto of Freisinger that a great victory had recently been won over the infidels by a king called Prester John, who was a Christian ruler and the descendant of the Magi. It now seems likely that at one time there really was such a ruler somewhere in central Asia. He was a powerful khan, who had been converted by Nestorian Christian missionaries, and who was known as the "Presbyter Khan"—the Priest King. His son, who is reputed to have succeeded him, was attacked and overthrown by Gen-ghis Khan toward the end of the twelfth century, which put an end to the Christian khanate in that part of the world.

Inevitably, rumors of this Christian kingdom in Asia, which had reached Europe in the eleventh and twelfth centuries, be-came inextricably confused with other rumors about the Chris-tian kings of Abyssinia. In the fourteenth century a Franciscan friar, writing of Abyssinia and Nubia, says that "the Patriarch of these countries is Prester Juan who rules over many lands and cities of Christians." He is also referred to by Marco Polo as ruling a kingdom somewhere near the Great Wall of China, while that old spinner of travelers' tales, Sir John Mandeville, placed his kingdom in upper India.

There is no smoke without fire, and we see now that medieval Christians in Europe were not so far from the truth when they believed that somewhere to the south and east there was a Christian king and country. Their hope was to establish com-munication with him, form an alliance against the heretic Mohammedans, and thus be able to take them in the rear. In this they were doomed to disappointment.

The lure of Prester John was something that inevitably ap-pealed to two sides of Prince Henry's temperament. As grand master of the Order of Christ, he clearly had the duty to estab-lish contact with this "lost" Christian ruler. It was practical politics for him, as a prince engaged in war against the Mo-hammedans, to try to establish a powerful alliance behind their backs. Prince Henry must have been further spurred in this quest when his brother Peter returned from his travels in 1428, bringing with him a copy of Marco Polo's book, which the Venetians had given him.

How often in his long conversations with travelers and sea-farers Prince Henry must have heard that name, Prester John.

The search for this long-dead, or nonexistent, monarch played as important a part in the history of navigation and discovery as the quest for the philosophers' stone in the history of chemistry.

8

❀

Henry was often alone these days. He was beginning his apprenticeship to the world of sea and silence. Below him in the bay a few ships drowsed at anchor. Around him lay the beginning of his palace, his fortress, and his naval base.

"How many times did the rising sun find him seated where it had left him the day before, waking all the hours of the night, without a moment of rest, surrounded by people of many nationalities. . . . Where will you find another human body capable of supporting, as his in battle, the fatigue from which he had so little rest in time of peace! I truly believe that if strength could be represented, its very form would be found in the countenance and body of this prince. It was not only in certain things that he showed himself to be strong, but in all. And what strength is there greater than that of the man who is conqueror of himself?"

The stern devotion to religious duties, which his mother had taught him, had disciplined him to long hours, and days even, of self-denial. As grand master of the Order of Christ he was dedicated to a chaste and ascetic life—but these were obligations that many a prince or nobleman would have taken lightly.

In Henry they were as binding as his mother's dying command, and the banked-up fires of sexuality provided the immense reserves of energy that astounded his fellow men. During those first months at Sagres he spent many a night vigil engaged in a contemplation that was part religious and part scientific. It was after one of these long nights alone that the period of inaction was suddenly broken.

It was early morning and the headland was cool, damp with the night dew and heady with the northern wind. He could hear the sound of the sea where it made up against the headland, a sound that had become part of his silence. The light was just beginning to bring color back into the world, and the dark water in the bay was like pewter. His attendants, his sailors, and the strange people who made up his stranger court— sea captains, Jewish cartographers, Moors, adventurers, and men-at-arms—were asleep. They were awakened by the Prince himself. With drawn face but shining eyes, he came among them like a strange spirit, and the simple, superstitious men were frightened by the power they saw in him.

"Two ships are to be prepared at once," he said. "They are to set sail and go as far south along the Moroccan coast as possible."

He must know more about that coast. He must know which way it trended, and how the capes lay, and whether there were anchorages safe from storms.

It was as if, during the night, he had seen a vision. This was to be no marauding expedition against Moorish shipping. This was to be the first of hundreds of voyages of exploration, voyages that seemed pointless and dangerous to the sailors, and a gross waste of money to the courtiers.

They were all a little afraid of him, though, for his anger could be terrifying. Normally a quiet and gently spoken man, one who would always listen with reason to the excuses and complaints of the men who worked for him, there came a moment when his face would freeze and his eyes become like ice. The anger that seized him then was a cold anger of the will—unlike the hot words or blows of other men.

"To sail south," murmured the sailors. "What is the point of that? How can we possibly pass beyond the bounds that are established? What profit can the Prince gain from the loss of a few poor sailors? There have been other princes who have tried to find out more than man was meant to know—and what did they achieve? Nothing."

They knew that beyond Cape Bojador there were no human beings. The land was as barren as the deserts of Libya, and there was no water at all. The sun baked men black, and the sea was so shallow that ships could not pass. And the tides were so strong—that eternal rush of great waters—that no ship could ever return.

"You will go south," said the Prince.

They went down to the ships, and made them ready for sea.

These first two ships to sail on a voyage of pure exploration were not caravels, but small square-sailed barks of the type in which most of the trade was carried. They were about fifty tons, half-decked, with a high poop. They were admirable ships for running before the wind, but the sailors had good reason for fearing that they would have difficulty in beating back against it. In the summer months the prevailing wind from the north, which cools the hot plains and valleys of Portugal, blows almost steadily. It was this wind, combined with Portugal's geographical position, that made the country ideally sited for Atlantic exploration. The wind that had been blowing when Queen Philippa died was to boost the ships of Portugal down all the trade routes of the world. It gave them the initial "lift" off the rocky Atlantic coast of Europe. Once they had gone far enough south, beyond the Canary Islands, they would find the northeast trades, which would ultimately carry them to the South Atlantic and South America.

The men who manned Prince Henry's ships in these early days were not native to the sea, as their descendants became. Most of them came from a peasant background, strong stock that had survived centuries of Moorish domination, misrule, civil warfare, and the inevitable hardships of medieval peasant life. Some of them had an apprenticeship to the ocean, for coastal fishing had long played an important part in Portugal's economy. But there is a great difference between coastal work and deep-sea sailing, and that difference was even more pointed in days when navigation and ocean seamanship were in their infancy. If ancestry means anything, however, the blood that flowed in Portuguese veins came not only from Visigoths, Suevi, and Iberians, but from two of the greatest maritime peoples in history. The Phoenicians had used the Portuguese ports on their trading runs to England and the north, and after them had come the Vikings, bound for the Mediterranean. A Viking and Phoenician ancestry should be enough to give a man "an itch in the blood," but the most famous seaman of all was supposed to have founded Lisbon. Olisipo, Lisbon's ancient name, was derived from its legendary founder, Ulysses.

It seems only fitting that there should be a link, however tenuous, between Ulysses and Henry the Navigator. Lord Tennyson's poem about the Homeric hero could almost apply to Prince Henry and his navigators:

> . . . Come, my friends,
> 'Tis not too late to seek a newer world.
> Push off, and sitting well in order smite
> The sounding furrows; for my purpose holds
> To sail beyond the sunset, and the baths
> Of all the western stars, until I die.

If the human material with which Prince Henry had to work was relatively unacquainted with the sea, his sailors had one of the most important of all qualities—a deep inbred endurance arising from centuries of back-breaking struggle on a hard land and a harsh coastline. On this first voyage of exploration their endurance was to be tested, for within a few days of leaving harbor the two ships ran into an Atlantic gale. In the driving murk of blown nimbus cloud they lost sight of one another. While one of the ships battled with the storm, hove to or driving before it, the other was carried away to the southwest—out into the Sea of Darkness. This second ship was to make nautical history.

The days went by and Prince Henry, his attendants, and the sailors of Sagres waited to see the ships return. When dawn broke, the Prince strained his eyes over the lightening rim of the Atlantic. He saw the deep base of the midsummer clouds catch fire as the sun came up over the land behind him. He heard the hollow boom as the onshore swell piled up against the headland, and the long withdrawn sigh as the blowhole spouted water over the bleached rock. He was not always at Sagres, though, in these early days. While his new buildings were rising on the headland, he often lodged in a small house in the village of Raposeira, a few miles inland. At other times he was at Lagos, farther down the coast, supervising the construction of ships, listening to the reports of men who had returned from Ceuta, or questioning captured Arabs and prisoners from Moorish galleys.

At last, one summer morning, one of the ships came creeping back over the horizon. As soon as she had dropped anchor, her captain came ashore to report to the Prince. The news was bad. Running down toward the coast of Morocco, they had fallen foul of this gale from the northeast, and the two vessels had lost sight of one another. His own ship had been hove to for several days, and had put about as soon as the wind was fair. He had seen no more of his companion since the first day of the gale, and he thought it likely that she had been lost with all hands.

Such are the normal hazards of the sea. But Henry—after rewarding the men and paying tribute to their courage—knew that this first disaster would increase their reluctance to venture south again. And then—a few days later—the second ship was sighted, bearing up toward the bay. Even before her anchor was down, her captain's boat was being lowered. The men at the oars were shouting the news before their captain had stepped ashore. They had discovered an island!

Running under bare poles before the gale, they had been carried more than 400 miles southwest into the Atlantic beyond Cape St. Vincent. They had given themselves up for lost. The sailors had cried out that it was all true—the sea ran downhill, and there was no return! But one morning, after the gale had died away, they had seen something ahead of them. The dawn clouds were lifting, and there on the horizon lay a small mountainous island, with the sun bright on its bare beaches. They had dropped anchor in the sandy bay, and in gratitude for their deliverance they had called it Porto Santo.

It was in this way that the smaller of the two main Madeira islands was rediscovered. It was believed at the time to be a completely new discovery, but we now know (from an Italian map of 1351) that the Genoese had come across the Madeiras some time early in the fourteenth century. Beyond recording them on their charts, however, they had done nothing about them. The Genoese were traders running between the Mediterranean and northern Europe. The Madeiras meant no more to them than a navigational hazard, or a place in which a ship might possibly take aboard water and wood. If it had not been for the presiding genius of Prince Henry, there is little doubt that this second accidental discovery would also have been dismissed—as of no importance except to mariners.

He learned from the captain and sailors that the soil was good, and that there were plants growing on the island. Among them were the juniper and the dragon tree—the latter was much valued in Europe at that time as the source of an astringent medicine. Henry questioned them more closely about the position of the island. It lay southwest of Cape St. Vincent nearly 500 miles from Portugal. There was no doubt, then, that this island had no connection with the Canaries. The fact pleased him, for the ownership of the Canaries was bedeviled by conflicting claims, Castile having the major interest. He had already approached the King of Castile and inquired whether he would be prepared—for a sum—to cede his interests to Portugal, and had been politely told to mind his own business. So the news that this island was alone in the Atlantic, and entirely uninhabited, encouraged his dreams. He saw that it would provide another base from which his ships might carry on their exploratory voyages down the coast of Africa.

The masters of the ships engaged in this first expedition were two squires attached to Henry's court, João Gonçalves Zarco and Tristão Vaz Teixeira. They were young men, had served at Ceuta, and were members of the poorer nobility. They were very typical of the men who would lead expeditions for Prince Henry during the next thirty years, belonging to a class that had little opportunity for advancement in the settled Portugal of King John. Such men normally found their employment and wealth in warfare, but now that there was peace with Castile, and internal peace in Portugal, there was little for them to do but return to their farms and small holdings. (Men of similar caliber were the minor squirearchy and

younger sons of nobility who later served England so well in
the reign of Elizabeth I.) Bearing in mind his mother's injunction to look after the nobly born, Henry was always willing to employ men like Zarco and Teixeira in command of his
ships. They were sufficiently intelligent to understand the objectives that he set them, and later—as the science of navigation developed—they were more capable of learning the uses
of astrolabe, compass, and chart than fishermen sailing-
masters.

With Prince Henry, to think was to act. No sooner had he
visualized the potential importance of this new discovery
than he sent his two captains back again. King John, who had
been told the news—as well as reassured that there could be
no Castilian claim to the island—also saw the strategic value to
Portugal of a colony and outpost in the Atlantic. He gave his
son permission to go ahead with the colonization of Porto
Santo. It was in this matter of colonization that a new development began in European history. The Genoese might have
been content to record the existence of the Madeira group, but
it took the visionary of Sagres to see that an island with good
earth could be cultivated and populated.

A third ship, under the captaincy of another minor nobleman, Bartolomew Perestrello, accompanied Zarco and Teixeira. Perestrello was later to be made governor of Porto Santo.
His name will be remembered in history because a daughter
of his was one day to marry a Genoese, Christopher Columbus, and Columbus for a brief period of his life would live in
Porto Santo. There he would learn all that the old seafarer had
known of Portuguese navigational methods and cartography.
If Columbus has become one of those names with which the
whole world is familiar, the fact remains that the seed of his
knowledge was planted many years before by a Portuguese
prince who refused to accept legends as truth, or superstition
as geography.

Driving out into the Atlantic, the three small ships made their landfall successfully at Porto Santo. This time they took with them seeds and plants, and also a pregnant doe rabbit in a cage. (The introduction of rabbits many centuries later to the subcontinent of Australia was to prove a disaster that might have been foreseen if the history of Porto Santo had been better known.) On a small island where there were no predators, no other animals at all, the rabbits multiplied at an astronomical rate. For the remainder of his life Perestrello was to battle against the ever-increasing hordes, which devastated not only the native vegetation of Porto Santo but the newly planted crops as well.

The island was a little over six miles long, by three wide, and the ships did not take long to circumnavigate it. They charted its bays and coves, recorded its high peaks at either end, and sounded the small bay of Porto Santo, where they established their base. It was during this period that first one man and then another noticed the cloud. It looked rather like a fog bank lying across the sea, to the south of the island.

"That is where the vapors begin," whispered a sailor. "We are at the outermost limits of the world."

"That is no ordinary mist," said another. "Beyond it lies the darkness of which we have been told. Beyond that mist begins the great rush of waters that roar at the world's end."

The three captains in charge of the expedition also noticed the cloud. There was something curious about it, something that had perhaps evaded the sailors.

"This cloud," they told Prince Henry on their return from the second expedition, "is strangely shaped. And it stays in the same place—always southwest of Porto Santo."

Clouds mean islands. Clouds mean night mists rising off wooded slopes, or condensation from the ocean hovering above mountain peaks. Prince Henry knew this; so perhaps did his captains. But—whereas it was comparatively easy for him to command, "Go south! Go farther! I must know more!"—his captains had the difficult task of persuading superstitious and reluctant crews to sail into unknown regions. The sailors would have been only too pleased to be assigned to the ships engaged in harrying the Moorish coast and its merchantmen. They were familiar with the normal risks of warfare, and in warfare there was always the chance of plunder. It was the unknown that terrified them, and—as far as they could see—gave little in return except their poor food and small wages.

It was at about this time that Prince Henry may have heard the remarkable story of the Englishman Robert Machin. Among the sailors in the crew of João Gonçalvez Zarco there was a Spaniard named Juan de Morales, who had at one time been a prisoner of the Moors. During his captivity, so he told Zarco, he had heard from some English fellow prisoners of their accidental discovery of an island in the Atlantic. It was completely uninhabited, they said, fertile, well wooded, and quite large. This description aroused Zarco's interest—for no one could call Porto Santo fertile and well wooded, nor was it large. The Canaries, for their part, were all inhabited. This sounded like an unknown island. The English sailors told Morales that they had been serving aboard a ship out of Bristol. It had been chartered by a young man of good family, called Robert Machin, who was eloping with a married woman named Anne d'Arfet. Machin chartered the boat to take him and his mistress to Spain. Anne d'Arfet's family was a powerful one, and the lovers could not remain together in England. Robert Machin had already been imprisoned by her parents for refusing to cease seeing her.

Not far out from the Bristol Channel, their ship had run into a heavy gale from the northeast. Day after day they had run before it, until they were carried a long way off their course—well to the west of the Bay of Biscay. Then, one morning, after thirteen days at sea, they had found themselves bearing down on a large, well-wooded island. They had anchored there and stayed for several days, making good the damage arising from the storm. Robert Machin and Anne d'Arfet had gone ashore, together with some sailors from the ship, to explore a nearby beach. The ship meanwhile cruised down the coast to make a survey. It was at this moment that another northeaster sprang up, and unable to come back for those ashore, the ship had gone on her way to Spain. Juan de Morales's fellow prisoners were the same men who had been left behind on the island. Anne d'Arfet, they said, had died from exposure and mental distress, and had been buried at the foot of an altar, which they had erected on first landing. A few days later her lover, Robert Machin, also died, and the sailors buried him next to his mistress. Then, having embarked in the ship's boat from which they had landed, they had been carried south by the prevailing winds. They had finally fetched up on the coast of Morocco, where they had been taken prisoner by the Arabs.

If this extraordinary story had fascinated first Morales, and then Zarco, there is no doubt what effect it must have had on Prince Henry. A large, fertile island—and uninhabited— far out in the Atlantic! Such a place would make an ideal base for his ships. His ambitions were still centered on Africa, but already he saw how even an island like Porto Santo could help his purpose.

The combination of the story of Robert Machin and Zarco's report of the cloud on the horizon further determined Prince Henry to send his captain to investigate. It must be remembered that Henry had only the devotion of some of his followers and—to a limited extent—the support of his father in these early ventures. All the time there was a party at court that disliked and distrusted this strange recluse of a prince. His withdrawal to Sagres, his asceticism, and his interest in astronomy and allied sciences seemed an affront to people whose colorful lives were lived in the splendor of the moment. The common people too—even the sailors who worked for him—were uneasy with a personality so alien to their own ways of thinking. It would be many years before the tangible fruits of his genius would be seen in trade with islands and coastlines as yet unknown. By then, both court and commonalty would have acclaimed the "Prince Navigator," and would be eager to join his expeditions—always provided there was the possibility of making some profit out of them. "The genius raids but the common people occupy and possess," wrote T. E. Lawrence, a man who might well have felt some kinship with Prince Henry. But without the raids of genius, the unknown shores, whether spiritual or terrestrial, would never emerge from the darkness.

It was in June, 1420, that João Gonçalves Zarco, having Juan de Morales as pilot aboard his vessel, set sail from Porto Santo in the direction of the cloud. The wind was favorable, the sea calm, and the small ship soon began to drop the familiar island astern. As they drew nearer, the cloud ahead of them thickened until it seemed to the sailors as if it blotted out the whole horizon. They felt the humid mist on the decks and rigging, and crossed themselves. Zarco and Morales peered ahead. They were men of more intelligence and experience than the others, but they too had been brought up in a climate of legend and superstition.

"Do you hear anything?" asked one.

The ship had begun to lift in an uneasy way, as if she felt a new movement of the ocean. It was no longer the swell from the following wind. Her bow began to lift and bump.

"Surf?"

They were feeling the cliff wash from an unknown shore.
"The sea is boiling!" cried the sailors. "Turn back! The
sea is boiling!"

But one man, calmer or more phlegmatic than the rest,
shaded his eyes against the dazzle of sun on mist, and saw a
line of broken water.

"Breakers ahead!"

The mist began to thin and the flapping sail to draw again
in a new light air. The sound of breaking waves was all around
them now.

Suddenly they slid out into the sunlight, and the land was
warm ahead of them. Tall peaks were clothed with forest and
twined with cloud. Streams were falling in silver ribbons
down emerald green, and startled birds were rising in bright
clouds. In front of them lay the friendly arm of a bay. They
had discovered Madeira.

9

Zarco's discovery of Madeira was the first important step in the exploration of the Atlantic. It was the first gleam of light to be cast upon the Sea of Darkness. It would be many years before Prince Henry could induce any of his mariners to round Cape Bojador and sail south of the Canaries down the African coast, but the discovery of Madeira was like the lifting of a curtain.

They called the island Madeira from the Portuguese word for "wood," and it was the dense forests of this fertile, well-watered island that at first seemed to promise the major profit from the discovery. Wood for shipbuilding was essential for a maritime country, and its importance in a thinly forested land like Portugal had been recognized from very early days. So much was this so that, among early edicts, there is one that reads: "Whoever shall cut a pine tree, let them hang him"—pine, then as now, being of great value for the planking of boats.

Prince Henry and his father were delighted with the discovery—the former because he saw in it further proof that his ships could be made to sail where men had always maintained there was nothing but the horrors of ocean, the latter because it justified his trust in his son's endeavors. Zarco was made a count, and the island was divided between him and his fellow captain, Tristão Vaz. The southern half of the island, with Funchal (after the Portuguese word, *funcho*, for fennel, which was found there) as capital, was given to Zarco. The northern half, with Machico (reputedly called after Robert Machin) as capital, was given to Tristão Vaz.

It was not for some five years after its discovery that the colonization proper of the island began. In the meantime, vast areas of the virgin forest had been devastated by a fire which, started deliberately with a view to clearing land for cultivation, soon got out of hand. The fire, so one report has it, burned steadily for seven years. Although at the time this seemed a major disaster, it proved a boon in the end. On the mountain slopes where trees had once grown, the vine took root, and in the fertile valleys enriched by the potash from the wood, the sugar cane flourished. Both of these importations were due to Prince Henry. It was he who sent to Sicily for sugar canes, and it was he who sent to distant Crete for the hardy stock of the malvasia grape. The best wine was ultimately produced near Machico, and it was this malvasia Madeira, corrupted into "malmsey," that later became a favorite tipple of the English. It is an odd thought that countless Englishmen over the centuries have benefited from the foresight and wisdom of the nondrinking, ascetic grandson of John of Gaunt.

In his choice of sugar cane from Sicily and vines from Crete—two islands with climates and soils not so very different from those of Madeira—Henry again revealed the practical streak in his nature.

During the next twenty years, while he was devoting most of his energy to the exploration of Africa—and despite the calls made on his time by successive troubles in Portugal— he never forgot his islands. Monthly returns were expected from his captains, Zarco, Tristão Vaz, and Perestrello, as well as details of the trees, the rocks, the earth, and the progress of viticulture and sugar making.

Only twenty years after the beginnings of colonization the Venetian Cadamosto could write of Madeira: "The whole island is a garden!" The beauty and fertility of the island were such that even the first colonizers, faced with the arduous tasks of tree felling and land cultivation, were conscious that Madeira was something of an earthly paradise. One of them, Gonçalo Ferreira, the first man to have children born on the island, called his son Adam and his daughter Eve.

Despite the pleasure he took in this discovery, Prince Henry regarded it as no more than a by-product of his main ambition. It was still Africa that haunted him—Africa, and Prester John, and the building of a Portuguese Moroccan empire. For the next fourteen years, from 1420 onward, as soon as the summer season was established, he continued to send out a succession of ships. His captains' orders were always the same— to proceed as far south as they could and bring back news of the unknown African coastline. One after another they disappointed him, returning always with the same story that beyond Cape Bojador, "the Bulging Cape," no ship could pass.

For a man devoured by ambition Henry showed an astonishing patience. He knew the limits of his human material. He knew it was only to be expected that his captains, noblemen, and crews should wish to make a profit out of their voyages. He could hardly complain when they came back having captured and sunk Moorish merchantmen from Granada, or when they turned aside into the Mediterranean, called at Ceuta, and then went marauding among the traffic of the North African coast. It was his duty, as grand master of the Order of Christ, to harass the infidel as much as possible. As a man whose income never met his expenditure, he could not openly disapprove of captains who made their voyages pay their way.

"The Prince always welcomed the captains of his ships with great patience, never disclosing any resentment, listening graciously to the stories of their adventures, and rewarding them as men who were serving him well. But immediately he sent them back again to repeat the voyage—either them or others of his household—impressing upon them, more and more strongly, the mission he required them to accomplish. . . ."

Some historians have said that Prince Henry is undeserving of the title "the Navigator" because, except for his two voyages to Ceuta and his later expeditions to Tangier and Alcaçar there is no evidence that he ever went to sea at all. But to deny him the title is as absurd as to deny the title of "general" to a modern field marshal, on the score that he does not personally lead his troops into battle. Henry, as in so much else, was in advance of his time in realizing—perhaps unconsciously—that the controlling brain needs to be remote from the day-to-day strategy.

At Sagres he correlated and combined the talents of many men and welded them into a team. Without his steady perseverance, the Portuguese would never have discovered the Madeira Islands, the Azores, the Cape Verde Islands, or the Guinea coast of Africa. Noblemen financing expeditions—as well as their captains and crews—would have been happy to remain occupied in the lucrative game of piracy on the Granada and Barbary coasts. There was no obvious or immediate profit in Africa. It is these fourteen years of almost fruitless and disillusioning quest that reveal most clearly the iron caliber of Prince Henry's character.

10

The ships in which the early expeditions were made were either barks or *barinales*. The bark was a square-rigged trading vessel common to the period, while the *barinal* was a Portuguese compromise with the Venetian galley. It was an oared vessel, but one that could set a square or lateen sail when the wind blew from anywhere abaft the beam. The difficulty that Prince Henry's mariners experienced in returning to Portugal against the prevailing north winds led to the evolution of the famous caravel.

It was not a completely new type of vessel. Like most ships, it had a long ancestry behind it, and was the product of evolution rather than a startling departure from conventional ship design. One can see today on the Tagus and the Douro small sailing boats that have sometimes been claimed as descendants of the caravel. These are broad-beamed, shallow-draught craft, pine-planked on oak frames, and used for the transport of wine, oil, and general cargo. Sometimes, at sea off the coast of Portugal, one sees them stooping and soaring over the Atlantic rollers, their lateen sails curved above a short mast. They are open boats, or half-decked. Their sailors are short and swarthy, native to the sea, who tend to keep aloof and live some-what apart from their fellow Portuguese. Unlike the fishermen and sailors of most countries, they do not seem to have been assimilated into the twentieth century. Like the *mariniers* of the Rhône barges in France, they are aware of an ancestry and a dedication to a craft that go back over thousands of years.

It seems more likely that these modern craft are not so much a descendant of the caravel as an ancestor. Although beamier, they are very similar to the feluccas of the Arabic Mediterranean, and the dhows of the Red Sea. The lateen sail itself is an Arabic invention.

The vessel native to northern Europe is the high-pooped bark, and to the Mediterranean the oared galley. Both of these have little in common with the caravel, either in rig or in hull shape. The felucca and the dhow, however, do seem closely related. It is very likely that the caravels of Prince Henry's day were derived from these ancient Arabic types of sailing vessel. An early sixteenth-century painting by Gregorio Lopez in the Convent of Madre de Deus, shows a vessel that is prob-ably similar to the caravels in which the early navigators made their epic voyages. The stem is quite graceful, almost yacht-like, with a certain amount of overhang. The general line of the bulwarks shows a gentle sheer. The stern is built up into a poop with an aftercastle, in which is stepped a mizzenmast. The mainmast is a little abaft the center line of the boat, and the vessel has two lateen sails.

Sailing with a lateen rig is comparatively easy compared to working with square sails, with gaff-rigged sails, or even with the modern Bermudian rig. The long wooden yard, which sup-ports the head of the sail, is hoisted on a simple block and tackle. The sail is easily controlled, and one or two men can handle quite a large area of canvas.

Caravels had no topsails to worry about. They had no complicated system of braces as did square-rigged ships, and no intricate sheeting of sails. It was—and is—an efficient rig, as anyone who has ever seen an Arab dhow can confirm. Until the introduction of the fore-and-aft sail plan many centuries later, the lateen was the most efficient rig for small boats. As the Venetian Cadamosto remarked of Prince Henry's caravels, they were "the most seaworthy vessels of their time."

The word "caravel" has passed into modern English usage as "carvel," the term used to denote boats built with flush planking as opposed to "clinker" (with overlapping planking). Caravels were small vessels, and the name was applied to ships of one hundred tons or less. (Columbus applied it to ships of forty tons.) The word "caravel," denoting a small sailing ship, is found as early as the thirteenth century in a Portuguese naval classification. Historians often seem to have been amazed at the smallness of these vessels in which the early navigators made their ocean voyages. The fact is, they were well designed and seaworthy, with a good, easily worked rig. Size has little to do with seaworthiness. (Yachts of ten tons and less quite often cross the Atlantic nowadays.)

The pine, with which they were built, had long been a protected tree in Portugal. This was partly on account of its use in shipbuilding, and partly because the land of Portugal, without its defensive barrier of pine trees, would be invaded by the sand, driven inshore on the steady Atlantic winds. The stone pine was native to the country, and it was particularly suitable for ribs, strakes, and curved pieces. The cluster pine was an importation, traditionally supposed to have been introduced by Isabella, the wife of King Diniz, "the Farmer King," in the thirteenth century. Valuable for its resin, which was used in calking the hulls, the cluster pine also provided good straight wood for planking. As in England, oak was used for the keels. Lisbon, Porto, and Lagos—close to Sagres—were the main shipbuilding centers, noisy with the thud of adzes on wood, and lively with attendant trades like sailmaking and ropemaking.

The early caravels were probably between forty and one hundred tons. But, even before the death of Prince Henry, they had increased in size, and when they exceeded one hundred tons or more, often stepped a third and even a fourth mast. These later vessels had a composite rig—lateen on the mizzen and main masts, and square sails on the foremast. Sixty to ninety feet long, with a beam of twenty to thirty feet, caravels were well-proportioned ships. Their broad beam allowed them to be comparatively shallow-drafted, and this was to prove an enormous advantage when working along the African shore in uncharted and often shallow waters. So efficient were they that in later years a legend grew up that only Portuguese-built ships were capable of navigating off the African coast. It was a legend that remained unassailed until the Elizabethan adventurers took their West-country ships into those waters, and challenged the Portuguese supremacy.

If the caravel owed something of its rig to the Arabs, and its hull form to the working boats of the Tagus and Douro, it probably owed its axled, hinged rudder to the north. (This great advance in ship design seems to have originated in the Baltic.) The axled rudder made for easy maneuverability, and the helmsman could be sited below, or under cover. The caravel seems, in fact, to have been a brilliant composite: adapting local shipbuilding methods and hull design to modifications learned from both north and south.

The two-masted caravel was very similar to the modern ketch rig, with its divided sail area, and the ketch—as amateur sailors can confirm—is perhaps the best design for ocean-going small boats. In windward work, the caravel was far superior to any sailing vessel of its time. It was this that enabled Prince Henry's ships not only to coast down Africa, but also to sail back again against the prevailing winds. Once Cape Bojador had been rounded, and once the caravel had been evolved, its windward ability must have increased the sailors' confidence. They no longer felt that they were condemned to blow down in front of the wind without hope of return.

What instruments and what charts had these early seafarers? For centuries, Mediterranean sailors had practiced coastal navigation in known waters. Rarely out of sight of land, they had reasonably accurate charts of the Mediterranean, and they relied on those three stand-bys of pilotage—log, lead, and look-out. For centuries too, seamen had been running between the Mediterranean and northern countries like England, Holland, and the Baltic states. Again, the shape of the Atlantic coastline of Europe was well known. But when it came to venturing south into the Atlantic, along a coastline of which there was no verbal record—let alone any charts—the problems became increasingly difficult. As the ships ran ever farther and farther south, the question of knowing their latitude accurately became all-important.

In the Mediterranean, most of the sailing was east and west. The sea being comparatively narrow from north to south, latitude had never been a major problem. Again, on the northern route between the Spanish peninsula and Britain, the ship's captain knew that so long as he did not diverge too far west from his north-south line, he was bound to sight the expected coast. (It was a divergence too far west that, if one credits the story, led to Robert Machin's discovery of Madeira.) But latitude was a problem that Henry's navigators had to solve. Longitude did not trouble them so much—and longitude in any case would not be accurately measured until the eighteenth century, when the English horologist John Harrison perfected his marine chronometer. Apart from the need to know their latitude, ships' captains also had to know their compass course.

By Prince Henry's time the compass was quite efficient. Many countries have laid claim to being the birthplace of the magnetic compass—Arabia, China, France, Greece, Italy, and Palestine, among them. All that can be said with any certainty is that it probably originated in the Orient and that the knowledge of it infiltrated from the Levant throughout the European maritime nations. England, curiously enough, which has never made any claims to being the compass's country of origin, has left us the first written description of a compass. It is to be found in the work of the twelfth-century monk Alexander Neckham. In two of his treatises he describes a pivoted compass needle, and it is probable that he gained his information at the University of Paris, where he studied between 1180 and 1186.

Prince Henry's navigators would have had a simple magnetic compass in a binnacle—*bitácula* is the Portuguese word, probably from the Latin *habitaculum*, "a little dwelling." They were also familiar with the constancy of the Pole Star as a northern reference point, for men had been using the Pole Star in navigation since classical times.

The compass in a caravel was kept in a small wooden binnacle, lit at night by a lamp burning whale or olive oil. Nearby, and often enclosed in the binnacle itself, was the hourglass—the only time-keeping device then available at sea. Clocks had been in use for over a century, but they were still rarities —and still totally unsuited for use in a small vessel. A ship's boy kept a watch alongside the helmsman. It was his duty to maintain the lamps and the binnacle light, as well as to watch the hourglass; reversing it when the sand had run out and calling out the hour. A grave offense, and punishable by flogging, was the trick of "warming the glass," when the boy either held the hourglass near the lamp or put it inside his shirt to warm.

The result was that the thin glass expanded, the sand ran through faster—and the long, tedious watch was shortened.

The Pole Star was known to sailors as the *Stella Maris* (Star of the Sea), and this name was often given to the compass itself. Felix Faber, a monk writing about twenty years after the death of Prince Henry, described a voyage he made to Palestine, and the way in which the vessel was steered. ". . . They have a compass, a *Stella Maris*, near the mast, and a second one on the topmast deck of the poop. Beside it all night long a lantern burns. There is a man constantly watching the Star (the compass card) and he never takes his eyes off it. He sings out a pleasant tune, telling that all goes well, and in the same chant directs the man at the tiller, telling him how to turn the rudder. The helmsman dares not move the tiller in the slightest degree, except at the orders of the man who watches the Stella Maris. . . ."

If the compass was a familiar instrument in Prince Henry's time, it was still held in some awe by the superstitious seamen. Many legends were attached to the lodestone itself. If it was placed beneath the pillow of an adulterous wife, it would make her confess her guilt. It was also used in the treatment of various illnesses, and was reputed to be efficacious as a contraceptive. It was sometimes maintained that the lodestone's powers were nullified by garlic, and it had even been suggested that sailors should be forbidden to eat that sovereign plant, so dear to Latin hearts.

If the compass still retained something of its aura of legend, the craft of the navigator was suitably dignified by being termed an art and mystery. Reasonably accurate charts of the Mediterranean and of the Atlantic seaboard of Europe had been current for a good many years. The oldest surviving maritime chart is the *Carta Pisana* dated about 1275. Even by this time, a scale and a wind rose were provided by the cartographer, so we know that a ruler and dividers had already become part of the navigator's equipment.

By the early fourteenth century the chartmakers of Genoa were well known throughout Europe, and the Catalan Jews of Mallorca were equally famous for their scientific knowledge and accurate draftsmanship. An outstanding figure of the period just prior to Prince Henry was Abraham Cresques of Mallorca, described as *"Magister Mappamundorum et Buxalorum,"* a "master of charts and compasses." His son Jaime Cresques was one of the leading cartographers whom Henry induced to come and settle at Sagres. Jaime Cresques joined the Prince's court a year or so after the discovery of Madeira. From then on he was engaged in research, in chart making, and in helping the Prince to correlate the information brought in by his sea captains. There is no doubt that he would also have brought with him from Mallorca mathematical tables, similar to those mentioned by Ramon Lull a century earlier, with which—by the calculation of rhumb lines—sailors could work out their mileage while at sea.

Henry's captains and navigators had in the seaman's astrolabe a fairly efficient instrument for obtaining their position by sun or star altitudes. Like so much else connected with the mathematical sciences, the astrolabe may have originated with the Arabs. We know from Marco Polo in the early fourteenth century that the Arabs had long been using a simple instrument called the *kamal* for star observations.

The astronomer's astrolabe was a costly and elaborate but accurate instrument. It was well known by the fifteenth century, but was unsuited for use at sea. From it was developed a seaman's version, with a simple scale of degrees for measuring the height of sun or star. It was this type of instrument that the Portuguese navigators used in their Atlantic and African explorations.

This was the beginning of a new era of navigation. At Lagos, Lisbon, or Sagres, the navigator became familiar with the tools of his trade, and took altitudes of the sun or stars at his home port. Then, as he sailed south, he noted the changing altitudes at various points along his route. As new capes, headlands, and bays were discovered, so Prince Henry's navigators "fixed" them for latitude. At a later date, they were also provided with a table of daily solar noon altitudes at their point of departure. By comparing the difference in the sun's altitude at noon between his home port and his present position, he was able to work out his difference in latitude. For longitude he was still compelled to rely on dead reckoning—his own estimation, from log and sea knowledge, of his ship's position.

The Portuguese navigators still hugged the coast as much as possible. Their instruments were not reliable, they were constructing their charts as they went along, and their shallow-draft vessels allowed them to work close inshore. When they came to a new point or headland, the obvious thing was to go ashore, with astrolabe and tables, and take the sun's altitude at noon from dry land. The heaving deck of a caravel was no place for accurate measurement with an awkward instrument. Even today, with the simple modern sextant, easy astronomical tables, and accurate charts, taking a star or sun sight can be difficult in a small boat.

These were the ships and these the navigational aids with which the Portuguese opened up the world. With each new voyage, their captains were gradually learning their deep-sea trade, and their crews were growing used to the wide spaces of the unknown ocean. Yet fourteen years went by, and the success of which Prince Henry dreamed continued to evade him. Cape Bojador, the Outstretcher, still barred the way, and still his seamen maintained that beyond that point no ship could sail.

11

Farther from the mainland than any other group of Atlantic islands, the Azores lie 800 miles almost due west from Cape St. Vincent. They lift their rocky, volcanic heads out of the depths of the Atlantic. Part of neither Europe, nor Africa, nor America, they are the peaks of immense volcanoes rising sheer out of the sea. Like Madeira and Porto Santo, their existence had been known in the fourteenth century. But they too had remained as no more than a hazard marked on one or two charts —a hazard that had been forgotten until Prince Henry's cartographers brought it to his notice.

It was in 1431 that he sent out Gonçalo Velho Cabral, with orders to find the missing islands. It was the fair summer season with the northerly winds broad on the beam, an easy point of sailing, so seamen call it a "soldier's wind." Hour after hour they sailed due west into the Atlantic, and every evening the sun went down ahead of them, in line with the ship's bows.

Several days and nights went by and the crew grew uneasy. Then, one morning, they sighted curling mists, and heard the hiss of breakers on rocks. They had chanced upon the easternmost of the Azores, the lonely barren rock of Formigas. Cabral circled the area cautiously and then put about. He returned to Sagres and reported that he had found only this rocky outcrop. He suggested that the large islands of which they had been told must be a myth. Now Gonçalo Cabral was a man of courage and ability, and he had every reason to believe that the Prince's instructions were based on solid fact. It seems more than likely, therefore, that it was a reluctant or mutinous crew that forced him to retire after this first encounter with the outriders of the Azores.

Prince Henry thanked him, rewarding him and his company for their discovery.

"But next year you must go back again," he said. "Now that you know land exists in that part of the ocean, you must search farther."

Rich and fertile Madeira had been discovered only after the small and somewhat disappointing island of Porto Santo. If there were rocks out there in the ocean, then that was an indication of some land mass rising to the surface. No doubt, before he left Formigas, Cabral's sailors would have taken soundings round the rocks, and everywhere they would have reported "No bottom." This might have convinced him that it was an isolated peak. But the absence of soundings would not really have been surprising, for the volcanic peaks of the Azores rise almost sheer out of two and a half miles of ocean.

In 1432 Cabral sailed for the second time into the summer Atlantic. He had been urged to try farther west. He made his landfall correctly—proof of the accuracy of his navigation, for Formigas is only the smallest spot in the Atlantic. (It would hardly be a disgrace for a small-boat sailor to fail to make such a landfall today.) Then they freed the sheets, and cast off a little to the southwest. Soon they saw cloud ahead of them, the soft drifting cloud that denotes land and humid earth. Twenty miles west of Formigas they found a fertile island. It was warm under the sun, barren of life save birds, but rich like Madeira in trees. Water came tumbling down the hillsides, and there were valleys where corn and crops might ripen. They raised the new island on August 15, the feast of the Assumption, and they called it Santa Maria.

Santa Maria was the first of the nine principal islands of the Azores to be discovered by Prince Henry's navigators. It may well be that Genoese, or other seamen on the northern route, had sighted the islands centuries before. The fact remains that it was not until Cabral and his successors reached them that the islands were accurately charted, made use of, and colonized. The Portuguese called them the *Açores,* from the word for "hawks," for which they mistook the sea birds that were hovering over the headlands.

During the years that followed, first one island and then another was dredged out of the uncertain limits of the Atlantic. As in the case of Madeira, Prince Henry's policy was a completely practical one. Cattle, crops, and men were sent out to populate the islands. Within a few years, not one ship, but many, grew to know the way the clouds swaggered over the mountain peaks. The men became familiar with those soft warm seas where the whale and porpoise foam out of the wave crests.

By 1457, three years before Prince Henry's death, the last of the main islands—the northern group of Corvo and Flores —had been added to the charts. While the colonization of Madeira went steadily ahead, and while Henry was often involved in campaigns abroad or in home politics, the Azores continued to be transformed. From virgin soil, benefited by an indulgent climate, they became rich in cattle, fruit, and vines. Small towns grew up, the port of Horta in Fayal—the best natural harbor in the islands—and Villa Franca (later to be destroyed by earthquake) in San Miguel. The volcanic

soil was excellent for vine growing, and in the extinct craters
of the islands there were lakes of crystal-clear water. As well
as whale, porpoise, and dolphin, the sea was well stocked with
tunny, bonito, and mullet. The pine, introduced from Portugal,
the poplar, elm, and oak took root and flourished. Life was
harsh for the early settlers, and the volcanic nature of the islands often made it terrifying, but the mild climate compen-
sated for many things. Peasant farmers found the land as easy
to work as their native fields, and the fishermen learned that—
except when the westerlies blew—it was ideal for coastal fishing. The islands were steep-to, gales comparatively rare, and
the light land and sea breezes, drawing between one rocky
island and another, made small-boat sailing easy.

In 1433 King John of Portugal died. He was seventy-seven.
His reign had been one of almost continuous success, not only
on the field of battle, but also in domestic politics and in the
increasing prosperity of Portugal. In some respects he resem-
bles Henry VII of England for the way in which he welded
together a nation, and created security for his country. His
achievements in other spheres were equally important. He
had founded some of the finest buildings in Portugal: the
Church of Our Lady of Batalha, in memory of the victory of
Aljubarrota; the palaces of Cintra, Lisbon, and Santarém; and
the Franciscan monastery of Carnota. He had reformed the
country's laws, caused the gospels to be translated into Portuguese, and had been a Latin scholar in his own right. He left
behind him five sons who were respected and loved throughout
the country. His private life had been happy. His death came
at a moment of further achievement, when his favorite son's
ships had just uncovered new islands in the Atlantic. Legend
has it that, with his last words, he exhorted Prince Henry to
continue his explorations into Africa and the war against the
infidel.

Henry had loved his father, but he had felt his ambition increasingly restrained by him in his later years. That canny ability to know just when "enough is enough" had served King John in good stead all his life. It had also become—to Prince Henry's mind—a die-hard conservatism that militated against his own ambitious schemes. It was King John who had ordered him to leave Gibraltar alone after the second expedition to Ceuta. It was King John who had prevented him from making an armed expedition against the Canaries and winning them for the Portuguese crown. Now that the restraining influence of his father was removed, Prince Henry saw in his brother Edward a king who was more pliable.

After King Edward's coronation, Henry returned once more to Sagres. He was thirty-nine years old, in the prime of his life, a man of power—Governor of Ceuta, Governor of the Algarve province, Lord of Covilham, and Duke of Viseu—and a man with a mission. In his maturity he felt even more the certainty of purpose that he had known so many years ago when, as a young prince, he had urged his father to the conquest of Ceuta. Azurara, who entered the Royal Library early in the reign of King Edward, described Prince Henry at this period of his life:

"He was a thickset man, of medium height, with large powerful limbs and thick hair. His skin was white, but the hardship and battles of life altered it as the years went by. Those who met him for the first time were struck by the austerity of his face. When he was seized by anger—which happened rarely—his expression was awe-inspiring. He had intelligence and strength of mind to a high degree, and his desire to achieve great deeds was without comparison. Avarice and lust never obtained a hold on his heart. As for the second of these vices, he was so continent that he preserved the most perfect chastity all his life. His body was virgin when it was

laid in the earth. What can I say of his magnificence, which
was exceptional among all the world's princes! In his house
every man of the realm who had any merit was always welcomed. This was equally the case with distinguished foreigners, for he nearly always had men from different countries in
his company. Some of them came from very distant lands, and
all of them held him in admiration. Nor did any of them ever
leave his service without receiving many benefits.

"All his days were filled with ceaseless labor. I am sure that
among all the nations of mankind one would not be able to
find another man so trained in self-discipline. It would be
hard to count the nights during which he never slept, and his
body was so subjected to self-denial that it seemed to find a
new nature for itself. His perseverance in his work was such
that, even as the poets have imagined Atlas sustaining the
heavens on his shoulders, so the people of Portugal regarded
the labors of this prince as surpassing even the highest mountains. Things which seemed impossible to other men were rendered easy by his steady persistence. A man of excellent
counsel and of authority, he was slow in certain things—perhaps because his nature was phlegmatic, or because those about
him did not always understand his motives. Quiet in manner
and calm in speech, he was constant in adversity and humble
in prosperity."

The ideal of the ascetic life, which Prince Henry held before him, is remote from our own age. More and more the
world inclines to the view that the aim of human life is comfort, sensual pleasure, and material acquisitions. The medieval
Christian belief that mortification of the flesh, asceticism, and
celibacy were aids in training the spirit, tends to be regarded
as a mental aberration in the twentieth century. But without
some knowledge of the climate of thought in which Prince
Henry was raised, it is impossible to understand him. Although

the achievements of his life played an important part in the Renaissance of Europe, he was medieval in his faith. He would almost certainly have agreed with Honorius of Augsburg, who described the economic life of man as "nothing but the struggle of wolves over carrion"—Honorius, who thought that men of business could hardly be saved, for they lived by cheating and profiteering. Henry would no doubt also have agreed that "it is monasticism par excellence which, by repudiating the prizes and temptations of the material world, is the true life of religion." If he sought a material empire in Africa, it would not be untrue to say that he sought it largely because in that way he could win souls.

It was in the summer after his father's death that Prince Henry called before him a native of Lagos, Gil Eannes, a squire in his court at Sagres. Gil Eannes had been sent on a mission of exploration the previous year. Like so many of the Prince's captains, he had disappointed his master, turning aside to carry out a little piracy in the Canary Islands and to capture some of the unfortunate natives. Gil Eannes, and others before him, had already disproved the old legends attached to the once invincible Cape Nam or Not. He had sailed past it by 30 miles, but he had shirked his prince's order to continue south and round Cape Bojador.

It is easy to deride the superstitions and credulity of these early sailors, yet even today the Sahara coast is one of the bleakest and most uninviting parts of the world. Under the burning sun of noon the vast plateau heaves and shimmers with mirage. Barren and burned, devoid of almost all vegetation, the land runs down in a glow of ocherish sand to the sea. In places it ends in sandy cliffs, which, disturbed by strong winds, fall with a rumbling crash into the Atlantic and stain the sea with red. The waters are shallow, the depths constantly shifting, and ships still give the coast a wide berth. After one of the constant cliff falls, the sea seems to boil until the debris slowly dissolves. Currents are strong and uncertain, the winds light—or hot and violent, when the harmattan whirls off the desert. It is a cruel landscape, and it is not difficult to believe that in this region life has come to an end. There is no indication that hundreds of miles to the south a green and well-watered land surrounds great rivers like the Senegal.

Eannes, no doubt, produced the arguments with which Prince Henry had long been familiar—how the sea was too shallow for navigation, and how the water boiled as you neared Cape Bojador. As is often the case with old legends, there was a substratum of truth to this—for the sea does sometimes seem to boil just off Cape Bojador. At the foot of the cape there is a reef over which the sea breaks even in calm weather, and—when the northerly swell meets the offshore breeze—the breakers burst and spout in high foaming clouds. Running down from the north, with the land quivering with heat on the one hand and the limitless ocean on the other, it is easy to understand how the lifting swell and foam off the redoubtable cape seemed like an ocean that was steaming. The second curious phenomenon along this part of the coast is due to the great shoals of sardine that suddenly rise, bright and silver, to the surface. The dappling hiss and flicker of a large sardine shoal can be heard and seen some distance away, and the sea seethes like water in a caldron.

Gil Eannes had probably seen some of these occurrences along that desolate shore. He would certainly have heard of others. No doubt he produced them all in support of his argument that the cape was impassable.

Prince Henry heard him out and replied:

"If there were any authority for these stories, I could find some excuse. But I am amazed at your taking them seriously! What surprises me is that you should pay any attention to the reports of a few sailors—the type of men who know only the coast of Flanders and one or two well-known ports—men who are too ignorant to be able to navigate by compass or by chart!"

He reminded Eannes it was because he had confidence in him that he had given him the captaincy of this ship.

"Go back again," he said. "I want only one thing from you —that you pass Cape Bojador. If you do no more than that you will have both honor and reward."

In the summer of 1434 the ship slipped away from Portugal and sailed for Cape Bojador. After a few days the long and level coast came up ahead. From Sagres to Cape Not is 500 miles, about a week's sail in the small *barcha* commanded by Gil Eannes.

Day by day as they drew farther south, the sun stood higher overhead at noon, the pitch turned tacky in the deck planking or rose up in shining black bubbles along the topsides. Under the shadow of the sails the men took their rest and ate their meals. They had lemons and olives in barrels, wine, dried fish, salted meat, cheese, and ship's biscuits. Biscuit was a staple part of the sailor's diet, and the royal ovens at Lisbon produced a thousand tons yearly—a man's daily ration of biscuits being about two pounds. It was a thirsty diet, but not too ill-designed for hot weather, for the fruit and wine balanced the salty meat, and fresh fish could always be caught.

As they neared Cape Not, Gil Eannes and his veterans knew where they were without reference to chart or sights. The water took on a red, muddy color as if they were off shoal ground, although the leadsman continued to report plenty of water under the keel. Just below the cape, a river, spawned in the Atlas Mountains 500 miles away, washes down the red Sahara sand into the sea. The daily offshore breeze adds a further sprinkling of sand, so that a ship's track is visible in the water, like the mark of a stick dragged through mud.

They noticed now how the current set them down toward the cape, and they altered course seaward to clear it. The nights were fine and the stars brilliant. Their wake was a milky pathway of phosphorescence, and porpoises leapt alongside the ship with long snorting sighs.

The water changed again as they ran farther down and neared the high sand hills of the next cape. Here it was a strange bottle-green in color, for the sea bed was formed of a dark, almost black, sand—quite unlike the rest of the coast-line. Day and night the flying fish were with them. They saw few birds, though, until they were near the latitude of the Canary Islands. Then they sighted the nearest island, Fuerte-ventura, dark as a whale's back on the western horizon. To the east the sand still shimmered, and the heat blew off the desert in hot dry blasts like the opening of an oven door.

Now they were at the limits of man's knowledge, bound for the dreaded Outstretcher, Bojador, the last arm of land in all the world. One hundred miles south of the Canary Islands it lies, a low sandy cape, deep red under the sun, and sliding into the sea in a confusion of breaking waves.

When the cape came in sight, Gil Eannes gave the orders for the ship to stand well out from the coast. Whatever un-natural hazards might lie ahead, at any rate he was not going to lose his ship through running onto a sandbank. So they sailed on a day and a night further, and then altered course and tacked back toward the shore. As they ran in again, on a hot midsummer day with only the sound of the sea and the sigh of the wind in the shrouds, the sailors gathered in the bows and shaded their eyes. Slowly the coast came up ahead of them, the same coast it seemed that they had known for days. As they drew nearer and nearer, they saw that there was one great difference. Away to the south of them the land ran on, flat, sandy, and shining under the sun—a level land with no cape breaking its steady sweep. They looked north and saw that they had passed the impassable limit! They had rounded Cape Bojador!

It was almost as if a wall had fallen down—a barrier to man's progress that had held him back for centuries. Sailing down this coast today, Cape Bojador seems to be no more than another bleak headland interrupting a coastline that is as monotonous as the desert dunes. But it was what the cape had represented that was important. If the discovery and charting of Madeira had marked a great advance in man's knowledge of his planet, the rounding of Bojador altered his whole approach to life. More than a cape was passed by Gil Eannes. A whole era of superstition fell away—much as the sand cliffs along this coast collapse and vanish without trace into the ocean.

They crossed the hundred-fathom line and came into soundings. The leadsman stood on the swaying deck of the small ship, while Gil Eannes and the helmsman watched the compass. They looked ahead and saw the water change color—first deep blue, then blue, then pale, then sand-and-white where the swell burst on the shore. They dropped anchor off the silent beach. The ship turned and swung, lying part to the wind and part to the current that sweeps along that coast. A boat was lowered and Gil Eannes was rowed ashore.

There was no sign of life. As far as the eye could see, the desert shook under the sun. The boat's keel scraped a thin wavering track in virgin sand. They looked about them and saw nothing. And then, clustered along a ridge of sand, Gil Eannes noticed a line of frail plants twisting in the wind. He went over to them, stooped—and recognized them. They were the plants known in Portugal as the roses of St. Mary. They seemed little enough return, perhaps, for all the effort, the expense, and all the fear that rounding Cape Bojador had entailed. He bent down and picked them. They were proof at any rate that, barren though the land was, it was still a land, not so unlike his own. He showed them to the sailors.

"St. Mary's roses!"

Eannes could not quite understand why it had been so important to round Cape Bojador, but he knew that in some way it was. He felt slightly ashamed of the fears that had possessed him. It was only another cape after all. He knew that the sight of the plants would please Prince Henry. He ordered the sailors to box them carefully and keep them safe until their return to Sagres.

12

The rounding of Cape Bojador inspired Prince Henry's captains, navigators, and sailors. It also confirmed his trust in the scientific approach to exploration. From 1434 onward—the year of Gil Eannes's achievement—we hear no more of "impossibilities" in the conquest of the ocean. Gradually, as cape after cape was left behind, and as the men became more and more familiar with deep-sea voyaging and with the tools of their trade, the chronicles of their voyages assume an almost matter-of-fact tone.

The "boiling" ocean, the flood of waters at the world's end, the magnetic rocks that drew the fastenings out of ships—all these stories were soon forgotten. No doubt too, in the normal way of human nature, the sailors were eager to forget the superstitions that had once oppressed them. Later generations forgot them altogether, or, if they read of them, laughed at the credulity of their forebears. But one thing that should not be forgotten is the debt the world owes to the man of Sagres. Without his encouragement, and without his passionate belief in the rational explanation of natural wonders, the course of history would have been different.

Some historians incline to the theory that the "great" men of history are no more than gifted figures standing at the head of general and popular movements. But this is not the case with Prince Henry of Portugal. He represented no general trend of thinking, no popular movement—the antithesis, in fact. Until a little profit began to come back to Portugal from Madeira, the Azores, and the African ventures, he was generally held to be a fanatical monomaniac. No group of courtiers or of merchants backed his enterprises.

There was not even any population pressure in Portugal driving the race to seek new lands. It was the reverse, in fact, for the country was very much underpopulated. One of the chief criticisms leveled at Prince Henry in his lifetime was that he took men away from a country that urgently needed them, to populate remote islands and to engage in apparently unproductive ventures by sea. From the Portuguese point of view the criticism is well justified. The nations that later benefited from the Portuguese pioneers were Spain, France, England, and Holland—which had men and money to spare on overseas adventures.

In the histories of these countries, Prince Henry usually occupies no more than a few lines, or a footnote. It is time perhaps that history was rewritten and revalued—from a world, and not from a national, point of view. Such an action would certainly lead to some strange changes in the Hall of Fame. This fifteenth-century Portuguese prince, little known in English-speaking countries, might well stand higher than Francis Drake or Christopher Columbus—two men who reaped where he had sown. Prince Henry's real achievement, which begins to be apparent from the year in which Cape Bojador was doubled, was that he set in motion the process of continuous exploration. It is a process that takes on a new meaning today as man reaches out toward the stars.

The activity at Sagres continued. Now that more and more ships were bound south for Africa, the importance of this southern base increased. It had always been Henry's hope that he would be able to establish at Sagres a new port that would gradually monopolize the African trade. He had visualized the merchandise from Ceuta and Morocco being landed in the bay, and being distributed from there all over Portugal. For two reasons, this never took place: Sagres was too near Lagos, which was already established as an efficient port and ship repair yard; and the Bay of Sagres was unsuitable for ships other than galleys or light-draft caravels. These could anchor here during the summer months, with adequate shelter from the north. But for nearly six months of the year the bay was dangerously open to the strong southerly gales. Apart from this, the trade that he had hoped would flow through Ceuta to the benefit of Portugal never came. It dried up at source as the Mohammedans diverted it to Tangier. Prince Henry had always realized that this might happen, and it was for this reason that he had for so long pressed his father to allow him to complete the operation by taking Gibraltar, and then Tangier.

The fact that Sagres was doomed to failure as a trading port escaped most people's notice for a long time. So redoubtable was the Prince's reputation for making a success of everything he put his hand to that the Genoese—hearing he was building a port at Sagres—were quick to make a bid for it. Azurara comments drily: "And the Genoese, as you know, are not people who venture their money unless they have great hope of gain." Prince Henry ignored the offer, but a treaty was concluded with Genoa, making Sagres an open port for Italian shipping.

Meanwhile, the long walls of the fortress went up. After 1437 a chapel was built for the mariners. A hospital was added, and quarters where seamen, merchants, and other attendants of the court could live. It is doubtful whether there was ever a navigation school, as such, on Sagres. There was indeed an austere building that no other prince would have called a palace. There were chart makers, instrument makers, and men from many countries who had information to give in return for the Prince's hospitality. There is little doubt that at Sagres Henry's sea captains learned from men like Jaime Cresques how to use their navigational instruments efficiently, and how to plot the positions of the new capes and bays that they were uncovering along the African coast. But Sagres was always more of an advance headquarters (a "field G.H.Q." one might almost term it) than a true permanent base. After Prince Henry's death, work on the buildings was abandoned, and the "City of the Prince" stood half finished until its destruction was completed in the sixteenth century when Sir Francis Drake stormed the citadel and carried away its guns as trophies. The trade with Africa and the East, which developed so rapidly in the last part of the century, went to Lagos or Lisbon.

Today the bleached bones of the buildings, the susurrus of the sea, and the rinsed air driving off the Atlantic induce a feeling of melancholy:

> My name is Ozymandias, king of kings;
> Look on my works, ye Mighty, and despair!
> Nothing beside remains. . . .

But then, turning seaward and gazing out across the Atlantic, one sees a monument to Prince Henry more lasting than any buildings, or any statues of bronze or stone. There, a few miles away, off Cape St. Vincent, the ocean trade routes of the world converge. Liners, merchantmen, and vast oil tankers are passing. Outward or homeward bound, they come from every ocean and every country—a living monument to Prince Henry.

If Sagres failed as a port, it was a useful anchorage for ships fitting out for, or returning from, the summer explorations of the African coast. The fact that the Genoese were interested in the Prince's new city and harbor must have reached the ears of the merchants of Lisbon and Porto. Certainly in later years, when the importation of African slaves had begun to make such voyages profitable, these merchants were eager to put their capital into ships and expeditions. If they always expected their own voyages to pay their way, they had a good reason for hoping that the Prince's more remote expeditions would succeed. It was no secret that he was trying, among other things, to establish contact with Prester John and the countries of the East. The merchants' interest in such possibilities was neither theological nor geographical, and Henry himself must always have been aware that if only his seamen could establish contact with the Orient, he would no longer be worried by the financing of his expeditions. If trade could be established by sea direct with India and the Spice Islands, then Portugal would become the richest nation in Europe.

The economic reason that prompted these voyages was the great demand for spices in Europe, where they were essential for preserving meat during the long winters. Spices were important as seasonings for varying the monotonous diet of the time, and also for their supposed value as medicines. Pepper, for instance, was used as a preservative for meat, and was also highly valued as a sovereign remedy for colds and similar complaints. So valuable was pepper, in fact, that it was often used in negotiations instead of money—a fact of which we are reminded in the English expression "a peppercorn rent." Camphor, cloves, ginger, nutmeg, and mace were all valued by the apothecaries of the time. Camphor taken in red wine was reputed to be an excellent aphrodisiac, and ginger was prized as a remedy for stomach ailments.

The European demand for spices placed the Mohammedan powers in a happy position, for nothing could pass from East to West except by their permission—and at their price. Early in the fourteenth century, the Sultan of Egypt had passed a decree making it compulsory for all spices to be transmitted through Cairo, and shortly after this he had granted permission to the Venetians to trade in Cairo and Alexandria. The price paid in Europe for spices was controlled, then, firstly by the Mohammedans, and secondly by their Venetian intermediaries. Apart from causing the cost to soar, it was also a long time before the spices from the East arrived in their European markets. (It took two years, from leaving the Moluccas, for cloves and nutmeg to reach the merchants of Mincing Lane in London.)

Long before the Portuguese merchants saw the economic point of their Prince's attempts to establish contact with the East, Henry had realized in what a fine strategic position his country would stand if only he could outflank the Venetian traders. He knew well how many Mediterranean cities had grown rich on the profits of the spice trade—not only Venice herself, but also Amalfi, Marseilles, Genoa, Barcelona, Narbonne, Nîmes.

Seven years before Prince Henry's death, when the Turks captured Constantinople and imposed an edict forbidding all trade with Christians, the situation in Europe became acute. It is difficult to imagine nowadays how desperate it was, and the only parallel one can draw is to imagine that some foreign power is suddenly able to prevent the sale of 75 per cent of our medicines and drugs, and nearly all the means whereby we conserve our meat. The situation was finally remedied when first Bartolomew Dias, and then Vasco da Gama, rounded the Cape of Good Hope and made contact with India and the East. Gil Eannes, when he rounded Cape Bojador, sounded the knell not for Venice alone, but for many a Mediterranean maritime state as well. Once the superstitions attached to the Atlantic had vanished like a mist before the trade winds, it was only a question of time before the ocean routes of the world were open to all adventurous seamen.

As an essential step toward his ambitions, Prince Henry saw that he needed another base on the coast of Africa. True, he had Ceuta, but Ceuta was in the Mediterranean and he needed a port somewhere on the Atlantic coast of Morocco. Tangier was clearly the ideal place. It was a good anchorage in almost all weathers, the city was prosperous, and it commanded the western approaches to the Strait of Gibraltar. Even before his father's death he had had his eye on Tangier, and now with his brother Edward on the throne he saw his way to getting his desires translated into action.

King Edward was not averse to the idea of a further expedition against the Moors. A pacific man by nature, he was at the same time eager to add glory to his reign and to emulate his father's achievements. He remembered too that King John in his last years, and even on his deathbed, had urged his sons to prosecute the just and holy war against the infidel. Edward knew that Ceuta was already a drain on the country's economy, and he saw that only by extending their conquests could the Portuguese hope to derive any profit from Morocco. He may at times have considered giving up Ceuta, but no doubt dismissed it as unthinkable in the light of its prestige value. What would the courts of Europe say if he gave away the crowning glory of his father's life?

There is no doubt that his brother Peter urged him to this course. Peter had returned in 1428 from several years of travel throughout Europe and the Near East. In 1429, the year after Edward married Leonora of Aragon, Peter also married, intending to settle down on his estates. It was to him that King Edward looked for advice and help on the many problems that confronted him in ruling the kingdom. On the subject of Moroccan enterprises, Prince Peter was adamant. They were a drain on the country's manpower and resources, and they brought no benefit to the peasants—even if they did enable the nobility to distinguish themselves and gain a certain meretricious glory. On the subject of discovery and exploration he agreed with Prince Henry, but when it came to the dream of a Moroccan empire, he could see no benefit in it. The two elder brothers were thus divided on the question, and during the years 1433 to 1436, when the proposed expedition against Tangier was being canvassed among the family and their advisers, it was around Prince Peter that the opposition rallied.

It was unfortunate for family relationships that Prince Peter had married a daughter of the Count of Urgel. The Count of Urgel had been a claimant to the throne of Aragon and the rival, therefore, of Queen Leonora's father. In the balance of conflicting interests that surrounded the Tangier expedition, the hostility of King Edward's wife to her sister-in-law proved important. Queen Leonora was also jealous of the influence that this much-traveled brother exerted over her husband. Prince Peter's references to the manners and customs of other countries, his suggestions as to how various matters might be changed in the court or in Portugal, all seemed to her to infringe on her husband's authority. For the recluse of Sagres, on the other hand, she had nothing but admiration and affection.

Henry was courteous, polite, and unfailingly respectful to women. Also, like many confirmed bachelors, he doted on children. He—who wrote in his will, "I have no child of my own, nor do I expect to have any"—played the indulgent

uncle to Leonora's children. He was already godfather to her
second son, Fernando, and in 1437 he took the small boy as
his adopted son. The way to a mother's heart is through admiration of her children, and this, coupled with her respect
for Prince Henry, made the Queen his devoted ally in any
enterprise. Another fact, which perhaps made her view Henry
in a more favorable light than Prince Peter, was that Henry's
ambitions and interests in no way conflicted with the day-to-
day running of the country and the court. Prince Peter, on
the other hand, was always ready with advice and with long
letters on the principles of government, culled from Latin
authors, his experience in other countries, and his own reflections on the subject.

Peter was probably the most intellectually distinguished of
the brothers. He was a Latin scholar like his father. He had
translated one of Cicero's works, as well as Colonna's treatise
on the principles of monarchy, and Marco Polo's book of
travels for Prince Henry. Something of a philosopher, a poet
in his own right, and a moralist, Prince Peter was a navigator
in the ocean of the mind—a more treacherous ocean than his
brother's Atlantic. In politics and affairs of state he represented the liberal "golden mean," strengthening King Edward
where he was irresolute, and attempting to moderate Prince
Henry where he was impetuous. The fact is that to his contemporaries Henry—especially in his youth—seemed to be a
fire-eater who needed a lot of restraint. It was only after the
burning drive of youth was spent, and after a bitter taste of
defeat, that Henry dedicated himself entirely to the conquest
of the sea.

Prince Peter had something of Henry's strength without his
fanaticism, and something of King Edward's sensitivity without his weakness. If he was intellectually the most developed
of the brothers, he was also the best balanced. But, like many

intelligent men who can see both sides of a case, this ability was to prove more of a curse than a blessing. Of life itself he had written: "We should consider the archer with his frail arrow who, if he wishes to hit his target, must aim high so that it fall in the right place. But we and our desires, we always fall short of our noblest dreams. . . ."

Such a philosophical acceptance of human weakness would not have appealed to Henry. Yet even if they disagreed about campaigns in Morocco, they had much in common, and Peter's knowledge of the Levant and the Middle East must have been unfailingly stimulating to Henry. Prince Peter had much to say of Prester John, of the spice trade, and of what he had learned about the Far East from merchants and princes who traded there. As the Spanish poet Juan de Mena wrote of him:

> Never was there before or since
> A man who knows
> The silks and secrets of the East,
> Its islands, hills, its heats and snows,
> Like you, my Prince.

The Count of Barcellos was one who rallied to Prince Peter's camp in opposition to the Tangier expedition. So too did Prince John, the fourth of the brothers, who had won his spurs under Henry's command during the second expedition to Ceuta. Prince John had noted on that occasion how eager his elder brother had been to attack Gibraltar, and how he had been stopped only by the command of the King. In contrast to his devout family, John was something of a cynic, and distrusted the religious justifications for a crusade against the Moors. If King Edward or Henry raised the argument that the Pope looked favorably on such enterprises, Prince John retorted, "Send a thousand gold coins to any of the cardinals and he will give you papal indulgences with far greater blessings!"

Their sister, Princess Isabel, was in no way involved. She

had married Philip the Good of Burgundy in 1429, and was now far away in the rich and splendid court at Dijon—whence she wrote, asking Prince Henry to come and stay with her. It is fascinating to speculate on what would have been Henry's reactions to the pleasure-loving and cultured court of his brother-in-law. The two men would certainly have had one thing in common, a devotion to the medieval concept of chivalry. (Philip the Good founded the Order of the Golden Fleece in the year of his marriage, and was engaged in preparing an expedition against the Turks at the time of his death.)

While the royal family was almost evenly divided over Tangier, the youngest son of King John, Prince Fernando, was an active advocate of it. Born in 1402, Fernando had been too young to take part in either of the previous campaigns in Morocco, and it was his eagerness to earn himself knighthood as his brothers had done that precipitated the crisis. It was he who repeatedly pressed King Edward to sanction the expedition, and it was after one of these outbursts that the King pleaded with Prince Henry:

"For the love of God, do not arouse Prince Fernando! But try rather to calm him down!"

His words fell on deaf ears, for it seemed natural to Henry that his youngest brother should wish to earn knighthood on the field of battle. It also coincided with his own plans.

"Africa!" he cried. "The Romans knew its value. Africa is the gateway to the empire of the world! Ceuta is nothing by itself—but once the whole coastline is ours, we shall have a second Portugal!"

More than a year of argument and controversy followed before King Edward finally agreed to the expedition. Unlike the first great venture against Ceuta, the preparations for Tangier took place in an atmosphere of doubt, skepticism, and reluctance. Most important of all, the secrecy with which King

John had so brilliantly shrouded his objective in 1415 was totally ignored by his successors. It was common knowledge that Tangier was the objective, and the Moors were prepared accordingly. Sala-ben-Sala, who had been governor of Ceuta in 1415, now held a similar post in Tangier. This time he was unlikely to be deceived about the Portuguese intentions.

13

Even while the preparations for Tangier were occupying him, Prince Henry did not neglect to follow up the success of Gil Eannes. Courtiers at Lisbon might laugh and say that he had discovered nothing more than a farther stretch of desert. But while they still derided his expeditions, they were uneasy—unwilling, perhaps—to accept that their small, easily comprehended world might only be part of something infinitely greater. In the year immediately after the rounding of Cape Bojador, he sent Eannes back again, accompanied this time by an oared galley under the command of Affonso Gonçalves Baldaia, his cupbearer.

"Go farther!" he ordered.

After long days at sea they passed the cape once more. The small square-rigged bark stumbled in the long swell, and the galley's crew were uneasy at their oars. Neither of the ships was really suitable for this type of work, and it was experience gained in early voyages like this that led to the evolution of the caravel.

Beyond Bojador the coast still trended to the southwest. As far as the men could see, there was nothing but the monotonous red-bronze sand, rising here and there into small hills, which seemed to smoke when the wind came scorching off the desert. They dropped anchor in a small bay 80 miles south of Bojador, a desolate place without vegetation or any sign of life. And then the first sailors to land on the beach came running back with the news: "There are tracks in the sand!"

Men and camels had passed along this coast. It was the first hint the Portuguese had had that there was any life beyond the dread cape. If they brought nothing else back to the Prince this year, they could at least confirm that he was right in his belief—there were other men living south of the Moroccan Moors. There was another compensation to the voyage. They found the bay full of gurnards, their ugly, angular heads at variance with the goodness of their firm flesh. *Angra dos Ruivos,* Gurnard Bay, they called it—a name it bears to this day—and turned homeward with their news.

Next year only one ship was sent out, the galley under Baldaia's command. Prince Henry could spare no more, for there was a great shortage of ships. Every available vessel was being fitted out and made ready for the assault on Tangier. This time Baldaia was determined to bring back something more tangible from the mysterious coastline. Henry had again ordered him to go farther south.

"Tracks of men and camels," he had said, "suggest that there is a town not far away—or else they were merchants on their way to some seaport. Go as far south as you can. Try to bring me news of the land. If you can capture one of the inhabitants, bring him back with you."

Dropping Cape Bojador 170 miles astern, the galley came down the shimmering coastline and anchored in a large inlet. From its shape, Baldaia and his men assumed that they were in the mouth of a river, so they called it the Rio de Ouro, "River of Gold." They thought that at last, perhaps, they had reached the fabulous lands where spices and precious metals were as common as prickly pear in Portugal. The bay where they anchored they called the Bay of Horses, for it was here that they disembarked the two horses that Prince Henry had provided for the exploration of the coast. Two young noblemen volunteered to make the first reconnaissance, and rode away down the sandbanks of the inlet. Baldaia and the seamen watched them as they disappeared into the unknown country. They saw the dust cloud behind their horses spurt up and hang yellow in the still air.

The scouts were away all that night, and in the morning when they returned, it was seen that one of them was wounded in the foot. They had a strange and exciting tale to tell. About ten miles inland they had come upon a group of nineteen men. Remembering the Prince's orders to try to bring back a captive, they had at once given chase. But the natives, who were armed with assegais, had fought them off all day, wounding one of the Portuguese in the course of the skirmish. It was an inconclusive affair, but it certainly confirmed that the coastline was inhabited.

Next day Baldaia and some of the crew went ashore, determined on capturing one of the strangers. They found nothing but the trampled sand where the fight had taken place, dried blood on the hot stones (some of the natives had been wounded), and a few pathetic belongings. The Africans had wisely taken to flight. They might indeed have cried with Rimbaud:

"*Les blancs débarquent. Le canon! Il faut se soumettre au baptême, s'habiller, travailler.*"

The first Europeans had made contact with the first unknown tribes of Africa, and the visitors came, as they would nearly always come, with swords in their hands. Not that these natives were at all peaceful by nature. They were Berbers, "the tawny Moors," as the Portuguese were to call them—tall, good-looking men with dark hair and hazel eyes, with sometimes a blond among them. They were a "white" and not a Negro race. Traders and farmers, they lived, as they do to this day, in houses of untrimmed stone, often in mountain districts among fields laboriously terraced out of the parched slopes. A warlike people (they have never been completely subjugated), they showed a hostility to the early Portuguese navigators that added a further hazard to the passage of Africa. It is interesting to see that in the current *Africa Pilot* (1953), published by the Admiralty in London, this stretch of coast is one of the few places in the world that is still described in those words dear to romantic writers: ". . . The natives are reported to be hostile to strangers."

Baldaia returned to Sagres with little to show for this first contact with the natives of the continent except for a few nets found farther down the coast, and the skins of some sea lions killed in the Bay of Horses. If Prince Henry was disappointed, he did not show it. After all, it had taken nearly fourteen years for him to find a man who would round Cape Bojador. The astrologers' assessment of his character was accurate: "His rising sign was Aries, in the House of Mars . . . therefore, Mars was in Aquarius, which is the House of Hope, signifying that the Prince would occupy himself with brave discoveries and conquests, and especially with the unraveling of those secrets which are not for the eyes of other men." It was in the exercise of the war god Mars that he now prepared to take the Portuguese fleet and army against the fortress of Tangier.

Before leaving Portugal, he was burdened down with advice from King Edward, some of it good, and some of it curiously irrelevant. What, for instance, could the King hope for by counseling Prince Henry "to make it your business to protect the virtue of chastity"? Prince Henry stood in no need of a reminder. One can only suppose that King Edward was afraid the Portuguese soldiers and sailors would behave in foreign ports as soldiers and sailors always have done.

"You know well how much Our Lord is pleased with this virtue," the King went on, "and I would call to your attention the English habit in this matter. For, as you know, in time of peace they are very much occupied with their women, having them always around them—yet in time of war, to protect them the better, they will not allow them to come anywhere near the battlefields." Presumably the King, with his eye on his English cousins, had noticed that—unlike the Continental armies—the English discouraged a long train of camp followers. This was for the practical reason that they would hinder their progress through the countries where they were campaigning. (Like so many other English habits and customs, it was based not on a love of virtue but on a sense of realism.)

Some of Edward's advice, however, was pertinent. He suggested that his brother should divide the fleet into three, sending one part to Tangier, and the other two to nearby Alcaçar and Arzila. In this way the Moors might have been made uncertain of the ultimate objective, and diverted their forces accordingly. What the King ignored, though, was the fact that Prince Henry's fleet and army were too small to be successfully divided. He had asked for fourteen thousand men—and he got six thousand. He had asked for almost as many ships as the armada that had gone to Ceuta—he got a scratch fleet made up of what trading vessels could be spared, and as many as could be chartered from other countries.

One piece of advice that the King gave his brother might be engraved in letters of brass in every military academy of the world: "Keep one flank on the sea," he ordered. "Whatever you do, you must maintain your lines of communication with the fleet. To receive provisions and reinforcements, and to be able to retreat if necessary—keep one flank on the sea."

The importance of the long and meticulous planning that had gone into the assault on Ceuta was forgotten by King John's sons. Twenty-two years had gone by, and they no longer remembered how nearly that first expedition had ended in disaster. If Prince Henry remembered Ceuta, it was only as the golden moment of youth when not only Africa but the whole world had seemed to lie within his grasp. His years of solitude, and his constant absorption in his dream of Africa, had increased a natural arrogance—acceptable in a young man, but not in a mature leader upon whom everyone depended. King Edward with his doubts and hesitations, Prince Peter with his balanced and profound mistrust of the scheme, were more adult in their approach to the campaign. Their brother was in many ways something of an adolescent. Obsessed with the fiery dream that God was with him, he still felt that the whole world could be taken by the sword in his right hand.

14

The fleet set sail in the last week of August, 1437. The north-
erlies were blowing, the same wind that had taken them to
Ceuta, to Madeira, to the Azores, and down the coast of Africa.
It was late in the year, though, to start a sea-borne invasion. Unless Tangier fell to them quickly, they were in danger of finding
the Atlantic spiked with autumn gales when they turned for
home. But the wind stayed fair for the passage, and the fleet
was anchored off Ceuta four days after leaving Portugal.

The sight of the Christian armada bearing down upon the
coast caused a panic among the nearby Moors. The garrison
of Ceuta, however, lost heart when they saw how small was the
army, and how few the ships. Count Pedro de Menezes, who
was still governor after twenty-two years on African soil, welcomed Prince Henry and his brother Fernando. Menezes, the
veteran of many African campaigns, was now an old and sick
man, unable to lead out his forces in company with Prince
Henry. But he and his advisers were the only ones present who
could claim to a real knowledge of the Moorish forces and their
dispositions. Their immediate advice was to postpone the expedition against Tangier until King Edward could follow up

with reinforcements. In the meantime Henry's forces would
be a useful addition to the garrison, and could be of service in
Morocco as raiding parties. Prince Henry would not listen to
the suggestion. Now that he was back in Africa again, with an
army under his command, nothing would content him but to get
to grips with the enemy.

"Our forces are small, I know," he said. "But even if they
were smaller we should have to attack! It is the will of God!"

Against such fanaticism, a fanaticism reinforced by the
Prince's great reputation, Count Pedro de Menezes and the
veterans of Ceuta could find no more to say. The Prince possessed the magnetic quality of leadership that compels men
to follow into any danger and to fight against the most unequal
odds.

Tangier is only about 40 miles by sea west from Ceuta.
The plan of attack was for the main body of the army under
Prince Henry to strike overland toward the city, while the ships
with their supply parties went round and anchored in Tangier
Bay. Henry's aim was to capture Tetuán, another Moorish
stronghold inland from Ceuta, and proceed from there by the
valley road that led to Tangier. At first all went well. On
September 10 his forces entered Tetuán, whence the Moors had
fled and destroyed the gates of the city. Wasting no time, they
moved on again next day and encamped on the outskirts of
Tangier on Friday the thirteenth. If the day seemed ill-omened
to some of the troops, their fears were strengthened when a
gust of wind carried away Prince Henry's banner as it was
being unfurled.

Deciding that even if the men were tired, it was better to
commence the assault at once than wait for dawn, Henry gave
the order to advance. A rumor had reached the Portuguese that
the city's gates had been left open and the population fled. They
were to be sadly disillusioned. As the first horsemen spurred

down through the orange groves above the city, clattering through the Roman ruins of ancient Tangier, they found the gates closed, the wall ominous and strong, and lined by a determined garrison. Even so, in the first wild rush of the assault they managed to burst open two of the gates. No sooner were they inside than the spearhead found itself fiercely opposed and driven out. This was no Ceuta.

Realizing that the city could not be taken by a simple frontal assault, the Portuguese began to draw off to their base. Skirmishes took place as the Moors came out of the stronghold and followed up the retiring horsemen. Alvaro Vaz de Almada, a nobleman who had fought with Henry V at Agincourt, was wounded by an arrow. A number of men and horses were killed, and there were casualties among the foot soldiers. Sobered by their reception, but not disheartened, Prince Henry's forces gathered round their campfires and reviewed the situation. It was clear that Tangier was likely to resolve itself into a protracted seige. They would have to strengthen their own positions, and make use of the fleet to bring up whatever arms and ammunition were necessary to reduce the city's walls.

Next day Prince Fernando came ashore to confer with his brother. He was ill with a fever, which was the reason he had gone round with the reinforcements by sea. He concurred with all that Henry said, for he trusted implicitly in his judgment: "We must prepare for a long siege." Cannon must be brought from Ceuta, scaling ladders for the walls, and mantelets—movable covers under which troops could advance to break down the gates.

A week went by in preparations, and in ferrying reserves by sea from Ceuta. On Friday, September 20, the assault for which they had waited so impatiently began. This was the first major attack on Tangier, and it proved a disaster. Despite the gallantry of the Portuguese—Prince Henry leading the attack on the citadel, Fernando besieging the main gate, and the warlike Bishop of Ceuta leading a scaling party against the walls—the Moors held firm. Henry, clad in black chain mail, was like the war god himself, always in the forefront of the battle. But bravery is not enough to win victories, and the planning of the assault had been inadequate. There were insufficient ladders, the artillery was too light, and (the decisive factor) they were faced by a determined garrison of about seven thousand men protected behind thick walls. The Moors were equally inspired by their determination not to yield Tangier, and to avenge the capture of Ceuta. With the loss of over five hundred men, Prince Henry called off the attack.

Ships were sent back to bring up two large cannon and longer scaling ladders. While the Portuguese army sat down to wait, Sala-ben-Sala could afford to relax. Every day that the Portuguese spent in front of Tangier gave his reinforcements more time to gather in the hinterland of Morocco. A week later, when the second attack was made, the Portuguese were again driven off. But this time they were fighting on two fronts, for the first of the Moorish reinforcements had begun to strike down from the hills behind them. Henry found himself compelled to fight a rear-guard action with half his army, while the other half went to the assault on the city's walls.

At this stage of the campaign a more cautious man would have decided to retire and wait at Ceuta until the spring. As September drew to a close, the weather was worsening, Henry's troops were tiring, and the supply of food and ammunition by sea was proving a difficult piece of logistics. But the qualities of perseverance and obstinacy (which were the secret of his success in the realm of discovery) were to prove fatal in the art of generalship.

King Edward in his instructions had laid down that if Tangier was not taken in three attempts, the army was to withdraw to Ceuta at once. "Do not remain there another hour," he had written, "but leave for Ceuta and await me there." It was his plan that if this should happen, he would come down from Portugal with a large army in the spring.

In any event, Prince Henry had no idea of giving up the campaign until he had attempted the third assault. More scaling ladders were constructed, and a wooden tower from which it was hoped the attackers would be able to swarm over the walls. While they went ahead with their preparations, the hills behind them began to fill with the enemy. Night and day the pressure on the Portuguese camp increased. There were skirmishes, cavalry charges, flights of arrows in the night—all the signs that, with every hour, the force that was building up against them was gaining heart from the steady influx of new troops. Prisoners reported that the kings of Fez and Morocco were on their way to the relief of Tangier. It was under these conditions that the third assault on the battered walls of the city took place. It was another failure.

Now the besiegers became the besieged. They had waited too long while the tribes gathered in the mountains behind them, and had expended too much energy in fruitless assaults on the city. The camp, which through Prince Henry's disobedience of his brother's orders had been pitched a few miles inland, gradually lost its lifeline to the sea. With a hostile city on one flank and Moorish troops to the rear, they found that the tide had encircled them. Like men standing on an offshore rock, they had kept their eyes fixed too long in one direction. To their fear and dismay, they found that they were cut off.

"Keep one flank on the sea!" King Edward had urged, and Prince Henry had neglected this salient piece of advice. In the first great Moorish attack, when the enemy horsemen swept right up to the city's walls, he had lost his cannons, ladders, and bombards. His horse was killed beneath him, and he himself was saved only by a stroke of luck. His troops, wearied by over a fortnight's campaigning and unrelenting work, were now being worn down by the continuous pressure of fresh foot soldiers and cavalry.

The siege of Tangier was over, the siege of the Portuguese had begun. The sailors from their anchored ships watched impotently as the wild horsemen and the flickering robes spilled round the Portuguese camp. The enemy swirled up and dashed like spray against the improvised defenses. But still Prince Henry's men held firm.

The few thousand troops under his command were now surrounded by tens of thousands of Moors—forty thousand horsemen and thirty thousand infantry, says one contemporary historian. Another estimated that half a million tribesmen gathered out of Morocco to relieve Tangier. From the moment that the enemy had re-established contact with the city and had cut off his camp from the sea, Prince Henry's position was hopeless. Despite the gallantry with which he and his men defended their barricades, they were doomed. It was only a question of time before their supplies ran out, and—worst of all—there was no fresh water in their encampment. They killed and ate their horses. When showers of rain swept up off the Atlantic, the men drank from the puddles or sucked the brackish sand and mud of Morocco. Henry decided that the only solution was to make a withdrawal by night. Under cover of darkness they would hack their way out of the camp and back to the beachhead.

It was while they were preparing for their midnight dash that their plans were betrayed in an astonishing way. It was astonishing because the traitor was none other than a Portuguese priest, Martim Vieyra by name. A traitor among the rank and file might have been conceivable, but that a priest should betray his Christian fellow countrymen to the infidel still seems almost inconceivable. Martim Vieyra was Prince Henry's own chaplain, a fact that in itself makes one pause. Could it have been some personal animosity that made him betray the Prince's plans? What words, what confession, perhaps, had he heard from his master that made him play the Judas? Had he detected in Henry the deadly sin of pride—a pride that would have preferred to see all the Portuguese go down fighting in their efforts to reach the sea rather than surrender? History tells us no more of Martim Vieyra, nor what became of him in after years. A Christian renegade serving in the Moorish army was so disgusted when he learned of the betrayal that he deserted that night and warned the Portuguese that their plan to escape had been revealed. Their only chance of success had lain in the element of surprise, and now that this was gone, they abandoned their attempt.

The next day was the nadir of Prince Henry's life. The sun came up over the desert, and the vultures were wheeling in the sky above the battlefield. The Moorish army was encamped all round. On every side of the Portuguese defenses, though, the great piles of dead told of the high cost to the victors. It may have been these losses, but more likely it was the thought of being able to conclude a favorable armistice, that prompted Sala-ben-Sala and the Moorish kings to propose a truce. Their messengers were admitted through the Portuguese defenses, and Prince Henry learned the harsh terms of peace. He and his army would be permitted to regain their ships only on three conditions. They must give back Ceuta to the Moors. They must leave all their arms behind them. They must exchange hostages—either Prince Henry or Prince Fernando—and in return Sala-ben-Sala would give them his own son as a surety of faith.

Abandon Ceuta! Lay down his arms! Deliver himself or his brother as a hostage! The terms were as bitter as death, but

the alternative was unthinkable. There was no doubt that since
his small force was short of food, water, and weapons, and ex-
hausted into the bargain, it was only a question of time before
it would be overrun and annihilated. It seemed as if God had
failed him.

While Portuguese emissaries were discussing the terms with
Sala-ben-Sala, the truce broke down. Neither the Governor of
Tangier nor the Moroccan kings could control the wild desert
tribesmen who had ridden so far to avenge Ceuta, to kill
Christians, and to enrich themselves with plunder. Once again
the great wave of horsemen and soldiers rolled round the
Portuguese barricades, and once again they were repulsed.
Prince Henry was at every point where the fight was thickest.
Alongside him, cross in one hand and sword in the other, the
indomitable Bishop of Ceuta gave absolution to the dying
Christians while he spread death among the infidels. Throughout the long hot day, while the desert shook under the sun and
the old tawny walls of Tangier mocked their lost hopes, the
Portuguese fought off the attack. After seven hours the tide of
battle ebbed, leaving behind it mounds of dead that were already beginning to swell and stink in the Moroccan heat.

This second reversal confirmed the Moorish leaders in their
decision to conclude an armistice, and next morning Sala-ben-
Sala sent word that his terms remained unaltered. This time
no further attacks followed the truce. The Moorish tribesmen
had lost heart before the indomitable courage of the be-
leaguered Christians.

Prince Henry accepted the inevitable. Only one point remained to be settled: should he or his brother be the hostage?
The disaster, he realized, must be laid at his own door, and it
was only right, therefore, that he should be the one to be delivered up to the Moors. But this was something that neither
Prince Fernando nor Henry's advisers would permit. It was

bad enough that they had failed to take Tangier and had been compelled to accept Sala-ben-Sala's terms. How much worse it would be to hand over their commander in chief! Prince Henry learned that day not only the bitterness of defeat, he learned the utter loneliness of high command.

On October 15 the treaty was concluded, and two days later the Portuguese began their retreat to the sea. Unfortunately—and it was to have an important bearing on later events —the terms of the treaty were not respected by the Moors. Unable to control the tribesmen whom he had summoned from the desert in his defense, Sala-ben-Sala watched his enemies fight their way slowly back to the shore. The Portuguese, for their part, had complied with the terms, and Prince Henry had seen his brother ride back to Tangier, accompanied by several of his servants, into captivity. There was no treachery by Sala-ben-Sala (the Portuguese had his own son as hostage with them), but the fact remains that by contesting their departure the Moors had given them the opportunity of saying that the treaty had been broken. It need no longer be respected.

Under the biting lash of arrows and javelins they gained the shore. Behind them the ruins of their encampment smoked and burned as the Moors carried off the equipment that had been abandoned. The walls of Tangier were thronged with the victors. Inside them the youngest of Henry's brothers was a prisoner. Prince Fernando was never to gain his knighthood with honor. He was never to know the bright moment of victory as Henry, Edward, and Peter had done so many years before at Ceuta. If Ceuta were not handed over, nothing remained in front of him but long years of imprisonment and an ignominious death.

On October 20 the Portuguese fleet weighed anchor and sailed for home. Prince Henry did not accompany it. Unwilling, perhaps, to face King Edward, or determined to effect his brother's liberation by an exchange of further hostages, he sailed for Ceuta. It was there, for the first and only time in his life, that his iron will and his immense reserves of physical strength deserted him. He savored the bitter knowledge that even the most ambitious and determined of men are subject to fate and failure.

15

It is difficult for a man to be completely dedicated to a dream, or to an idea, without sacrificing something of his humanity. In Prince Henry's attitude and conduct during the years immediately following the disaster of Tangier, the struggle between the man of simple human feelings and the man of ambition is painfully apparent. For he was far from being cold and insensitive by temperament. Incidents in his early youth show that he was more sensitive than most men of his time. After the capture of Ceuta, for instance, he had hardly been able to face the mother of one of his companions who had been killed in the struggle. His distress had been so great that the bereaved mother had herself to comfort the man who brought her the news. There is every evidence that he was more gentle and compassionate in his relations with other persons than was considered normal in that age. Azurara's comments on this aspect of his nature are very relevant to the tragedy of Tangier and the fate of Henry's youngest brother.

"Hatred or ill will toward others was never known in him, even though heavy faults had been committed against him. In this matter his generosity was such that practical men re-

proached him with weakness in dispensing justice, for he made
no distinctions among persons. They thought this particularly
the case because he inflicted no punishment on some of his
servants who had abandoned him during the siege of Tangier.
But, more than this, he even received them back into his service
and gave them privileges, as many or more than those he gave
to the men who had served him well. This is the only weakness
which I have found possible to relate of him. . . ."

If this was his attitude toward servants who had left him on
the field of battle, it can be imagined what his feelings must
have been in connection with Prince Fernando—the young
brother entrusted to his care, who was now a hostage of the
Moors. It was true that such things were the normal fortune of
war, but Prince Henry was intelligent enough to realize that it
was he alone who, by neglecting to "keep his flank on the sea,"
had jeopardized the Portuguese army. Added to the bitterness
of failure, he was now faced with the terrible problem of
weighing Ceuta in the balance against his brother.

He hoped at first that in some way or another an exchange
of hostages might be made with Sala-ben-Sala. The Moorish
Governor's son was held by the Portuguese, and surely he
would be willing to effect an exchange if gold was added to the
balance. Sala-ben-Sala quickly disillusioned him on this score.
One son meant little to him; he had plenty of sons, he assured
the envoys. If King Edward and Prince Henry set so great a
store by this brother of theirs, then they must hand over Ceuta
as they had agreed to in the terms of the treaty. But the treaty
had not been kept, Henry protested. The Portuguese had not
been given safe passage to the sea. They had had to cut their
way back to their ships, losing a great many men in the process.
During the long months of negotiations, while envoys and emissaries passed out of the gates of Ceuta to contact Sala-ben-Sala,
Prince Henry hoped desperately that some ransom other than

Ceuta might be found acceptable. Sala-ben-Sala remained adamant.

The first of these negotiations was undertaken by Prince John. He had arrived with reinforcements on the very day that Henry, broken and dispirited, retired to Ceuta. Prince John took Sala-ben-Sala's son aboard his ship and sailed at once for Tangier. The second Portuguese fleet arrived off the triumphant walls of the Moorish fortress only to find that Sala-ben-Sala had already transferred the royal prisoner and his attendants to Arzila on the Atlantic coast. The weather was worsening as they set out for Arzila, rounded Cape Spartel, and came out into the long rollers of the ocean. They anchored in the exposed roads opposite the small port, and Prince John immediately attempted to effect the exchange. Sala-ben-Sala maintained that he was interested only in the return of Ceuta, but—with one eye on the weather—he protracted the negotiations. After a few days, as perhaps he had expected, a southwest gale came rolling up out of the Atlantic, and the Portuguese, exposed on a lee shore, were compelled to up-anchor and stand out to sea. The autumn weather was now growling into winter. Prince John had no choice but to save his ships and run back to the coast of southern Portugal. The first of the many attempts to rescue Prince Fernando had failed.

The return of the defeated army to Lisbon was a crushing blow from which King Edward never recovered. Never over-enthusiastic about the expedition, he had been swayed in its favor mainly by Queen Leonora, by Fernando's eagerness to win his spurs as his brothers had done, and by Prince Henry's desire to add Tangier to Ceuta. Now it seemed as if even Ceuta must be sacrificed. Prince Peter, who had opposed the scheme from the start, was quite clear what action should be taken— hand back Ceuta. It was only a drain on the Portuguese purse in any case, keeping a garrison there. King Edward would have liked to consult with Henry, but there could be no easy communication with a man hundreds of miles away in Africa.

Early in 1438 Edward convoked the Cortes, the representatives of the nation, and asked for their opinion. The Cortes were divided but, on the whole, their verdict was against returning the city. Another doubt now harried King Edward—had he the right, in any event, to hand back Ceuta to the Moors? Its capture had been hailed as one of the great achievements of Christendom in the long war between cross and crescent, and Ceuta had been the greatest glory of his father's career. He applied to the other kings of Europe, and they answered with one accord that Ceuta must never be surrendered. The Pope, as might have been expected, pointed out that Ceuta was more than Portuguese, it was a Christian possession. Its consecrated churches and its importance as a Christian bastion in infidel Africa were things that could not be exchanged for the life of one man. Unless some other means could be found to effect his release, Prince Fernando was elected to martyrdom.

Throughout the winter Henry remained in Ceuta. Grief, illness, and nervous strain had at first prostrated him. But gradually he won through to a balanced estimate of the position. All was not lost, only a battle. He had been at fault in the means whereby he had tried to capture Tangier, but not in the object itself. He would gladly have taken his brother's place as the hostage, but such a comparatively easy road had not been marked out for him. He accepted his destiny, as willingly as he would have accepted his brother's. One thing he knew—under the circumstances, he would never have countenanced the return of Ceuta for his own life.

"Whatever the world thinks, he who hath not much meditated upon God, the human mind, the *summum bonum*, may possibly make a thriving earthworm, but will most indubitably make a sorry patriot and a sorry statesman" are words with which he would have agreed. In the long months of that North African winter he had tried to effect his brother's release, and had failed. He still believed that it could be achieved, but he knew now that the task would not be easy.

He returned to Sagres in the spring. King Edward had been pressing him to come back—for how could he come to a decision about Ceuta without consulting the principal actor in the drama? But it was not until Henry had spent nearly three months at Sagres that, in June, 1438, he agreed to come north and meet the King.

Henry's behavior throughout the months and years that followed the tragedy of Tangier was never that of the hard-hearted man of ambition to whom a brother is only a pawn in the great game of power. This was immediately apparent on his return to Portugal where, rather than face his brothers Edward and Peter, he had taken refuge at Sagres. His behavior may be called cowardice, but certainly not unfeeling arrogance. The fact is, he had come to the conclusion that nothing short of a further—and successful—expedition against the Moors could save Fernando. When Prince Henry finally journeyed north to meet King Edward at Portel, some 70 miles from Lisbon, he had made up his mind.

King Edward saw that his brother was in deep mourning. (It may have been for the death of many brave men at Tangier, or it may have been for Fernando. Perhaps he already knew he would never see him again.) Henry listened to all the arguments that had been put forward on the subject of exchanging Ceuta for the young prince, and when King Edward had finished, he made his reply. It was simple, and to the point. Ceuta must never be given up. There was only one answer, he said. If Sala-ben-Sala would not treat (which appeared unlikely), then they must prepare a bigger expedition. Only this time, let the King and the Cortes of Portugal give him what he had asked for in the first place—a large army and a large fleet. With twelve thousand foot soldiers, six thousand cross-bowmen, and an equal number of cavalry, he would guarantee not only to take Tangier, but to subdue the whole Moroccan coastline.

King Edward was appalled at his brother's attitude. To talk of a further expedition at a moment when the country was still reeling from the loss of the last one! The fact remains that in theory Prince Henry was right, even if his theory was impracticable. Given a well-equipped army and fleet, such as his father had had for the taking of Ceuta, he would more than likely have succeeded with Tangier. Whether he would have ever recovered his brother from captivity is another question. What he forgot —and he was blind to it all his life—was that a small country with a population of about three million could not afford to wage large-scale wars. The loss of a few thousand able-bodied men, who might have been employed on the land or in coastal fishing, was of grave importance to Portugal.

Meanwhile, Prince Fernando—"the Constant Prince," as he was to be immortalized in Calderon's play *El Principe Constante*—had been transferred from Arzila to Fez. He had been ill throughout the winter, and now his fate was sealed. The kingdom of Fez was administered by a violent anti-Christian, the Vizier Lazurac, who derived great pleasure from having among his slaves and servants a son of the same Portuguese king who had humbled Moorish pride at Ceuta. He determined to degrade his princely and Christian hostage. At night Fernando was compelled to sleep in a cell that housed ten others. Verminous, weak from dysentery, and aware that with every day his prospects of deliverance lessened, he bore his lot with a fortitude that seemed praiseworthy even to his captors.

He had been a prisoner for nearly a year when in the late autumn of 1438 the news reached Fez that King Edward was dead. The Vizier personally showed the document containing the news to Prince Fernando. Lazurac knew that his chances of reaping a rich reward were now greatly lessened, and Fernando's reaction confirmed his views.

"If he is dead, then I shall remain a captive till the end of my life!" the Prince cried.

Fernando was well aware that the succession of Edward's six-year-old son would lead to many problems in the court and country. His own importance was inevitably lessened, now that his brother was dead. He knew perhaps that Prince Peter would still try to save him, but as for the feelings of Prince John or his half-brother, the Count of Barcellos, he could only hazard a guess. Where Prince Henry was concerned, he knew that this brother would have suffered any torture rather than have Ceuta handed back to the Moors.

It was the failure of the expedition to Tangier and the loss of his brother that largely contributed to King Edward's death. "An unparalleled sorrow, and acute distress resulting from the misfortunes of Tangier" were the reasons given by his doctors for a death that might nowadays be described as due to a broken heart.

Edward had been too gentle, too weak perhaps—certainly too sensitive—for the position to which fate had called him. A prey to conflicting opinions, he had spent most of his brief reign listening to the advice of brothers and ministers, of his wife even, and failing of his own accord to make the firm moves required of a king. His character is most clearly revealed in his treatise *O Leal Conselheiro*, the Loyal Counselor, where he paints a moving picture of the dignity and affection that existed among Queen Philippa's sons. He had many of his mother's virtues, but the great thing that he lacked was his father's strength of character. At the time of his coronation astrologers had prophesied a brief and unhappy reign. He had been king for five years only, and he died leaving his youngest brother a prisoner of the Moors and a child as heir to the throne.

Apart from the Queen, only Prince Peter was with him at his deathbed. Prince John and the Count of Barcellos were away on their estates. Prince Henry, after his summer meeting with Edward at Portel, had retired again to Sagres.

There, beneath the ramparts of his rising fortress, he watched the long undulating plains of the Atlantic. Ships were busy in the bay beneath him. They brought him news of the Azores—of further islands being uncovered out of the obscure ocean—and of the steady progress in Madeira. At Sagres he still felt the pulse of Africa. From his own ships returned from raids along the coast, or from Moors come to do business with him, he tried to assess the extent of his defeat and the possible chances of rescuing his brother.

Some men are crippled by failure. With a few it happens that the broken limbs heal harder and stronger than with the others. Tangier had brought Henry to the only physical and mental collapse in the course of his life. When he came back to Sagres after the long months in Ceuta, it was seen, though, that it had not weakened him. His failure in generalship had taught him a lesson; it had not led to his retirement from the field of action. The loss of his brother had caused him acute suffering; it had not weakened his resolve.

However much the common people might dislike him for what they saw as his inhumanity, he knew that one man was not worth a city. If he had been asked by Sala-ben-Sala why he would not give up Ceuta, he would have replied that the city was not his to surrender. His answer would always have been the same: "It belongs to God, and not to me!"

16

The event seemed a small thing at the time, but it was to have an impact on European history, and to lay on almost all the maritime nations a burden and a guilt from which they still suffer. The first ship returned to Portugal with captive Negroes four years after Tangier. These were the first slaves ever taken by the Portuguese on the west coast of Africa.

In the summer of 1441 Prince Henry had fitted out a small bark and sent it south under the command of a young man called Antão Gonçalves. For once, he had not given any orders for a voyage of exploration, but had contented himself with telling Gonçalves to go to the Rio de Ouro. There he was to take aboard a cargo of oil and pelts from the sea lions that were plentiful in the bay. Gonçalves was young and inexperienced, and this was to be a "working-up" cruise for him.

Close on Gonçalves's heels Henry sent a second ship commanded by a tried veteran, Nuño Tristão. In his case the orders were as usual—to proceed as far south as possible, and try to capture some of the natives. Nuño Tristão's command was a caravel. This is the first time we come upon the word that ever afterward is to be associated with the Portuguese voyages of discovery. Azurara introduces the term "caravel" quite casually into his narrative. By the time he was writing his *Chronicle of the Conquest and Discovery of Guinea* in 1453, "caravel" had become a household word in Portugal. He also mentions that it was an "armed" vessel, so one may assume that it was not only built to the new design, but was intended further as a warship capable of attacking any Moorish ships it might encounter. Nuño Tristão's caravel was probably no more than fifty tons. She had the advantage over every other type of vessel that had so far sailed down the African coast, in her ability to work well to windward. With her ease of handling she could tack and go about quickly—an important consideration when working in uncharted waters. Her shallow draft was also a great advantage in the shoal waters off the sandy headlands of Morocco.

When Nuño Tristão brought his new ship down the coast and anchored near the bark, he found that young Gonçalves had anticipated him. Having taken aboard all they could carry in the way of pelts and oil, Gonçalves and his companions had gone ashore in a raiding party, and had managed to capture a Berber man and a Negro woman.

Prince Henry, with a view to getting immediate information from the natives, had sent a Bedouin Arab in the caravel to act as interpreter. It was soon found that neither the Berber nor the Negro woman could understand Arabic. Determined to capture some more inhabitants, Nuño Tristão organized a further raiding party. This time they were more successful, and after a skirmish in which four unfortunate natives were killed, the Portuguese managed to take ten prisoners. Among them was a tall Berber called Adahu. He was of superior caste and intellect to the others, had traveled in Morocco, and was able to speak Arabic with their Bedouin interpreter. Gonçalves was knighted by Nuño Tristão for his part in the affair and was then sent back to Portugal with his captives.

The caravel sailed on down the coast. Almost effortlessly they worked their way southward, leaving behind them Galley Rock, so called from its shape, and then another small cape, which ran out to break the monotony of the desert. As far as they could see, there was only the steady rise, dip, and fold of a waterless landscape. At length they raised a further headland, a real landmark this time. The coast here was rockier than it had been farther north, and a few dark shadings of desert grass showed up against the interminable sand. Beyond the rocks and the red glow of the shore, a long white plateau tumbled precipitously into the sea.

"The White Cape!"

Cape Blanco lies 320 miles south of Cape Bojador, a cliff of crumbling rock that changes shape year by year, as first one hanging ledge and then another crashes into the shallow sea. Beyond it opened out a large bay, one of the largest on the west coast of Africa, and scoured by crosscurrents. It was here that Nuño Tristão called a halt to the year's voyaging. He and his crew could feel pleased with the results. They had taken useful prisoners, they had gone farther south than man had ever been before, and their new ship had shown how adept it was in these waters. Easy to handle, sea-kindly in the long surge of the Atlantic, she was clearly the ideal vessel for circumnavigating an unknown continent.

They had another proof of the caravel's ability to voyage far from home ports when they found it necessary to careen her. They were well over a thousand miles from Portugal, and no vessel had ever before attempted any major repairs when away on the African coast. It may be they had touched a rock or sandbank; it may be that some of the calking had spewed out in the tumble of the Atlantic; or it may have been no more

than the fact that the hull was beginning to grow foul with
weed after long weeks at sea. At any rate, Nuño Tristão ordered
the caravel to be "drawn up a shore, where it was cleaned and
repaired while waiting for the tide. Just as though he had been
in Lisbon harbor. It was a feat whose boldness aroused the
admiration of his men." It would have been difficult, if not
impossible, with a *barinal* or with a bark. The *barinal*, built
on Venetian galley lines, was destined to be hauled ashore on
a cradle. The bark, on the other hand, was an awkward-shaped
vessel, which a small crew would have found difficult to careen
in those waters.

Not until men return from space, or from visiting other
planets, will anyone be able to experience the emotions of
these early Portuguese navigators. They were venturing where
man had never gone before. They were learning to adapt themselves to an unfamiliar element—the vast ocean. They were
experimenting with new designs in transport, and they were
using navigational instruments that were still in their infancy.
Every day, as the sails shook and the ship leaned to the wind,
they were seeing a new world.

At dawn they opened their eyes to the first sunrise over a
virgin sea. The capes and coves and headlands that lifted out
of the dew haze on a summer morning were being created by
their vision. The flare of sunlight on the water, the rushing
crystal of a wave—even these seemed new. Astern of them at
night the North Star began to settle lower in the sky. Homer
had written: "Alone of all the stars, the Pole wheels round and
round in one place, and never takes a bath in the Ocean." But
it is probable that there were some among Nuño Tristão's crew
who would be the first Europeans in history to catch sight of
the Southern Cross in the seas below the equator. Among them
were men of whom it could truly be said that they

> hove the Cross to heaven and sank
> The Pole Star underground.

They saw the moon over bare desert hills, and the sea like sheets of glass on a dazzling morning. At dawn the rigging hung with strands of light like a spider's web, and at night the ship's track was a sword across the water. The phosphorescence off that coast was even more vivid than in the summer Mediterranean. It swirled round the rudder, and when a wave lipped over the gunwhale and ran along the deck, it was fiery, and quick as mercury. At night Nuño Tristão consulted the first manual that had been drawn up for the use of navigators. (It was being altered and improved with every year that passed.) He grew familiar with the "Rules for Observing the North Star"—"the Regiment of the North," as it was called. At noon he waited for the sun's meridian altitude—the moment when the sun seems to tremble in the heavens before beginning its slow decline.

After several days at sea, beating to windward against the prevailing breeze, they came back again to waters that were already becoming familiar. They passed Cape Bojador, now only another headland on the chart—and soon they saw the outermost of the Canary Islands lifting out of the sea. (They kept clear of the Canaries, for the Prince had instructed his captains not to meddle in the affairs of Castile.) They ran on up the coast and passed Cape Not—it was difficult to believe that this had once been the outermost limit of the world. Soon they saw the wine-red glow in the shallows where the Sahara sand colored the sea. They turned more northerly, heading home for Portugal and leaving the coast at Safi, where the sardine shoals were leaping under the sun.

They found Prince Henry and the court at Sagres eagerly awaiting them. For four years there had been few voyages, and the initial excitement of discovering new islands and of rounding Cape Bojador had died away. But the arrival of the first captives changed everything. The visible proof that there were other men living in those remote regions aroused the interest of even the most skeptical, and the Berber chief, Adahu, became the focus of attention. Prince Henry was soon engaged in finding out from him all he could about the desert lands and those that lay beyond them.

Now he heard at first hand of the caravan routes that crossed the remote valleys and plains, as Adahu told him of the gold that came overland from Wangara, and of the fertile country that lay somewhere far to the south. Beyond the Sahara, he said, the sandy wastes were transformed into a rich green delta—land surrounding a great river. Henry heard the name of the mysterious city that was to haunt European imagination for centuries—Timbuktu. This was the "meeting place of the camel and the canoe," for on one side lay the desert caravan routes, and on the other were navigable channels leading to the Niger. Adahu knew of the gold trade that made Timbuktu rich, but he knew little of its source, and of the vast extent of Africa he was probably quite ignorant. But it may well have been from Adahu that Henry heard tales of how the Nile flowed westward into the Atlantic. (It had long been a belief that one branch of the Nile flowed across the continent and emptied into the western ocean.) It would be many years before the sources of great rivers like the Senegal and Gambia were discovered, but their existence was confirmed by early captives like this Berber chief.

". . . So the Prince learned many things about the country that Adahu inhabited. And realizing that armed ships carrying his men must often go there, Prince Henry immediately prepared to send an embassy to the Pope. . . ."

He petitioned His Holiness for all the new territory beyond

Cape Bojador to be conceded to the crown of Portugal. He also asked that the Order of Christ might have spiritual jurisdiction over these new lands, and over all converts made to the Christian faith. He asked that any of his men who died on these voyages of exploration might be granted the same indulgences as if they had fallen in a crusade. It was natural that Henry, as grand master of the Order of Christ, should apply to the Pope for his blessing on the expeditions. The Pope was head of Christendom, King above all kings, and God's representative on earth. Only he could say with authority to whom a particular territory belonged by right of conquest and conversion.

Pope Eugenius IV was deeply concerned at this time about the Turkish threat to eastern Europe. He was overjoyed, therefore, at the news of these maritime successes on the western flank of Moslem power. Tangier had proved a setback that Christendom could ill afford—which was the main reason he could in no way consider giving up Ceuta. But the fact that the ships of this Portuguese prince appeared to be sailing beyond the confines of the Moors was an immense encouragement. In 1445 he issued a bull confirming all that Prince Henry had asked.

The wind was set fair. It was more than twenty years since Prince Henry had first sighted the spray-whitened rock of Sagres and had known his destiny. They had been long years, calling for endurance and constancy in the face of many profitless voyages and popular skepticism. But now, as they always will when a great man has shown them the way, the people began to follow him. ". . . They confessed their former foolishness and admitted their ignorance of the very things which previously they had never taken seriously. Now they said openly that the Prince was none other than a second Alexander."

His brother Prince Peter, regent of Portugal, granted Henry

a charter, which allowed him one-fifth of the profit from the expeditions—a right normally belonging to the crown. Bearing in mind that for twenty years Henry had paid the whole cost of the expeditions, he also issued a mandate which stated that "no one might sail down the African coast without permission from the Prince Navigator."

In 1441 Prince Henry could feel the steady trade wind of success blowing behind his enterprise. Had it not been for the thought of his younger brother Fernando still a captive of the Moors, he would have had every reason to rejoice. He could look back on the four barren years that had followed the disaster of Tangier as no more than a desert through which he had had to make his way. Now he could see the promised land.

17

The years immediately following Tangier had been a testing
ground for his character. The succession of an infant prince
and the problems of the regency had greatly weakened the
state, and a conflict of interests had brought the country to
the verge of civil war.

Queen Leonora's dislike of Prince Peter was one of the main
factors that precipitated the crisis. Peter, whom the people of
Portugal would have been glad to see as undisputed regent,
found himself opposed at every turn by his sister-in-law. Her
claims to the regency were supported by the Count of Barcellos,
who for years had been nursing the grievance of his birth.
He now found himself in a position where he could play
Machiavelli in the politics of the country.

Drawn from his seclusion at Sagres, Henry arrived in Lisbon
to attempt the part of peacemaker. The country was divided
almost equally between the popular support for Prince Peter
and the group of nobles who were pressing Queen Leonora to
take the reins into her own hands. The strong reign of King
John had kept the nobles in check, and they had not dared
challenge King Edward, since he was backed by his four

brothers. But things were very different now. Prince Fernando was a hostage in Morocco, Prince John was ill, Prince Henry was living like a recluse at Sagres, and only Prince Peter, the popular choice for regent, stood in their way.

The arrival of Prince Henry temporarily checked the trouble. Although it was an uncongenial task, and very unlike those to which he was accustomed, Henry spent many weeks engaged in the hard task of peacemaker. He endeavored to calm public fears, to appease the power-hungry, and at the same time to ensure that the government of the country was carried on. His solution was to propose a compromise settlement whereby Queen Leonora and Prince Peter should share the regency. The Queen would attend to her children's upbringing and education, and retain power over all court appointments. Prince Peter, meanwhile, with the title of "Defender of the Realm," would have equal authority over any decrees that were made. The Cortes were to assemble once a year to give their advice on matters of policy, and Prince John and Prince Henry could be called on whenever necessary.

Like so many political compromises, it was a failure. Prince Henry's proposals were agreed to, but they did not solve the problem. They seemed logical and reasonable to him, but he failed to take into account the characters of courtiers, prelates, and noblemen for whom worldly power was all-important. His own dreams were so much vaster and more impersonal that he could hardly conceive how men could fight and conspire for the possession of a few more honors, a few acres of land, or an increase in their income. Prince Peter he understood, for he, like Henry, was an idealist and an honorable patriot. But the creatures who infested the court were beyond the comprehension of a man whose eyes were fixed on the Atlantic.

Queen Leonora was well aware that Henry's advice was disinterested. After a slight delay, she agreed to the proposed terms, and her brother-in-law left for the Algarves. It was not long before his peace was once more disturbed.

The struggle had begun again. Queen Leonora was urged to it by her supporters, and Prince Peter was reluctantly compelled to assert his equal rights in the government of the kingdom. This time Henry threw the weight of his authority wholeheartedly on his brother's side. He attempted a reconciliation between Peter and the Queen, but Leonora would have none of it. Seeing that the mood of the nation was completely against a shared regency, Henry made it clear that in his view Peter should be sole regent. The man from Sagres was the only one of the brothers with whom the Queen would now have any communication. Henry knew little about women's emotions. It would have seemed incomprehensible to him that the Queen's mistrust of Peter stemmed from the fact that she disliked his wife.

Queen Leonora finally overreached herself when in an attempt to win Prince Henry to her side, she wrote saying that Prince Peter was so determined on absolute power that he even intended to have Henry imprisoned. This was unthinkable, and Henry knew it. Peter was his favorite brother, the only one who in any way shared his dreams about the exploration of Africa, and with whom he had often pondered over charts and discussed the existence and whereabouts of Prester John. The bitterness that prompted Leonora's letter seems at last to have made him aware of the hatred she bore Prince Peter.

He rode north at once. He left behind the level country where he had made his home, with its coastal plains rich in grapes, figs, oranges, lemons, olives, and almonds. Aloes and dates grew there, and even the climate had something North African about it. He knew that warm land as well as he knew the sea surge round the cliffs of Sagres and the sliding panels of the Atlantic. But as he rode north, the hills began to limit the horizon. Trees and vines clung tenaciously along their terraced flanks, and he felt the world closing in on him—that world of conspiracy and intrigue to which he was a stranger. He longed for the time when he need hardly ever come north again.

A few days later he reached Coimbra, the graceful city on the banks of the Mondego. Prince Peter was there to meet him, and Henry hailed him with a laugh.

"See what the Queen writes to me!" he said. "See, brother, how afraid I am of you!"

"Evil times bring forth evil fruit," Peter answered wryly as he looked at the letter. "At any rate, you will find an honorable prison awaiting you!"

The whole family was assembled to greet Prince Henry. His reluctance to leave his mysterious fortress in the south, and his strange quest for unknown islands and continents, had made him something of a legend even among his relations. The fact that this was the second time within two years that he had hurried north served to emphasize the magnitude of the dangers confronting the kingdom. The esteem in which his father, King John, was known to have held him gave greater weight to his opinions. Even the Count of Barcellos, who was present, together with Prince John, was prepared to listen to his advice. Despite his personal ambitions, he had begun to feel that the present divided state of the nation could continue no longer. The Queen's growing arrogance—the likelihood that she would not be easy to control if she were sole regent—had disillusioned him.

The man who now added the weight of his authority to their council was in his mid-forties. His white skin, upon which Azurara had commented, was tanned and lined like a sailor's. His dark eyes were deep-set in a fine mesh of wrinkles.

They were eyes that had grown tired with watching the dazzle of sunlight on ocean rollers, and gazing night after night at the wheeling pattern of the stars. There was self-confidence in his speech and in his movements, but something also a little slow and ponderous. It was as if, grown unused to courts and cities, his nature had changed its rhythm to accord better with the remote world in which he lived. His hair was still dark and thick, but there were touches of gray in it. His shoulders were as broad as ever, and the deep barrel-chest showed where the strength lay that had made him a legend at Ceuta. The hands were strong, lean, and deeply tanned. Unlike his brothers, he wore no jewelry, and the dusty state of his traveling clothes did not seem to worry him. He drank no wine when it was offered, and ate sparingly. Prince Peter's family gazed with awe at this famous uncle, but with affection too—for his eyes were gentle, and he was notoriously indulgent with children. (In later years it was well known that Prince Fernando, King Edward's second son, whom Henry had adopted, was outrageously spoiled by his uncle.)

The conference at Coimbra produced the desired result. Queen Leonora, who had refused to come to meet Prince Peter and his brothers, was informed that the Cortes must be summoned immediately. (It was known that they were in favor of having Prince Peter as sole regent of the kingdom.) Soon afterward Lisbon and Porto both came out openly in favor of the same decision. The Count of Barcellos quietly withdrew to his estates and—while still making mischief whenever opportunity was presented—as quietly withdrew his support from the Queen's party.

Unwilling to accept second place in the kingdom, Queen Leonora retired from Lisbon into the country, and ultimately to Castile. The decision was reached that her two sons, Affonso, the future king, and Fernando, Henry's heir, should be

brought up by Prince Peter as well as by herself. It was agreed
that a woman's schooling was unsuitable for men who must
rule a country in a dangerous age. It was this that aroused
her impulsive pride. Rather than share the responsibility for
her sons' education and upbringing, she withdrew altogether
from their lives. King Edward's unhappy queen ended her
days an exile in Castile.

Whether the successful outcome of the affair owed much to
Henry's intervention at Coimbra is doubtful. It was the popular
voice of Lisbon and Porto in demanding a strong regent that
really decided the issue. There is no doubt, though, that it was
the united front displayed by the three brothers, Peter, Henry,
and John, that helped to prevent what might well have turned
into a civil war. It convinced the Queen's party of the futility
of their efforts. Perhaps in those difficult days the brothers
remembered Queen Philippa's words: "Take one arrow by
itself, and it is nothing. . . . But if you take many of them
together, it is beyond your strength to break them."

By 1441, the year in which the first Africans were brought
back to Portugal and Nuño Tristão in his caravel discovered
Cape Blanco, the country's affairs were becoming stable again.
For four years Henry had had little leisure to devote himself
to his chosen task. There had been little chance, either, of
redeeming the hostage of Tangier.

Prince Fernando had been right when he said that with the
death of King Edward his captivity would end only with his
life. Although his memory haunted his brothers, they were
impotent to help him, particularly when the country was
divided over the question of the regency. King Edward in his
will had asked that every possible means be used to secure
Fernando's freedom, even to the extent of surrendering Ceuta.
There is no doubt that Prince Peter and Prince John were
prepared to go to this length. King Edward had been deterred

by the unanimous advice of his fellow monarchs and of the Pope that Ceuta should never be surrendered. His two brothers did not feel bound by any similar obligations. Two attempts were in fact made to ransom Prince Fernando, offering Ceuta in exchange, but on both occasions nothing was concluded. The first time, a gale dispersed the ships that had gone to conduct the negotiations, and the second time the Moors themselves were unable to agree about the terms. Prince Henry may well have seen the hand of God in the failure of these two missions.

Condemned to martyrdom, the Constant Prince remained in the hands of the Vizier Lazurac. Day by day his hopes of freedom faded, and day by day Lazurac saw his chances of a rich ransom disappear. The Prince became no more than any other Christian captive—a slave, and not a hostage. Deprived of any concessions to his status or to his royal blood, he was set to work in the gardens of the palace of Fez. Later, when weakness and dysentery had made him unfit for work, he was confined to his cell. His constancy and his resignation remained unchanged, and his uncomplaining nature moved his companions. If they cursed their jailers, Prince Fernando only remarked that no better could be expected of men who had never heard the words of truth. If they called down malediction on all Moors, he reminded them that they ought, rather, to pray for their enemies.

His only comfort during these long years was the companionship of the attendants and friends who had followed him into captivity. For the last fifteen months of his life he was denied even this. Lazurac, discovering what pleasure the Prince found in talking to them when they returned from their work in the evenings, ordered him to be confined in a separate cell. Deprived of companions and of conversation, he was also deprived of light. For more than a year the youngest son of King John lay alone in a windowless cell. His only fault had been that he had hoped, like his brothers, to see the banners wave over a conquered city, and to earn knighthood on the field of battle.

In 1442 Prince John, who had been ailing for many years, finally succumbed to his illness. He had been a constant help and a faithful adviser to his brother Peter during the troubles of the regency. His death increased the burden that lay on the Regent's shoulders. Henry was too far away, and too little interested in the economy and politics of the country, to be of much assistance. From now on Prince Peter had the heavy task of reigning in his nephew's stead, and of educating the young Prince, and at the same time avoiding the snares laid for him by friends of the self-exiled Queen, or of the Count of Barcellos.

Prince John's death increased the hopelessness of Fernando's position. One brother was fully occupied in the internal affairs of Portugal, and the other was brooding over charts of Africa—still dreaming of a crusade that would deliver all Morocco to him as well as his brother. It was true that Henry would have paid a ransom for Fernando (which would have been acceptable to Lazurac), but Sala-ben-Sala had died. This further confused matters, and Sala-ben-Sala's brother, who succeeded him as governor of Tangier, was adamant that he would take nothing but Ceuta in return for the Prince.

In the summer of 1443, worn out by illness and privation, Prince Fernando died. He was forty-one years old, and he had been a prisoner for nearly six years. To the end of his life he maintained the nobility and sweetness of disposition that he had possessed in common with his brother King Edward. Even Lazurac was compelled to admit that he had borne his captivity nobly, and declared that had he been a Mohammedan, he would have been called a saint. The Moors blamed Fernando's family and his country for leaving him to die, unransomed and alone, in a foreign country. His body was disemboweled and hung up at the gate of the city, so that the mob might deride a Christian and a prince.

Prince Fernando paid the price of empire. He was the price of Henry's failure at Tangier, but he was also the price of Ceuta. The sons whom Philippa of Lancaster bore to King John of Portugal were more than worthy of their grandfather John of Gaunt. They were men in an age when the virtues of manhood were called for among princes, yet they never confused manhood with arrogant self-assertion. In a century when violence and corruption were commonplace, the brothers were unique, and they would be exceptional in any age.

Now, out of the five sons whom Queen Philippa had borne, only Peter and Henry were left. Prince Peter, busy with affairs of state, alternated between Coimbra, Lisbon, and Porto. His enigmatic motto *Désir* had led him a long way from the youthful triumph at Ceuta, throughout most of the Near East and almost all the courts of Europe, to bring him finally to the regency of Portugal. He was not ambitious for power, a reluctant philosopher-statesman rather, who would have been happier in his library than in court and council.

If Peter was deeply moved by the pathos and shame of Fernando's death in Fez, he had the comfort of a wife and children. It is not difficult to imagine the feelings of Prince Henry, alone on the promontory of Sagres. The words that Shakespeare makes the Duchess of Gloucester say to John of Gaunt might almost have been written for him:

> Ah, Gaunt! His blood was thine: that bed, that womb,
> That metal, that self-mould, that fashion'd thee
> Made him a man; and though thou liv'st and breath'st
> Yet art thou slain in him. . . .

From 1443, the year of Fernando's death, he rarely ventured outside Sagres and the province of Algarve. It was as if he were determined to efface the tragedy of Tangier in a victory not only over the ocean and Africa, but over himself as well.

18

The fame of Henry's ocean voyages, the news that his sailors were uncovering the coastline of the unknown continent, had now spread through the courts of Europe. It was rumored that far to the south on a lonely headland at the end of Portugal, something strange was taking place. Ships were being launched into the immensity of the Atlantic and were coming back with reports of unknown islands, of a huge coastline, and of races of men whom no one had ever seen before.

Something of the jealously guarded mystery that today surrounds Cape Canaveral was attached to Sagres. The knowledge gained in the Portuguese voyages was closely kept from the seamen of other nations. The additions to the charts were known only to the Prince, his captains, and his cartographers. The courses steered, the instruments used, even the new types of ship, were all Portuguese secrets.

In 1443 the mysterious headland attracted a German nobleman, Balthasar, a courtier in the household of the Emperor Frederick III. Throughout history the Germans have been drawn as if by a magnet to the sun and the south, and Balthasar was no exception. He had a good passport to Prince Henry's

affections, for he had taken part in the attack on Ceuta and
had been knighted for his services on that day. Balthasar had a
favor to ask of the Prince. Might he be allowed to go on one
of the voyages down to Africa? He wanted to see once more
that strange continent, and, above all, he wanted to see something of the ocean. He had heard of its great storms. He had
seen a little bad weather during those days when the Portuguese
invasion fleet had nearly come to grief in the Strait of
Gibraltar, but this time he hoped to see the Atlantic in the full
sweep of its fury. A romantic character, like many of his race,
he had courage too, as he hoped to prove again on a voyage
into the unknown.

Prince Henry readily granted his request. Balthasar was the
kind of man whom he was only too pleased to have in his
service. He often wished that there were more noblemen in
the Portuguese court ready to give up pleasure and place seeking for the profound excitement of going where no man had
ever been before. Balthasar was given a berth in the ship
belonging to Antão Gonçalves, who was on his way back to the
Rio de Ouro to put Adahu, the Berber chief, ashore and to
receive a ransom for his return. Adahu had been pining for his
native country for many months. He had no more information
of use to the Prince, and he had assured the Portuguese that
his people would be happy to pay a ransom for him as well
as for two young Berbers who had been captured with him.

In the early summer Gonçalves set off from Lagos in his
barinal. There was room aboard for about twelve men—a
small covered forecastle forward for the sailors, and cramped
quarters aft for himself, his sailing master, and his guest,
Balthasar. They spread an awning over the deck abaft the
mainmast, and there Adahu and the two young Moorish boys
spent most of their time. The *barinal* was an oared vessel, but
she also set two square sails, one from the mainmast and the

other from a small foremast near the decked-in forecastle. With the northeasterlies blowing from astern they had no need to row, and in the warm summer weather there was no discomfort in having to live mostly on the open deck. As they left Lagos, to the shouts and cheers of the dockside workers and the flutter of scarves from the houses, Balthasar recaptured something of the emotion he had felt that day, twenty-eight years before, when he had sailed from Lisbon for Ceuta. The sounds of the ship brought back the old memories. All the time there was the purring lisp of water, the creak of the tackles that restrained the full-bellied sails, and that strange smell of a sailing boat—a compound of tar, wet rope, canvas, and pitch pine.

They ran out from the coast and dropped the town astern of them. Looking back, he saw the shine of its white houses and the tawny walls of the two forts that guarded the approaches. Ahead lay the ocean. The *barinal* went well down-wind, but, as no doubt Gonçalves explained to his German guest, coming back to Portugal was another thing altogether. The seamen had to spend back-breaking hours sweating over the oars, while the master had to use every trick of current, and work every swirl round bay or headland that could help them against the wind. The caravel was the ship for this African work, he was told. He would see one later in the year when Nuño Tristão came down to join them off the Rio de Ouro.

Balthasar's wish to see a gale was soon granted. (One cannot help wondering whether he had been rash enough to mention this hope within earshot of the crew. He would certainly have earned the reputation of a Jonah if he had.) One evening, when they were well south of Portugal, they ran out of their favorable wind. An ominous swell began to lift under their bows, a slow deep-breathing movement of the ocean. It came from the southwest. An apricot light flickered along the cloud base, and the sea was the color of gun metal. It may be that Balthasar heard some of the old sailors' lore about wind and weather—sayings like those that King Edward had once collected and set down among his writings: "When the new moon is red, it signifies much wind," and "If the moon sparkle like the water raised by oars, it means there will soon be a storm."

They labored with difficulty into a rising sea, and then, a few hours later, the wind began to sound in the rigging. Before many hours were out, the small boat was staggering in a big sea. The spray whipped over the bulwarks like a handful of flint chips slung against the face. The waves gradually built up and came with a sliding rush, seeming to stand high over the boat's mast. There was that numbing minute when it seemed as if the *barinal*'s stern would never rise to the great mass of water, and then the quick glissade as she ran down the steep face of the sea. The sails were lashed down, and the oars had long since been boated and stowed. They were running back now under bare poles before the wind and weather. From the stern, perched uneasily some four feet above the water, Balthasar saw twenty-foot waves that looked like smoking gray walls. He looked up, but all he could see was the wild welter of the sky, and beneath him were two thousand fathoms of ocean. The helmsman braced his feet against the thwarts, steering to keep the boat's stern presented squarely to the following sea. Weeping streamers of nimbus cloud, the rain bearer, swept over them. Ropes parted, gear was swept from side to side in the dark rush of bilge water, and the Africans abandoned hope. Yet still the seas built up, and the wind came at them with a driving shout.

At times it seemed as if there was no hope. Only the experience of the crew, men who had learned their hard craft on the Atlantic coast, could bring them to safety. Balthasar learned the truth of the saying "It's not the ships that count, but the men in them." If the sailors had weakened or lost their heads, then the boat would certainly have been overwhelmed. If the helmsman had panicked as one of the great rollers swept under their stern, the *barinal* would have broached to. It would have been rolled over and over in the great mass of water, weighing hundreds of tons, that smoked and sizzled in every wave crest.

With their provisions ruined, and damage to boat and gear, they came running back to Portugal. The wind died, and the swell was easing by the time they raised the bleak headland of St. Vincent. Adahu and the two Berber boys were still prostrate with fear and sickness as they crossed the hundred-fathom line, and the sailors got out their oars to shape a course back to Lagos. It would be several days' work before the damage could be made good, and it would be many years before Balthasar would forget his baptism of fire at sea. The wind's high pipe in the rigging, the rush of great seas against their thin plank sides, the scouring rattle of rain on deck, and the sighing advance of the huge Atlantic rollers—these were things he would remember and tell to admiring circles in the Emperor's court on his return.

He insisted on staying with the ship when they set out again. He had been through a storm at sea, and now he was determined to see the hot sands of the Sahara and to pass the cape that had once marked the end of the world. This time they had no trouble, and Balthasar saw the flying fish rise in the fair weather, and heard the eternal rumor of the cliff wash off Bojador. The sea birds spread their wet wings to the sun along deserted beaches. He learned the dull, woody taste of water that has been long in cask, and the monotony of biscuit, salted cod, and meat—broken occasionally by a ration of fruit, or fresh fish. During the hot hours after noon, he lay and watched the shadow of the awning sway like a pendulum across the deck to the boat's steady roll.

One day Antão Gonçalves pointed ahead. A long sandy arm ran out from the coast, and inside it lay the deep well-sheltered anchorage of the Rio de Ouro. Balthasar was the first man other than a Portuguese to see this new world. They quickly lowered a boat and set Adahu ashore to arrange his ransom and that of the two young boys. For a whole week they waited swinging to the tides in the blue bay, while the sailors fished or went after the sea lions that lived in great colonies along the sandy inlet. Adahu did not return, and the Portuguese cursed themselves for having put their trust in a heathen. Then a caravan made its way across the desert and signaled them. There was no ransom for the man who had sat in Prince Henry's company and told him all he knew about the continent. (Perhaps Adahu felt he had more than bought his freedom by giving away this information to foreigners.) But ten adult Negroes were handed over in return for the two young Berbers. Some gold dust, a native shield, and a number of ostrich eggs completed the transaction. Gonçalves could, after all, feel pleased with the result of his voyage. He was not only the first man to bring back Negro slaves; he was the first to bring back gold from the new territory.

The attitude of Christian Europe to the slave trade is something that seems puzzling and profoundly depressing to a modern. With what justification could Christians take slaves back into their countries and feel apparently no twinge of conscience? Since it was the Portuguese who began to import West African slaves into Europe and into their colonies, and since Prince Henry has been harshly criticized by some historians on this score, it is important to try to understand the fifteenth-century outlook.

To begin with, slavery was nothing new. It had always existed in Africa and among the Arabs—and still does to this day. A raiding African tribe would appropriate what women they fancied from their neighbors, and would then sell the rest, together with the men and children, to the traders who came down from Morocco. The Roman Empire had been founded on slavery, and Christianity had grown up in a society that accepted the slave as the basic machinery around which civilization revolved. Slavery was a hazard that every Christian risked who sailed in Mediterranean waters, where the Moorish pirates had their eyes on the value of the captives almost as much as the cargo of a ship. Every man who fought at Ceuta or Tangier knew just what his fate would be if he were taken prisoner—unless he could find a ransom. We know from the story of Prince Fernando that there was no hope of anything but a life of slavery unless a ransom was forthcoming.

Prince Henry's own attitude to the slave trade is made abundantly clear in Azurara's chronicle. He knew that there was little or no hope of converting the Moors from the religion of Mahomet, but he saw every heathen Negro as a potential Christian. His aim was to create a Christian kingdom in Africa. It has been succinctly put by E. J. Payne in the *Cambridge Modern History*: "Dom Henrique was not a mere slave-trader. The capture of slaves was destined to serve a greater purpose— the conversion of Bilad Ghana (Guinea) into a Christian dependency of Portugal, to be administered by the military order of Jesus Christ . . . the project was in substance similar to that carried out by the Teutonic Order in conquering and christianising the heathen Prussians."

When the first Portuguese ships returned with Negro prisoners aboard them, there was rejoicing in their conversion and acceptance of the Christian faith. There was no conception of "color bar." The Africans were freely permitted to intermarry with the Portuguese, always provided that such marriages were Christian ones. It was not until much later that a cynical approach to the slave trade infected nearly all of Europe. But it was traders from Liverpool and Bristol, from Spain, and from the Breton ports of France who made the slave trade a stain on the European conscience. These later adventurers had no interest in their unfortunate captives except for their cash value in the slave markets of the West Indies and America. This was never the outlook of Prince Henry, whatever his individual captains may have felt on the subject.

It was in this same year, 1443, while Balthasar was embarked with Antão Gonçalves in his *barinal,* that Nuño Tristão set out again in his caravel. Tristão was the kind of captain Henry admired, for on every voyage he managed to go a little farther than before. He was not content to stay in familiar anchorages like the Rio de Ouro, and this time he went on to pass Cape Blanco, and to sail into one of the largest bays on the west coast of Africa. Lévrier Bay, which he discovered, is about thirty miles wide, with Cape Blanco at the northern end and the low hump of Cape St. Anna at the southern. Fierce tides disturb the bay, and even when the wind is light, the water is lumpy and snarls with tide rips. When the trade wind blows strongly from the north, the air is full of driven sand, the capes vanish, and leading marks are obscured.

Below Cape St. Anna another small bay opens out, and it was here that Nuño Tristão dropped anchor in the lee of an island. Arguim Bay they called this second of the two folds in the great land mass of Africa. It was to play an important part in Portuguese history, for it was here, on the main island in the bay, that Prince Henry began to build a fort and trading post in 1448. So small a thing was the beginning of colonialism in Africa—one mud-and-stone fort on an islet in an obscure bay —yet it marked the beginning of the vast colonial empires of the Portuguese, the Dutch, the English, and the Spanish. What must always be remembered about Prince Henry and his place in history is that he not only began the exploration and discovery of the world, but he set the pattern for all future colonialism. His dream may have been of the conversion of souls, but its outcome was the fort, the armed caravel, and the slave trade.

In the hot bleak bay, between Arguim Island and another, which they named the Isle of Herons, Nuño Tristão's men captured fourteen Negroes. They had been rash enough to paddle out in canoes to investigate this curious great bird that had dropped into their quiet world out of the Atlantic. On Arguim Island itself the Portuguese captured a further fourteen natives, and on Heron Island they took many royal herons and other sea birds. "So Nuño Tristão returned to Portugal with his captives, more pleased than the first time because he had taken more, and also because he was alone and therefore had no need to share with anyone else."

When Balthasar, Antão Gonçalves, and Nuño Tristão returned to Portugal, they were hailed as heroes. Now people could see some tangible profits accruing from the Prince's African expeditions. The slaves, the gold dust, even the ostrich eggs, were seen as an earnest of future, and fabulous, wealth. Some of the ostrich eggs were served at the Prince's table "as fresh and as savory as if they had been of domestic birds," though one feels that after a long sea voyage in the hot summer, only a palate prejudiced in their favor could have come to this conclusion.

A new type of hero now began to emerge, a hero who would dominate European life and literature until the collapse of colonialism in our own century—the adventurer-explorer, the warrior-colonist. How many young Portuguese, as they looked at men like Nuño Tristão, must have felt as Rimbaud put it centuries later:

"*Je reviendrai, avec des membres de fer, la peau sombre,*

*l'oeil furieux: sur mon masque, on me jugera d'une race forte.
J'aurai de l'or. . . ."*

Thus, after a quarter of a century's dour persistence in the
face of failure and discouragement, the dedicated policy of
Prince Henry began to yield results. Like many another man
of genius, he could have no idea what forces he had set in
motion. In exploration as in love, it is the first step that counts.
From now on, there could be no turning back.

Men who in the past would venture into the unknown only to
gain the Prince's rewards and favors now went willingly to
win themselves a private fortune. On Henry's orders, they
marked the new capes and bays with wooden crosses, and their
caravels flew the Cross of Christ on their sails. On Henry's
orders, the captives were instructed by priests in the Christian
faith. But the religion of Europe came hand in hand with the
sword and the culverin. Before long, many a lonely bay in
Africa would echo with the cries of captives, as a superior
technology and civilization were imposed upon them by force.

19

Henry was still eager for his navigators to sail to the fertile lands and the great rivers, which he had heard lay farther to the south of Cape Blanco. The fact that he was now able to find men willing to put up the money for these expeditions was a great relief. He had borne the whole cost for so many years that it seemed logical to allow others to fit out the ships. He could content himself with the knowledge that even if they went for personal gain, they were also serving his purpose. Whether they would or not, some of them were bound to advance the geographical knowledge of the continent.

Typical of these early expeditions was one fitted out by Lançarote, the King's customs officer at Lagos. Lançarote provided and provisioned six caravels, the captain of one of them being Gil Eannes, the man who had made all this possible by being the first to round Cape Bojador. In midsummer the raiding expedition came down the hot coastline, and into the steamy Bay of Arguim. Azurara cannot restrain a note of pity as he tells of what followed:

"Then you might see mothers abandoning their children, and husbands abandoning their wives, each thinking only how to escape as quickly as possible. Some drowned themselves in the sea, others sought refuge in their huts, and others hid their children under the mud—thinking that they might thus hide them from the enemy and be able to collect them later. . . ."

Yet he is able to go on, without any trace of irony: "And at length Our Lord God, who always rewards the upright, wishing to recompense them [the Portuguese] for their work during this day, ordained that they should have victory over their enemies and should capture 165 men, women and youths. This is without reckoning those that died in the battle or killed themselves."

It was a polite fiction to call these unhappy Berbers and Negroes "enemies." Although most of the Berbers were certainly Mohammedans—and therefore technically at war with Christians—the Negroes were primitive heathen. They were quite unaware of the conflicting merits or demerits of the two warring religions.

On August 8, 1444, the six caravels landed their prisoners at Lagos. The whole town was astir, and people had even ridden in from the surrounding countryside to see the black gold that was being mined in the distant south. Merchants, farmers, and nobles alike had been quick to see the value of cheap labor in their fields and houses. "Envy began to gnaw at them as they saw the houses of others filled with servants, and their possessions increased. . . ."

The manpower problem in Portugal was acute, and it was easy to see how these captives could help to solve it. The population, small in any case, had been drained by the Castilian wars of King John's time; men had been lost at Ceuta, others at Tangier, and yet others had gone to colonize Prince Henry's Atlantic islands. The almost annual recurrence of plague in the seaports of Lisbon and Porto caused a further steady drain on the country's population.

Seasick, homesick, and some of them wounded, the Africans were destined for the first of the Lagos slave auctions. ". . . Very early, because of the heat, the sailors began to fill the boats and take the captives ashore as they had been ordered. And when they were all assembled in this field it was an astonishing sight, for some of them were almost white, handsome, and with well-made bodies. Others were black as Ethiopians and as ugly. . . . But what heart even the hardest would not be moved by pity when seeing them gathered together; for some bowed their heads, with their faces bathed in tears; others groaned and raised their faces to the heavens as if to implore the Father to help them; others beat their faces with their hands and threw themselves full length upon the ground."

Without regard for racial or family ties, the captives were divided among their owners. One-fifth of them belonged to Prince Henry, for such were the terms under which the expeditions went to Africa. It is impossible to know what he made of the tragic scene. We know that he was there, on horseback in the midst of his people, and the only clue to his feelings can be gauged from the words: ". . . He parcelled out his share like a man who was in no way eager to possess great riches, since, out of the forty souls who fell to his lot, he made presents of them. He had no other pleasure than in thinking that these lost souls would now be saved."

His captains and the merchants of Lisbon may have been hypocritical, but it does not accord with what we know of Prince Henry's character. Azurara's comment in this case is probably accurate. He goes on to say that Henry's "hope was not in vain for, as soon as the Moors understood our language, they became Christians. And I, who write this history, have seen in the city of Lagos boys and girls, the children and grandchildren of these Moors, born in our country, as good and true

Christians as though they had been descended from those who were first baptised according to Christ's law."

Azurara calls all these first captives "Moors," but later in his narrative he makes the important distinction that "they were not hardened in their beliefs like other Moors and embraced the law of Christ without difficulty." Most of them, in fact, were Negroes from northern Senegal, who were of course heathen, not Mohammedan, and thus presented little resistance to conversion. Distributed like slaves, they were not treated as such, for none of them was ever chained. They were treated with kindness, were taught trades, and intermarried with the Portuguese. Within a generation they were regarded as little or no different from any Portuguese peasant. Harrowing though the description of their capture and disposal at Lagos is, it is important to bear in mind how different was their fate from that of later generations in Africa who were sold to slavers for the plantations of the West Indies and America.

The Portuguese attitude toward the Africans was determined by the Church's outlook on the subject. Color of skin was unimportant. So long as they embraced the Christian faith, they received far better treatment than would any Arab prisoner who remained adamant in his faith. Azurara compares these Negroes with the North African Arabs and notes four things that differentiate them: firstly, that after being for some time in Portugal they did not try to escape, but even forgot their own country; secondly, that they were very loyal and obedient and bore no malice; thirdly, that they were "less inclined to lewdness than the others"; and fourthly, that as soon as they had been given clothes, they evinced a marked taste for "baubles and gaudy colours." This first European assessment of the African character is curiously accurate, for amiability and a love of bright colors are still outstanding features of the African.

The Portuguese, to their credit, never overlooked their common humanity with their African prisoners. "Sons of Adam like ourselves," it was said of them. A number of the captives who fell to Prince Henry's lot were given to the Church to be educated. Among them was one young boy who later grew up to be a Franciscan friar and to serve in the monastery on Cape St. Vincent. Azurara commented with sincerity: "How great must be the reward of the Prince before the Lord God for having saved not these souls alone but many, many more in the course of his life!"

From 1442 to 1447, while Prince Peter was ruling Portugal as undisputed regent, Henry was able to devote himself almost exclusively to his African projects. It was easy now to find men willing to go raiding down the coast, but to find the kind of man who would devote himself exclusively to the Prince's search for knowledge was another matter. Henry not only wanted information about the continent; he also wanted, if possible, to maintain a friendly relationship with the tribes along the coast. With every year that went by, this became more difficult, for the natives now knew what a caravel portended when she slid round a headland and lowered her boats.

In 1445 Henry had an example of the way in which his captains were disobeying his orders. A squire of his household, Gonçalo de Cintra, was ordered to sail as far as Guinea and not to stop until he had reached the fertile country to the south. But Gonçalo de Cintra was like everyone else—once it had been raiding parties into the Mediterranean or the Canaries that had deflected the captains from their orders, and now it was the chance of making a slaving raid on the African coast. Gonçalo de Cintra paid for his disobedience with his life. He was ambushed and killed, along with seven companions, in the bleak bay north of Cape Blanco, which still bears his name. These were the first Portuguese losses of the West African expeditions, and they served to increase Henry's desire to make peace with the natives.

From now on the divergence between the Prince's intentions and the conduct of the ships sailing under his banner became more and more apparent. He could hardly forbid men like Lançarote from equipping expeditions, and he could no longer control them by withholding his rewards and favors. They were now able to find their own rewards, and as for favors—he was bound to honor men who brought back heathen souls for conversion. By the end of his life, however, he was successful in winning their friendship by peaceful means.

In the very year in which Gonçalo de Cintra lost his life, Prince Henry found a man who was prepared to serve him in the true spirit of adventure. He was a squire called João Fernandes, who went out in an expedition financed by the Prince. These ships had orders to treat with the natives, and to try to come to some peaceful arrangement for the exchange of merchandise.

João Fernandes volunteered to be set ashore in Africa and to stay there throughout a winter. His aim was to gather information about the climate, geography, and customs, and to make friends with the people. In view of the Portuguese behavior to date along this coastline, he was a brave man. It seems that the natives respected this quality in him, for no sooner was he put ashore than he went off in company with a group of Berbers who practically adopted him. Fernandes was the first European to bring back first-hand information of the Saharan region of Africa and of the customs of the Berbers and Tuareg Arabs. He landed in company with an old Moor who had been in Prince Henry's court and who was now returning to his own people. Fernandes had already acquired some Arabic, and possibly also a slight knowledge of the Berber dialect.

The following year Antão Gonçalves, who had now been given command of a caravel, picked up Fernandes at Cape Resgate. In company with him was a Berber chief who had befriended him, and who brought along some Negroes to barter with the Portuguese. Fernandes's account of his wanderings in the barren Sahara must have fascinated Prince Henry, for this was just the kind of information he was always seeking and so rarely finding.

It was a land without any grass except in the valleys, Fernandes told him, and the people were nomads speaking the Berber tongue, and of the Mohammedan faith. Their diet was largely milk, except for the coastal nomads who were fishermen and lived on raw, sun-dried fish. Wheat was a luxury, and the nomads ate it as a Portuguese would a sweetmeat. Most of the men were clothed in leather jackets and breeches, the wealthier wearing long woolen capes. "But the chiefs," said Fernandes, "have good raiment like that of the other Moors. They have fine horses, handsome saddles, and stirrups. Their women wear capes of wool which form a kind of mantle with which they hide their faces." It seemed that, like the ostriches, they thought that they were thus completely concealed, for their bodies were naked, and Fernandes concluded: "Certainly this is one of the things that show the brutishness of man. . . ."

Prince Henry heard further confirmation of the rich land of the Negroes that lay to the south, and how the Tuaregs raided them, carrying off the prisoners for sale to the merchants who came from Tunis. Fernandes told him that desert travel was rather like life at sea. The camel caravans were guided by the wind, the stars, and the flights of birds. Sometimes they would be traveling for days on end between one well and another, scorched at noon and frozen at night, for the desert got very cold as soon as the sun had set. But it was not all desolation; life existed in this strange world.

"There are many ostriches," said Fernandes, "antelopes and gazelles, partridges and hares as well. And the swallows which leave our country in the summer pass the winter among these sands. So do many other small birds." But he had watched the storks flying overhead, going south, even farther south. "They go to the Land of the Negroes and pass the winter there."

The Portuguese were on the verge of breaking through into this long-sought country. Only Henry's insistence that they should carry on had forced them as far as the Bay of Arguim and its populated shore. Now all the signs were that year by year they were leaving the barren desert behind them, and were nearing fertile land. Fernandes's account of his travels served to confirm other reports that Henry had been receiving ever since Adahu had first come to Sagres. There was no longer any doubt that not so many miles ahead lay a great river—the western Nile, he believed it to be—and possibly, not so far beyond that, the southernmost point of Africa.

It is important to remember that Prince Henry's conceptions of Africa were largely based on the stories of Arab geographers. The Arabs believed that the Senegal River originated in a lake in Central Africa, and that this was also the source of the Egyptian Nile. For this reason the Senegal was known as the western Nile. Prince Henry probably dreamed that by Christianizing this river up to its source, he would be able to link up with Prester John, or the Christian King of Abyssinia in his kingdom on the eastern Nile. By 1460, the year of his death, he may well have been under the impression that the end was in sight and that, after a few more voyages, Africa would be rounded. By this time the caravels had passed the Senegal, doubled Cape Verde, and were off the mouth of the River Gambia. But it was not, in fact, until 1487 that Bartolomew Dias, a descendant of one of Prince Henry's most skilled navigators, rounded the Cape of Good Hope and burst into the Indian Ocean.

It was in 1444 that Denis Dias, a Lisbon noble and an ancestor of the famous Bartolomew, discovered the green world that lay beyond the desert. Dias was older than most of Prince Henry's captains (he had been at the court of King John), but "he was unwilling to let himself grow soft in well-being and repose, for he was a man who wanted to see new things."

Denis Dias was given command of a caravel, and it is worth noting that from about 1442 onward, we hear no further mention of *barchas* or *barinales*. The ideal vessel for the Atlantic and for the exploration of Africa had been evolved, and caravels were building fast in the yards of Lagos, Lisbon, and Porto. In Madeira too, the colonists were felling trees and building the new design of boat on the beaches of Funchal and Machico. Wood from Madeira was beginning to supplement the timber of Portugal, and in the Azores the pines were already growing that would furnish later generations with planking for their ships.

Denis Dias scorned the easy pickings of the Bay of Arguim. As he sailed past, he could see other ships at anchor, busy sending raiding parties ashore. But he kept on south and dropped down the coast to pass Cape Resgate. Cape Blanco was 300 miles astern, when on a fair day he reached Cape Verde—the Green Cape.

The twin humps of Les Mamelles, "The Breasts," which broke the sky line above the cape, were pale with grass. All innocence, a native canoe came paddling out to meet them.

These were golden years. The troubles of the regency seemed over, and every new cape won out of the ocean helped to efface the memory of Tangier. This was true victory, this discovery of a continent. It was a victory of the spirit as well, for the prisoners were saved from that hell reserved for heathen, and converted to the true faith. Guilds of merchant-adventurers were formed in Lisbon and Lagos, and the shipyards were busy with orders for caravels. There was no longer anyone to be heard deploring the Prince's extravagance on useless expeditions.

Courted and flattered, he was greeted with acclamation when he rode between Sagres and Raposeira, or through the streets of Lagos. In 1442 King Henry VI of England had made Prince Henry a knight of the Garter. He was not changed by success. In the year that Denis Dias discovered Cape Verde he was fifty, an age at which men are set in their characters. For many years now he had drunk no wine, and he fasted almost half of every year. As he grew older he became even more devout. He "was obedient to all the commands of the Holy Church and attended her offices with great devotion. In his private chapel these offices were performed with as much solemnity and ceremony as in the chancel of any great cathedral. . . ."

Such a man was unlikely to be spoiled by success, any more than he had been deterred by failure. His dream was always of the next island—of the headland beyond the one that could be seen. In his dealings with the men who served him he remained just, and astonishingly patient—even when he saw that most of those who were commissioning caravels, and asking for his license to sail to Africa, were interested solely in their own profit. "To such a temper, all activities divorced from religion are brutal or dead, but none are too mean to be beneath or too great to be above it. . . ." Prince Henry never made the error of despising the human material through which he worked. Often, though, he must have wished that he could make the merchants, captains, and sailors see that peaceful commerce was preferable to warlike raiding parties.

But now that the whole coastline from Cape Blanco to Cape Verde was roused against the foreign invader, there seemed to be no other solution than to impose peace by force. Once that had been done, it would be possible for a permanent trading station to be established. The death of Gonçalo de Cintra brought matters to a head. A delegation from Lagos, led by Lançarote, asked for permission to send a strong force into the Bay of Arguim to subdue the islands.

"If you will allow us," they said, "we will arm our ships against them, and by death or imprisonment break their strength and power." They did not forget to add, "And if God wills that this undertaking ends in victory we shall be able to take a valuable number of captives."

The argument was cynical, but sound. Arguim Bay was the first and only place within a thousand miles of Portugal where ships could safely anchor, careen, repair, and draw water. On the barren coast of Morocco there was no other natural harbor. It was true that the caravels now used Madeira as a regular port of call, but Madeira was rapidly being left behind. What was needed was a base on the mainland of Africa, and Arguim Bay was the answer.

On August 10, 1445, a fleet of twenty-six ships sailed from Lagos and Lisbon to carry out the pacification of the bay. Times had changed greatly since the days when one or two ships were all that could be mustered for the Prince's voyages. Their arrival off the coast was a welcome sight to three other caravels, which had preceeded them. The sailors cheered when they saw the dipping lateen sails lift over the horizon.

The combined force soon cleared Arguim Island, the Isle of Herons, and the other off-lying islets and coastal regions of the bay. A number of captives were taken and sent back to Portugal on ships returning home. Within a year or two the fort on Arguim Island began to rise, the first of so many similar forts and trading posts that would mark Portuguese progress round the globe from Africa, to India, to the Spice Islands, and as far east as China. The policy they inaugurated in Arguim Bay was one that would be followed by the other nations of Europe. A century or so later nearly all the islands and continental coastlines of the world would be studded with these small stone-built fortifications, which symbolized power and trade borne on the lifelines of the sea.

It was nearly autumn when the great raid on Arguim Bay came to an end, and most of the ships turned for home. Only six caravels, one of them under Lançarote, who had played so large a part in financing the expedition, decided to continue on south to the land of the Negroes. Their wonder at the new coastline and at the marvels that confronted them every day still speaks through the quiet voice of Azurara. The historian, who had never been to these far shores, caught something of the excitement that gripped the men whose reports he heard. It was not only new bays and inlets, but new birds and beasts and fish that they were discovering. They watched the birds that had come south from Europe building their nests in Africa, and thus, as with the rounding of Cape Bojador, centuries-old legends about the migration of birds were dispelled at a blow. They saw the hornbills, "the neck so great that it can contain the leg of a man. . . ." They saw flamingos like elegant dancers, idling over their reflections in the lagoons; and curiosities like the remora, or suckerfish, which attaches itself to a large parent fish by the "crown" in its head.

After the salty cleanness of the sea wind and the dry dust of the Sahara, the scent of the fertile land seemed heavy, rich with fruits. ". . . On coming to it by sea the perfume gave them the impression that they had been carried into a beautiful orchard."

So they drew near the mouth of the Senegal, and a long way out from the shore they could see where the river laid its mark across the Atlantic. It stained the blue waves with a broad muddy track, and the change of color made the sailors think that they were nearing shoal ground. The leadsman ran forward and took a cast—no bottom! And then, happening to wipe his mouth with the back of his hand, he paused.

"Here is a new marvel!" he cried. "The water is fresh!"

They lowered a wooden bucket over the side.

"Sweet water! We must be near the mouth of the River Nile!"

The caravels turned and tacked toward the coast, following the brown stain of the river. It was the rainy season when they discovered the Senegal, and they had no difficulty in negotiating the river mouth. Had they arrived a month or so earlier, they would have been confronted by a great sand bar cutting them off entirely from the entrance. (Annually this bar builds up in the dry season, and annually it is washed away again when the rains come.)

Beyond the Senegal they sailed on south until they reached Cape Verde, and there they saw the sails of another caravel ahead of them. Landing on a small island near the cape, they found carved upon a tree the arms and the device of Prince Henry. It was a way the caravel captains had of telling their successors that the ships of the Prince had already marked and charted this point. Nowhere in his life's story does one feel more deeply the singular greatness of Prince Henry than in this scene of men landing on the beach of a tropical island off West Africa and seeing his arms carved upon a giant tree. *"Talent de bien faire!"* If ever a man justified his motto and aspirations, Prince Henry did. The words of William Mickle, the eighteenth-century translator of Camoëns's *Lusiads,* are not exaggerated: "What is Alexander in all his glories crowned with trophies at the head of his army, compared with Henry contemplating the ocean from his window on the rock of Sagres?"

The caravel that Lançarote and his ships had seen belonged to a nephew of João Gonçalves Zarco, the discoverer of Madeira. Zarco had built and fitted out the ship at his own expense. Unlike most others at the time, he had told his nephew to sail as far south as he could, and to bring back a useful report of the country to Prince Henry. In this way Zarco repaid the Prince for his trust in him in the early days, and for his governorship of Madeira. Zarco's nephew sailed on beyond Cape Verde, and about sixty miles to the south reached a cape, which he called the Cape of Masts, because it was covered with stark palm trees that had been stripped in a tropical tornado. Prince Henry's ships were now only about 14 degrees, 840 miles, north of the equator.

The dangers and hazards attendant on these early voyages are nowhere more clearly seen than in the tragic story of Nuño Tristão. The first man on record to have commanded a caravel, the discoverer of Cape Blanco and of Arguim Bay, Tristão was the ideal explorer—the man who is not content to rest until he has gone farther than all others. He sailed from Portugal in 1446, again determined to bring back news of unknown territory. Cape Bojador, Cape Blanco, Cape Verde—all the old landmarks were left behind. Day after day he worked his ship farther down the coast, making use of the diurnal onshore and offshore winds. He dropped the Cape of Masts astern and came down on a long, low coast, dense with umbrella trees and palms. A bald cape broke the western end of the shore, and patches of red cliff shone against the dark green of the jungle. The mouth of a great river beckoned him.

Dropping anchor just off the shore, and eager to explore the estuary, Nuño Tristão lowered two boats. He and most of his crew got into them and made off upstream on the flood of the tide. The trees closed over their heads. They saw for the first time the green darkness of Africa, and the river-light pearly with heat haze.

It was there, in the humid darkness, that Nuño Tristão came to the end of all his voyages. The two Portuguese rowing boats had not gone far upstream when they found themselves surrounded by canoes. A shower of arrows whispered through the air. They made a light sound like the mosquitoes of the delta, but they were twice as deadly. Nuño Tristão and his crew had discovered the mouth of the River Gambia—and the natives of that area steeped their arrowheads in poison. These were no simple natives like those of Arguim Bay, who could be rounded up like sheep. The inhabitants of the Gambia delta had no doubt heard, if not of the white men, at any rate of the Berber slavers who preyed along their boundaries. To them all strangers were enemies, and this first encounter proved that these white men were as mortal as any other.

Out of the twenty-two men who were in the boats, four were dead before they reached the safety of the caravel. Only two men escaped without injury, the others all being hit by arrows. Native canoes pursued them downstream, and further flights of arrows hissed about them as they clambered aboard. There were not enough unwounded to get up the anchors, so they cut the cables and let them go. Slowly the ship drifted away. Her decks littered with dead and dying, she floated out from the terrible river mouth, and gained the sea.

Nuño Tristão was dead. So were another knight, three members of Prince Henry's household, and sixteen sailors. Out of a crew of twenty-six, only five survived. One of them was an African boy, one a sailor, one a young clerk who had been sent along to keep the log of the expedition, and two were Portuguese ship's boys. They were 1,500 miles from home, a long way south of any other ships, and on a hostile coast. The first thing to do was to set some sail, and make an offing from the shore. It cannot have been easy working a fifty-ton vessel with only one able-bodied seaman, a youth, and three boys, but somehow or other they managed. The seaman, it turned out, had no knowledge at all of the art of navigation. At this point, by sheer good luck it turned out that the young clerk, Aires Tinoco, had been a personal attendant of Prince Henry. He had not been trained in navigation, but he had picked up enough to know that, once clear of the coast, their best course was a little east of north. So for two months the caravel stumbled back from the mouth of the river. They were too shorthanded to work the ship efficiently, and often her sails thundered when an unexpected squall hit them, or slatted idly

as they rolled in the long Atlantic swell. Sometimes they saw
the coast, but it was barren and featureless, and they dared
not approach for fear of the natives.

"North by east!" said Aires Tinoco. They watched the Pole
Star high over their port bow, and dawn after dawn they saw
the sun tilt over the hidden continent of Africa to sink at dusk
in the unbroken ocean.

Two months. They saw no ship, nothing—and then one day
they raised a sail. They had no idea where they were, and at
first they would have been glad to escape unnoticed. If they
were near a coast, they thought they were off Morocco—in
which case this was most probably a Moorish corsair. The unknown ship came out toward them, and then to their joy they
found themselves hailed by "a Christian—an honest corsair
from Gallicia." The ship was a pirate running out of northern
Spain, bent on plundering the Moors. They were just off Sines
in Algarve, they were told. The Gallician piloted them into
Lagos, no doubt receiving a reward for his services before
going on his way.

The epic voyage of Aires Tinoco was to be paralleled by
others in later years. It served to prove how fine a sea boat
the caravel was, if she could be handled by so small and inexperienced a crew. It proved, also, that young Aires Tinoco
had not wasted those years when he had served as a humble
groom of the chamber to Prince Henry.

The survivors were rewarded and taken care of, but Henry's
feelings of responsibility did not stop at that point. He had
known all the men, and some of them had been brought up
at Sagres in his court. He mourned Nuño Tristão as a companion, a sailor, and a man. The relatives and dependents of
all those who had lost their lives were at once taken under his
care and protection. In an age when kings and noblemen forgot

their retainers and men-at-arms on the conclusion of a campaign, and when ex-soldiers begged for bread as soon as their usefulness was at an end, Henry proved that he was no callous prince.

21

The Canary Islands remained an irritating and unsolved problem. It was one that troubled Prince Henry to the end of his life. Now that his ships were sailing ever farther down the African coast, the advantage of a base in one of the Canaries was obvious. Lying just north of Cape Bojador, they would have provided his ships with useful harbors and anchorages, and an advance headquarters for the exploration of Africa.

As early as 1424, just after the discovery of Madeira, he had fitted out a fleet and attempted to seize the islands by force. But the cost of maintaining so many ships and men, the angry protests from Castile, and—finally—an order from his father King John to leave the islands alone, had forced him to abandon the project. Castile's authority over the Canaries was only nominal, and the thing that must have profoundly irritated Henry was the way in which the islands were mismanaged. Only two of them, in fact, were colonized, and these were Lançarote and Fuerteventura, the two nearest the African coast. The other islands were still independent, ruled by their native Guanche chiefs, and raided periodically by both Spaniards and Portuguese. Prince Henry felt that if only he had control of the islands, they would all of them follow the pattern set by Madeira and the Azores.

The matter was brought to a head shortly after the great raid on Arguim in 1445. While some of the caravels had gone on to discover more of the Guinea coast, three of them turned aside on their way back to Portugal and made a raiding expedition into the Canaries. They captured some natives from Palma and then, by an act of treachery, took a number of prisoners from the island of Gomera, whose chieftain was friendly to the flag of Portugal. If these Portuguese captains expected a warm welcome from the Prince on their return, they were mistaken.

Henry was already engaged in trying to establish friendly relations with the tribes on the African coast and, if possible, to stop the slaving parties by substituting peaceful trade. It was bad enough that Canarians had been captured, but that most of them had been treacherously seized was enough to arouse the Prince's fury. Far from being rewarded, as perhaps they had hoped, the caravel captains concerned were severely taken to task. The Canarians, on the other hand, were made his guests, given rich presents, and sent back to their island.

The incident, nevertheless, brought the problem of the Canaries to the forefront again. Henry consulted with Prince Peter, who as regent was responsible for all matters of foreign policy. A charter was at once drawn up forbidding Portuguese subjects from going to the Canaries, either for war or for trade, without Prince Henry's permission. A further clause gave him the right to one-fifth of any imports from the islands. This was in consideration of the expenses he had incurred in his African ventures.

It was shortly after this that Maciot de Béthencourt, the heir of the French noble who had first colonized Lançarote and Fuerteventura, approached Prince Henry. He offered to lease him Lançarote, and Henry readily agreed. (An annual rental was paid from then on to Maciot.) Unfortunately, Henry was unaware that Maciot had also come to a similar arrangement with the Queen of Castile.

The complications arising from this piece of double-dealing led to many incidents between Portuguese and Castilian ships in the years that followed. Incensed by the general confusion that surrounded the rights to the Canary Islands, Prince Henry was on the verge of sending an armada to take and subdue all of them. But Prince Peter managed to dissuade his brother from any further involvement in a situation that had already brought Portugal and Castile to the verge of war.

The ownership of the Canaries was never properly resolved until nearly twenty years after Prince Henry's death, when an agreement was signed between the two countries, which laid down that all "the conquests from Cape Not as far as the Indies, with the seas and islands adjacent, shall belong to the Portuguese, but the Canaries and Granada shall remain in the possession of Castile." This is the reason the Canary Islands are Spanish to this day, while the Azores, Madeira, and the Cape Verdes are Portuguese possessions dating back to their discovery in Prince Henry's lifetime.

Although the Canaries never came within the Portuguese sphere of influence, they continued to attract Prince Henry's sailors. These "Fortunate Islands" of the ancients had many claims to interest, not least of which were the inhabitants, the Guanches. The captives from Gomera, whom Henry had treated so kindly and returned to their island, were of this stock. An offshoot of the Berber race, the Guanches were for a long time considered the aboriginal inhabitants of the Canary Islands. But nearly two thousand years before, when those forerunners of the Portuguese, the Phoenicians, came to the Fortunate Islands, they recorded that they were uninhabited, although there were ruins of buildings visible on some of them. These signs of a lost civilization served to add substance to the legends, perpetuated by Plato and others, that the Canary Islands were all that remained of the fabulous lost continent of Atlantis. Prince Henry, no doubt, was familiar with the story of Atlantis, which was believed to have once existed out in the Atlantic. It is just possible that if Henry had managed to capture and colonize the Canaries, he might have encouraged his captains to sail westward into the unknown, as well as south down Africa. But that was a project to be left to the son-in-law of his governor of Porto Santo, Christopher Columbus. Even so, Portuguese caravels of his time were capable of sailing as far as America, and in 1452 one of them did go as far northwest as the Newfoundland banks.

During the last twelve years of Prince Henry's life, when Lançarote was technically under lease to him, his ships often sailed to the island, trading also with the Guanches of Teneriffe and Grand Canary. Dragon's blood from the dragon trees of the island was one of the Canaries' principal exports. This red-colored resin was greatly valued as an astringent medicine, and one of the few substances known to fifteenth-century surgeons that could stop bleeding and assist in healing wounds. From these voyages Henry's captains brought back many strange stories of the customs of the Guanches, stories that retain their fascination, for these early inhabitants have entirely disappeared. Like the Caribs of the West Indies, they were decimated by the later Spanish conquest, and the strain of their blood is detectable today only by a darker coloring among some of the Spanish colonists.

Prince Henry, who described knowledge as "that from which all good arises"—a remark that in itself justifies his inclusion among the men of the Renaissance—listened with interest to reports of the manners and customs of these island dwellers.

"On Grand Canary," he was told, "it is the custom for the ruling knights (of whom there are about two hundred) to take the virginity of all young maidens. Only after he has done with her may her father, or the knight himself, marry her off to whom he pleases. But, before they lie with them, they fatten them with milk until their skin is as plump as that of a ripe fig—for they maintain that thin maidens are not as good as fat ones. Their belief is, that in this way the bellies of the fat maidens are enlarged so that they can bear great sons. When the maiden has been fattened she is shown naked to the knight who is to take her, and he tells her father when he considers she is fat enough. After that, the mother and father make her go into the sea for a length of time every day, until all the surplus fat is lost. She is then brought to the knight and, after he has taken her virginity, her parents receive her back again into their house."

The sea captains who brought these stories back to Prince Henry probably dined off them for months to come. But it is more than likely that the ascetic of Sagres only yearned for ships and men to subdue the islands, and teach the Guanches Christian morality. Of their other customs and methods of living, there were some that would have appealed to him—the fact, for instance, that these simple natives "disdain gold, silver and all other metals, making mock of those that covet them." Gold and silver Henry hoped to find in Africa, but he had little personal use for such things—except in so far as they were necessary for keeping his ships at sea.

"They have many fig trees, and dragon trees and dates," said his informants, "also a great number of sheep, goats, and swine. They shave themselves with stones, and they believe that it is a great wrong to slaughter and flay cattle."

Although the Canarians ate meat, they considered the trade of butcher a loathsome one, and would either hire a Christian,

if it was possible, or give the office to one of the island crim-
inals. The life of these primitive inhabitants resembled in
many ways that of the Polynesians of the Pacific in the days
before the Europeans came. Local wars and vendettas were
constant, but the indulgent climate allowed them to live without
much exertion. They made primitive huts or lived in caves. In
some islands they wore colored palm leaves to conceal their
sex, but on the island of Gomera they went completely naked.
"In Gomera," said the Portuguese explorers, "they even make
a mock of garments, saying that they are nothing but sacks in
which men tie themselves up. Their women they hold in
common. That is to say, when one of them goes to visit the
house of another, the latter at once offers him his wife as a
token of hospitality. If he fails to do this, it is taken as an
unfriendly act."

One wonders how many sailors deserted to live in indolence
among the Guanches. The life of a seaman in the caravels was
a hard one, and poorly paid. There must surely have been some
who were tempted to stay ashore in the lazy Lotus Land. Such
an outlook would have been inconceivable in the bracing air of
Sagres. But climate is a great transformer of manners and
morals. The Portuguese, as they sailed ever farther south into
the tropics, would be the first Europeans to learn the languor
of those blazing noons, the sudden flights of passion and
violence, and the dark aftermath of ennui and boredom that
follows so closely on their heels.

Throughout Henry's lifetime the Canaries remained un-
conquered, and mostly uncolonized. Within fifty years of his
death, however, the great wave of expansion and exploration,
which he had set in motion, engulfed them. The last of the
Guanches yielded to the swords and the priests of Spain. It
was of this tall, warlike race that Azurara had commented dis-
approvingly: "They spend the greater part of their time in

singing and dancing, for their vice is to enjoy life without labor. Their greatest happiness they find in fornication, for they have no knowledge of the law; they believe only in God."

Such a state of primitive innocence was not destined to last. By the end of the sixteenth century, the outermost islands of the globe would see the unfamiliar wings of sailing ships rise above their lonely horizons.

Prince Peter's regency ended in 1447. Prince Affonso was fourteen, an age at which he was considered old enough to govern by himself. He was married to Isabel, Prince Peter's daughter, and with his father-in-law at hand to call on for advice, and with the good wishes of the nation, he was formally declared of age in the palace at Lisbon. Prince Peter and Prince Henry were both present. So too was their half-brother, the Count of Barcellos, now aged seventy. But if King John's illegitimate son was an old man, he was active as ever in his quest for power. Old age may deaden the lusts of the flesh, but the lust for power is something that nothing but death can extinguish.

All his life he had been jealous of his half-brothers, and now, with a youth on the throne, he saw his chance to strengthen the House of Bragança. The dukedom of Bragança was an honor that he owed entirely to Prince Peter. Peter had sensed, perhaps, that the Count of Barcellos had always resented King John's omission to make him a duke after the battle of Ceuta (as he had done for both Prince Peter and for Henry). But far from healing old wounds, this act of consideration was probably regarded by the Count of Barcellos as a piece of insufferable patronage. It is always hard to love those to whom we are obligated. Now that the old man saw Prince Peter retiring from the office of regent, he felt it was time that the influence of his own party was strengthened in the court. This was not so difficult to achieve as it may seem, for the young Queen was little more than a child, Affonso was known to have a pliable character, and Prince Peter had many enemies.

It is difficult at any time to rule justly and honestly in the name of another, but it was doubly difficult in a fifteenth-century country where every nobleman was scheming to aggrandize his own family. Prince Peter had never sought the office of regent, but had had it thrust upon him by the Cortes, and by the people of Lisbon and Porto. During the six years of the regency the country had prospered and the power of the nobles had been kept in check. The success of Prince Henry's recent expeditions had added a new luster to the name of Portugal, and it was felt that the disaster of Tangier had almost been erased by these new conquests. In theory, there seemed to be no reason why this prosperity and stability should not continue.

But there was one fact that boded Peter's downfall: the hostility of the great families to a strong central rule. Peter was not a man of iron as his father had been—a type of man the nobility feared as well as respected. He had been a man of action in his youth, but for many years now his principal interests had lain in his library, his family, and the progress of his brother's work. If the powerful nobility did not find him *simpático* as a man, they had resented even more a regent trying to carry on the repressive policies of King John. They saw their chance, now that a fourteen-year-old boy was proclaimed king, and they found a natural leader in the Count of Barcellos, Duke of Bragança.

It is not difficult to trace the hand of the Duke in the long sequence of tragic events that followed. For many years now he had bided his time. Where there had once been five strong brothers allied together, and united in the defense of Portugal and of its throne, there were now only two. King Edward, Prince John, Prince Fernando—all were dead. There remained the young King, the fifty-four-year-old Regent, and the recluse of Sagres. In any struggle for power, Prince Peter was clearly the man who had to be eliminated. Prince Henry scarcely stirred from the province of Algarve, and his knowledge of politics and court intrigue was hardly greater than that of his nephew. It was true that Prince Henry had great prestige, but with whom? Sailors and sea captains, and merchants. Many of the nobility had hardly ever seen him, and when they did meet, his brown eyes had an uncomfortable way of looking right through them. Bragança and his friends knew that Henry had been a fire-eater in his youth, but the failure at Tangier seemed to have altered him.

During the months that followed Prince Peter's resignation from the office of regent—months that seem to move forward as inexorably as an Aeschylean tragedy—how could Henry have failed to realize what was happening? While the country slipped into a state of civil war, and while his brother's fall was being cunningly contrived, Henry spent most of the time at Sagres. To understand his blindness to what was happening, it is essential to realize that he was fully occupied with what to him seemed the most important thing in the world. Once before, during the crisis which preceded the regency, he had been constantly summoned north to act as peacemaker. The present course of events may well have seemed to him somewhat similar, another quarrel over pride and position, which would blow over just as the previous affair had done. In any case, although in 1440 he had been able to spare the time to attend to affairs of state, it was quite different seven years later. At last Africa was beginning to yield its secrets. He had been entirely dedicated to his quest for so many years now that it was impossible for him, at the age of fifty-two, to take an active interest in home politics. In the past there had been King Edward, Prince Peter, or Prince John to look after the affairs of the kingdom. It was they who had given Henry complete liberty to devote himself to that world whose pulse he felt when he leaned from his window at Sagres.

The years from 1447, when Peter resigned the regency, until the battle of Alfarrobeira in 1449 were years when Henry was completely engrossed in external affairs. He was involved in leasing Lançarote in the Canaries from its ruler Maciot. He was also being drawn to the verge of war with Castile over the conflicting rights to the island and the Canaries generally. He was beginning to build the fort in the Bay of Arguim. He was also trying to establish a policy of friendly trading with the natives of the coastline. In addition to all this, he was absorbed in the progress of his ships, which were now sailing beyond Cape Verde. During these years they were bringing him back regular news about the newly discovered land of Guinea, and he thought that he was on the verge of establishing communication by sea with the Indies. It is hardly surprising that by the time he realized what was happening, his brother's fate was sealed.

Within a few days of formally accepting the responsibility of government, Affonso stated to the Cortes that he wished the Regent to remain in office a little longer, since he did not feel that he "could as yet manage so heavy a task." The Cortes were quite agreeable—the regency had been well managed in the past six years, and an extension of it for another year was perfectly logical. Whatever Prince Peter felt on the subject (and it is quite likely that he was in sympathy with the fourteen-

year-old boy's reluctance to assume office at once), the reaction
of the Duke of Bragança was immediate and violent. He chose
to see in the action a deep-laid scheme, whereby the Regent
would retain his hold on the country. He was afraid that by
the time Affonso really assumed power, the policy of repressing
the nobility would have become so fixed that nothing could
change it.

He came out into the open and protested to the Cortes against
the decision. When this had no effect, he began to play on
Affonso's vanity—never a difficult thing with an adolescent.
Bragança also had an ally among the King's entourage, a court
secretary named Barredo, who daily prepared for the young
man two sinister intellectual poisons: flattery of his own
abilities and mistrust of his uncle.

It was not long before the combined influence of Barredo
and the Bragança faction among the courtiers began to produce
the desired effect. Affonso gradually became convinced that
Prince Peter was not only trying to keep him from ruling his
kingdom, but that he was a tyrant who had mistreated the
people during the regency. It was time, said the voices around
him, that he claimed the authority to rule on his own behalf.
He was a king, he must start to be a king—not a child listening
respectfully to his uncle and his father-in-law. The Count of
Ourem, eldest son of Bragança, was largely instrumental in
what followed. He advised Affonso to go at once to Prince
Peter and demand his rights. If his uncle refused, or argued
that the further year of regency was not yet at an end, then
Prince Peter should be expelled from the kingdom.

"It is time," said the Count of Ourem, "that you prove your-
self a man in the eyes of the court and of all Portugal."

Betrayed by his youth and his soft-speaking circle of
insincere friends, Affonso went to see Prince Peter. If he
expected, from what he had been told, that he would meet

with any resistance to his plans, he was mistaken; and if the Bragança clan had expected any show of reluctance on Peter's part, they were to be disappointed. Immediately and willingly, Prince Peter resigned his authority.

"In your interest," he said to Affonso, "I have neglected my own for ten full years now. I am happy to surrender my position. All I ask is that I may be allowed to go in peace to my estates and look after them."

There seems no doubt of Prince Peter's sincerity in these words. If this young man felt that it was now time to assert himself and set his own house in order, so much the better. Even so, Peter was well aware that the growing influence of Bragança and of the nobles was not in Portugal's best interests. In the fifteenth century, strong rule by a single man was the secret of a country's prosperity.

Prince Peter had visited the courts of Italy and France, and he knew how much Portugal had benefited by his father's firm autocratic rule. Many of the finest navigators, sailors, cartographers, and scientists were in the courts of Italy, yet it was Portugal that was beginning to reap the benefit from the exploration of the Atlantic. This could never have come about if Portugal, like Italy, had been divided into a mass of petty states, each one warring against the other. Prince Peter knew the secret strength that had enabled his brother to continue with his voyages of discovery—it was the internal security of Portugal. Unfortunately, Henry on Sagres had had his eyes fixed for so long on the sea and Africa that he had become unaware of the roots that sustained him.

With Prince Peter's resignation, the Bragança faction became all-powerful at court. Peter was slandered, accused of innumerable crimes—among them the exile of Queen Leonora. His enemies harped on the Queen's unhappy fate, her years in Seville, and her death in a foreign country far away from her son Affonso, who was now king. Gradually the young man began to hate his uncle as the persecuter of his dead mother. It was not enough for the nobles to have had Prince Peter removed from the office of regent; they longed for his complete downfall. When that happened, his lands and the lands of all his followers would be available for redistribution among themselves.

After a time, the rumors from court were so persistent that they even reached Prince Henry. He was busy with an expedition to the Canaries, and with a further voyage of exploration to the Guinea coast. But the news was so disturbing that he left Algarve at once and rode north to the court at Santarém.

The historian Ruy de Pina, who wrote the life of King Affonso, says that Henry at this time did not defend Prince Peter "with the fortitude that his brother deserved." But Ruy de Pina's evidence can have been only hearsay, for at the time of these events the future historian was only seven years old. The fact is that the events leading up to the death of Prince Peter were such a stain on the young King's reputation that they were never quite effaced. It was natural, therefore, that his biographer should try to pass some of the blame on to Prince Henry's shoulders. This bias is quite clear in de Pina's history, and for this reason his evidence should be treated with reserve. Azurara's evidence (which would have been biased in favor of Prince Henry) does not exist, for his work ends in 1448—the year before Prince Peter's death. After saying that there was always great love between these two brothers, Azurara tells us that he intends to reveal all the circumstances leading up to Prince Peter's death, and that "Henry did everything he could to save him." Unfortunately, this account, which would have been of the greatest value, was never written.

When Henry reached the court, he found his nephew set in his hostility toward Prince Peter and surrounded by sycophants and self-seeking nobles. Henry quickly abandoned any attempt at personal influence. He realized that if the young King was poisoned against Prince Peter, whose son-in-law he was, it was unlikely he would listen to his other uncle. He sent instead for Alvaro Vaz, Count of Avranches, who was in Ceuta. He hoped that this was one counselor who would be able to instill some sense into the young monarch's head. It seemed likely that he would pay some regard to Portugal's foremost soldier. Alvaro Vaz had fought with Henry at Tangier, had been given the honor of the Garter by King Henry V of England for his part in the battle of Agincourt, and was at the moment prosecuting the war against the Moors from Ceuta. He was a legendary figure in his own country, and his arrival in court must have temporarily upset the plans of the Duke of Bragança. Alvaro Vaz was a man whom a youth of fifteen was bound to idolize.

Prince Henry, thinking perhaps that he had neutralized the opposition to his brother, returned once more to Sagres. If he was blameworthy in the events that followed, it was because he had no conception of how corrupt the court of Portugal had become. The court in which he and Prince Peter had grown up, modeled by his father's strength of character and his mother's Christian virtues, had been superseded by one that might have found its parallel in any of the small kingdoms of Italy.

Alvaro Vaz's influence on the King did not last long. Before many months were out, he was branded as one of Prince Peter's men. Peter himself was forbidden access to the court, the office of constable was taken away from his eldest son, and even Alvaro Vaz found himself deprived of the castle of Lisbon, which had been his for nearly ten years.

It was at this time that Prince Peter wrote to the younger son of the Duke of Bragança, who was not involved in the intrigue, and who was, in fact, one of the few who were trying to make peace. The letter gives us a good insight into Prince Peter's character and into the motives of his opponents. ". . . Many were ill-content during my tenure of office, some because of jealousy and others because they could not circumvent justice. . . . While I was Regent, I said several times that I would abdicate willingly if the King asked for it. I said, though, that I would not do so while there were so many planning and scheming to get rid of me—not for the good of the State but to further their own interests." It is a sad letter, for one sees in it the eternal tragedy of the honest man who has no means to protect himself from his detractors.

In the spring of 1449 the Duke of Bragança deliberately brought matters to a head by marching south, on the pretext of visiting the King. He had a whole army behind him, and his route was so designed as to involve passing through Prince Peter's land. Alvaro Vaz by this time had left the court and had rallied firmly to Prince Peter's side. His opinion was that if the Duke of Bragança persisted in crossing Peter's land with armed followers, he should be met with force. By now even Prince Peter's normally quiet temper had been tried beyond endurance. It was an unbearable position for him, with his enemies everywhere in control and even his daughter powerless to help him. Women's advice was not greatly reckoned with in those days, and in any case she was too young to have any real influence.

Prince Henry wrote to his brother, warning him to give the Duke of Bragança no opportunity to say that he had been provoked. Throughout this tragic period, Henry's counsel to Peter was always to "do nothing that could be construed as an affront to the King." He advised him to stay quietly on his estates until the outcry against him had died down. What Henry failed to realize was that the party hostile to the ex-Regent had no intention of allowing him to remain in peace. Unfortunately

also, although Alvaro Vaz was an outstanding soldier, he was
no politician. His reactions were a soldier's—if people were
conspiring against you, subdue them with the sword. But there
was nothing Bragança's party wanted more than for Prince
Peter to come out into the open and declare himself a rebel.

In any event, an open clash between Prince Peter and the
Duke of Bragança never took place. Many of the Duke's men
were in sympathy with Prince Peter, and Bragança, finding
himself in a position where he could neither attack nor retire
without losing face, abandoned his followers. At the moment
when it seemed inevitable that the two forces must come to
blows, Prince Peter is reported to have said, "Please God that
they may retire without fighting." It seemed as if his prayer
had been heard.

Alvaro Vaz did not share his elation. With their enemies'
army dispersing, and with the Duke himself taking the road
back home, Alvaro Vaz advised Peter to make the most of his
opportunity.

"Now," he cried, "is the moment to follow up your enemy
and take him prisoner!"

If Prince Peter had been as unscrupulous as his enemies had
made him out to be, such would undoubtedly have been his
action. Being what he was, a philosopher who had reluctantly
become involved in affairs of state, he was happy to let his
enemy go. He assumed, wrongly, that after such a sorry debacle
the Duke of Bragança would leave him in peace. Alvaro Vaz's
advice was more to the point:

"He who spares his enemy dies at his hand!"

Shortly after this, Prince Henry came north again and went
straight to Santarém to plead his brother's cause with Affonso.
His intervention proved futile. He found himself tarred with
the same brush as his brother. The King's mind was sealed
against both his uncles, and Prince Peter was openly branded

as a traitor. It was even being suggested that he had been responsible for the deaths of King Edward and Prince John, as well as for the exile of Queen Leonora. The atmosphere of the court must have sickened and repelled Henry. He stayed, though, for it seemed that the least he could do was try to protect his brother against these calumnies.

"I will not allow it to be said," he protested on one occasion, "that any son of King John would conspire to do an injury to his King and Lord!"

Peter, ignorant that his brother was doing all he could to save him, thought that even Henry had betrayed him and had gone to Santarém to side with his enemies. The situation was further confused by the fact that letters between uncle and nephew were being intercepted. Prince Peter's letters, couched in reasonable tones and asking that the charges against him be openly discussed at a meeting between himself and the King, were altered so as to convey a completely different impression.

The conspirators finally turned the knife in the wound by making the young Queen the means of conveying Affonso's decision as to Prince Peter's fate. It was from his own daughter that Peter now heard how the council had given him the option of three choices—death, imprisonment for life, or banishment from the kingdom. They had forced him into a situation from which there was no escape.

"I choose death," he said.

Some of his advisers were in agreement with Prince Henry. The King, they said, was only a youth, and the crisis would pass in a year or two. Prince Peter should fortify his castle in case of any attack, and should remain quietly on his lands. Alvaro Vaz, on the other hand, was for war. If only they had killed the old Duke of Bragança when they had had him at their mercy!

"It is better to go down fighting than to live a life of ignominy," he said. He felt that men like Prince Peter and himself, both knights of the Order of the Garter, could not, and should not, put up with unjust accusations of disloyalty and treachery.

Peter made one more attempt at reconciliation. He wrote to his daughter, saying that he was prepared to accept any blame rather than to allow the present situation to continue. The letter achieved nothing. The enemies of Prince Peter and of King John's house were too powerful now. He was a dissident subject, a murderer—no calumny was spared.

As for Prince Henry, he had always been something of a wry joke to the elegant courtiers of Santarém. This old man with his dreams about Prester John, the Indies, Africa, and unknown islands—he would achieve nothing by continuing to insist on his brother's innocence. Why did he not go back to that desolate land of his in the south, to that madman's dream of a castle, perched on a rock, overlooking the Atlantic? Prince Henry with his abstemiousness that seemed to them an insult, with his devotion to the Church that mocked their irreligion, with his ascetic life and manner that were more suitable to a hermit than a prince—it cannot have been difficult to turn him into a figure of fun.

In the plot and counterplot, even the young Queen was not spared. She was charged with infidelity, but the conspirators had overstepped themselves, and the case against her supposed lover fell through. Affonso's faith in his wife remained unshaken, but his faith in his uncles was now completely corrupted. He saw Prince Henry as an eccentric, possibly even insane, and he was convinced that everything he had been told about Prince Peter was true. This man who had trained him for kingship, his uncle and father-in-law, was the persecutor of his dead mother and a rebel who wanted the throne of Portugal for himself.

In the spring of 1449 King Affonso took the road with his army and marched north to Coimbra to beseige Prince Peter in his castle. Still determined to prevent bloodshed, and to reduce everything to a rational level, Prince Henry followed. Peter, despite Alvaro Vaz's protestations that the whole thing could be settled only by the sword, seems still to have hoped for a peaceful outcome. These were the events leading up to the battle of Alfarrobeira, the battle that should never have been fought.

Hearing that the King was advancing on him, Prince Peter spent the night in prayer in the abbey of Batalha beside the tomb of his parents. It was here, in the Gothic church with its golden-brown limestone spires, that King John and Queen Philippa lay at rest. Here his father had prepared a place for all his family to be buried. Three of his sons were dead already (but the body of Prince Fernando lay far away in Fez), and now the fourth son knelt beside his parents' tomb. Above his head shone the intricate stonework. It had been carved by English masons, whom Queen Philippa had brought over to give to her last resting place a memory of the cool Gothic of her native land.

On the morning of May 5 Prince Peter left Batalha. Together with his sons and about five thousand troops, he went forward to meet the King's forces. If only he had stayed behind at Coimbra, the battle could never have taken place. If he had followed Henry's advice, the worst that could have happened was a siege of his castle—during the course of which it might still have been possible for the two sides to come to terms.

He pitched his camp on a tree-lined bank near the river of Alfarrobeira and waited for the arrival of the King. Outnumbered by nearly ten to one—for the King had called up all the available royal forces—it does not seem possible that Prince Peter can ever have intended to give battle. What seems most likely is that he wished to meet the King in person, and answer the charges that were being made against him. Ruy de Pina, however, says that bets were being made among the royal troops on who should kill Prince Peter, so there can be no doubt that the Prince's enemies had determined to conclude the matter with his death.

The fatal skirmish and the events that led to Prince Peter's death are best described in the memoirs of Olivier de la Marche, a Burgundian noble who was not present at the battle, but who heard the reports of eye-witnesses. Unlike Ruy de Pina, he was not prejudiced in favor of either side.

"The Duke [Prince Peter, Duke of Coimbra], when he saw the King coming, closed his ranks and put his troops and artillery in good formal order. . . . And several Portuguese noblemen who were present have told me that he did this with no other intention than of sending some of his principal followers as emissaries to the King. They were to go in full humility, to recommend him to the King's good grace, and to ask the reason why he found himself in dispute with His Majesty. They were to make his humble vows to him, and to remind him of the services he had done the King in his youth —as well as for the good of the realm—and in conclusion to offer him his services again. But it happened by chance that the crossbowmen of the King of Portugal came near his camp in large numbers. And in this way a fight began between the hotheaded on both sides. In the course of this, a crossbow bolt struck the Duke of Coimbra [Prince Peter] in the chest. He died of this wound within the hour. Not a single other man was wounded in this first affray, only the Duke. . . ."

So died Prince Peter. The friend of princes and kings throughout Europe and the East, he had been the only brother who had comprehended Prince Henry's dreams. He had been too honest and too scrupulous for the age in which he lived.

His death was the signal for a confused and foredoomed action. In the battle that followed, Alvaro Vaz, Portugal's hero and supreme soldier, was killed. Fighting to the last against the soldiers of his king, the hero of Agincourt was stripped of his armor and his head cut off. The forces of Prince Peter were overrun and cut to pieces. His castle and estates were seized, and his family forced to flee. In the years that followed, his widow and his sons wandered as exiles through the courts of Europe.

Prince Henry found himself surrounded by the men of Bragança and the creatures of the court, rejoicing over the death of his beloved brother. If he had sickened and died a little at the news of Fernando's death, it was nothing to this moment of utter disgust.

The battle of Alfarrobeira severed his last link with the world of courts and courtiers, almost even with Portugal. We know nothing of his reactions, except that he asked that he might be permitted to leave the country forever, and to retire to Ceuta.

In Ceuta he had known his greatest happiness and triumph. In Ceuta there were no politicians. He asked that he might be allowed to end his days there, and devote his last years to fighting against the Moors. The simple world of the soldier, and even of the infidel enemy, was preferable to that of his fellow countrymen. His request was refused.

23

Henry was now fifty-six. His life was set in grooves that were cut as deep as the wave-chiseled stone of the headland. As a young man of twenty-three he had dedicated himself to this life of sea and sky, where nature imposed a pattern as austere as any of the orders of the Church. But the youth who had come here so willingly had turned into a man who now found in this self-imposed isolation the only sanity and peace that were left to him.

Sagres was no longer a testing place for his character, but a refuge from the world of men. He saw things in simple terms of black and white, not the multitudinous shades of gray that, for most people, make up the palette of living. On the one hand there were the infidel Moors, and on the other the Christians. On the one hand there were the unhappy heathen, and on the other there was the Order of Christ designed to bring light into their darkness. It must have been with something of this feeling that he had applied for permission to withdraw to Ceuta. There, under the North African sun, life was like the noonday streets of the old town—a blinding vivid white, or shadows as dark and thick as tar. Refused permission to leave

Portugal and end his life in Ceuta, he rediscovered his peace at Sagres.

He was more alone now than ever before. The deaths of his brothers starred his years and marked the different phases of his life, much as the wooden crosses that his mariners erected marked the coastline of Africa. An outcome of his failure at Tangier had been the death of his eldest brother, King Edward. Then had followed the three troubled years when the question of the regency was in dispute. The death of Prince John from illness, followed shortly afterward by the martyr's death of Fernando in Fez, had ushered in the beginning of the conquest of Guinea. Prince Peter's death came at the end of this phase of exploration. If Henry had sacrificed himself to his quest, he had sacrificed others too. Edward, Fernando, and even Prince Peter might all be considered in one degree or another victims of his ambition. If he had not ventured on the capture of Tangier, two of them would probably still be alive. If he had not been so completely absorbed in Africa and his islands, his brother Peter would almost certainly have been saved. Greater than Alexander perhaps, Prince Henry like all conquerors left death in his wake—in his case the death not of thousands but of those nearest to him by blood and affection.

After the tragedy of Alfarrobeira he was rarely seen outside the Algarves. Between his villa at Raposeira, his town and fortress at Sagres, and the busy shipyards of Lagos, there moved this dark enigmatic figure of the last of King John's sons. In the great painting by Nuño Gonçalves, which shows the courtiers, the noblemen, and the seamen of King Affonso's court kneeling before Saint Vincent, there is an unforgettable portrait of Prince Henry in these last years. It is a tribute to the whole of Henry's life's work that the dominant figure in one of the panels should be an old fisherman kneeling in prayer, with gnarled hands held up to a white-bearded face, and the mesh of a fishing net suspended behind him. In what other country at that time would it have been conceivable to introduce the figure of a workingman and the tools of his trade into a gathering of the nobility? Prince Henry had shown his country that its destiny lay on the sea.

There are many faces in Nuño Gonçalves's masterpiece: the young Affonso, his Queen, knights and nobles, priests, and men in armor with swords and pikes. Close to the youthful form of Saint Vincent (as close as Sagres to the cape that bears the Saint's name) there is a figure like a dark rock. In contrast to the jeweled clothes, the caps sewn with pearls, the elaborate armor of the men, and the gem-set pendants of the women, Henry wears the robes of mourning. His hair is cut short, and on his head he wears a dark barret cap with a long trailing fold that lies on his right shoulder. Most of the faces around are pale, his is brown and weathered. The forehead is furrowed, there are lines under the eyes, and the eyes themselves gaze on, and out of the picture. They are fixed on something far away. A heavy mustache in the English fashion shadows his upper lip. The mouth itself is curious. The lower lip is quite full, but the upper lip has a sad, almost sardonic, twist, and the right corner is turned down. This was Henry in the last years of his life, clothed in mourning for his brother Peter, and wearing the impenetrable reserve that had become part of his nature.

It may well be that the reason he was refused permission to retire to North Africa was that Affonso and his advisers felt they could not risk the interpretation that the other courts of Europe would put on this act of self-banishment. For within a few months of Alfarrobeira the storm broke. The Duke of Bragança and his party had not been slow to help themselves to the castles and estates that now lay vacant, and this seemed further proof of their guilt—and of the dead man's innocence —in the eyes of the other European countries. There was an immediate protest from the Duke of Burgundy, the husband of Princess Isabel, King John's only daughter. His ambassador even came to the Portuguese court and read out a formal indictment of the action, and of the dispossession of Prince Peter's wife and heirs that had followed. The Pope published a bull declaring Peter's innocence of the charges that had been made against him. King Henry VI of England did not approve of the dishonorable way in which Affonso's uncle—a knight of the Garter, England's most ancient and honorable order—had been hounded to death. The young King was held to blame by nearly all the courts of Europe for an atrocious act. If Prince Henry had been allowed to leave Portugal at that moment, it would have seemed the crowning disgrace on Affonso's reign.

There was only one compensation in the two sad years that preceded Alfarrobeira and the rise of the House of Bragança —they had not been fruitless in the field of exploration. With Henry's orders and permission, ships continued to sail between the Canaries, Arguim Bay, and Guinea. Arguim was settled, and the fort was built. Prince Henry's policy of trading and dealing fairly with the natives had already begun to take effect, so much so that Azurara, concluding his narrative in 1448, adds: "The sequence of events (in exploration) which followed later did not call for so much effort and endeavor. For, from this date onward, the affairs relating to these countries were effected more and more by negotiation and exchange of merchandise than by force of arms."

Some idea of the difficulties and hazards that beset the sailors in the caravels is seen from the story of Vallarte, or Abelhart the Dane. Like the German Balthasar, Abelhart was an adventurous nobleman who had heard tales of the wonderful new world being discovered in the south, and had come to Sagres in the hope of taking part in one of the expeditions. Henry, as always, was only too pleased to have this type of man enlisted under his banner. He gave Abelhart command of a caravel, with a Portuguese knight, Fernando Affonso, as co-captain, since "the stranger was not sufficiently familiar with the usages and customs of these people." Fernando Affonso was also ". . . to have command of the mariners and other matters relating to navigation."

The voyage from Lagos to Cape Verde, a distance of about 1,500 miles, should have taken a few weeks at the most. But head winds and storms delayed them, and they were forced to run into the island of Palma for shelter. When they finally reached Cape Verde, they had been six months away from Portugal. The end of this voyage was as sorry as its beginning. Abelhart and a boat's crew were ambushed on the coast, and only one man escaped by swimming back to the caravel. When last seen, Abelhart was still alive, sitting in the stern of the boat, surrounded by natives. A year later a report reached Prince Henry from some natives captured off the same stretch of coast. They said that there had been four survivors of the boat's crew, and that they had been taken to a fortress in the interior. One of them had died, but three were still alive, prisoners in the heart of Africa. The fate of Abelhart, as of so many others in these early years of exploration, remains unknown. But eight years later a Genoese traveler reported that he had seen a European Christian in the interior of Africa, and it is just possible that this was one of the survivors from Abelhart's ill-fated expedition.

Hostile natives, the natural hazards of wind and weather, uncharted coasts, navigational errors, all of these took their toll of the Portuguese seafarers. But still the voyages went on, and still the Prince asked that, before anything else, men should try to sail "always a little farther."

By now all the courts of Europe had heard of what was taking place. The discovery of Madeira in 1420 and the rounding of Cape Bojador in 1434 might have gone unremarked except by seafarers and cartographers. But the arrival of black slaves from Africa, of gold from the Rio de Ouro, of wine and sugar from faraway islands, were things that aroused the interest of everyone in Europe. On a headland at the far end of Portugal, in a place that Henry described as "remote from the tumult of men," a revolution was taking place. Artists, philosophers, and scientists, living obscure lives in remote places, have often initiated the great changes that alter man's conception of the world and of the universe, but few have done so more decisively than Prince Henry on Sagres.

By the time he was fifty-six, even distant parts of Europe had heard of the discoveries. In the same way that, today, we hear of giant galactic systems being discovered by radiotelescope in outer space, so they heard of new islands in the Atlantic and of a great continent stretching to the south. Sailors who had called at Lagos or Lisbon, or who had anchored for a night in the bay below the Prince's austere palace, brought confirmation of the stories. By 1448 nearly one thousand Africans had been shipped to Portugal. The sailors had seen their faces in the streets of Portuguese ports; tall Berbers, coffee-colored half-castes, and ebony Negroes from the land of the Senegal and Gambia.

There were parrots and other strange birds on sale in the booths of Lagos: canaries, hornbills, and many singing birds captured on the African coast. In the jewelers' shops gold was being worked that had come, not through the markets of North Africa, but direct from caravan routes leading to the new trading post in Arguim Bay. There were sugar cane and wine from Madeira, salted fish from the Azores, and quantities of sardine and gurnard from the fishery that had been set up in Gurnard Bay. In the carpenters' and shipwrights' shops, where the scent of resinous wood hung on the air, they were cutting and planing unfamiliar trees for which they were only just inventing names. In the pharmacists' stores dragon's blood from the Canaries was on sale, and spices that had come from Ceuta. There were sailors swaggering through the streets who had been hundreds of miles south of Cape Bojador. There were men who had seen the fertile lands beyond the desert, and the great river that was probably the mouth of the western Nile. They told of poisoned arrows, of long-legged flamingos, and of the hot heavy smell of Africa.

British, Dutch, French, and Scandinavian sailors, who were on the northern run between the Mediterranean and the Channel, had seen these new Portuguese vessels called caravels. They reported them small boats compared with their own trading craft, but with fine lines, and looking rather like the Arabic sailing boats of the Levant. The Portuguese captains and navigators, they said, were secretive about these new islands and the African coastline. The courses they steered, the charts they used, the wind and weather south of the Canaries, and the nature of the coastline were almost impossible for foreigners to discover. It was even rumored that only caravels could sail in these unknown regions.

Strange gifts—presents between sea captains, or between one courtier and another—began to circulate throughout Europe. Ostrich eggs arrived in Italy and in England, and the silversmiths of these countries cut them carefully in halves and mounted them as two matching goblets. One of the strangest gifts of all was brought back by João Fernandes, the man who of his own accord had once spent seven months living in the Sahara among the Berbers.

Fernandes was the first European on record to have penetrated the interior of Africa, and his travels in some areas anticipated those of the Scottish explorer Mungo Park by over three centuries. On this particular voyage, which took place in

1447, Fernandes went down to the Moroccan coast in a caravel, taking eighteen captive Moors to exchange against Africans in one of the ports north of Cape Not. Fifty Africans were considered a fair ransom price for the Moors, and having put them aboard, Fernandes then bargained for a suitable present for Prince Henry. A live African lion was added to the deck cargo. But at this point "the wind began to blow so strongly from the south that the caravel had to make sail and return home at once. So they brought back the lion to the Prince, who afterward sent it to a place called Galway, as a gift for one of his followers who lived in that country. For it was known that such an animal had never been seen there. . . ."

Tangible proofs like this began to open men's eyes to the world that lay beyond their small villages, their local fishing ports, and their familiar coastline. Cartographers, navigators, and men of education might understand what Prince Henry and his pioneers were doing, but it took something like a lion in Galway Bay to bring the reality of it home to ordinary people.

24

The fame that Prince Henry's explorations brought to Portugal was reflected on Affonso's reign. The birth of a son in 1455 ensured the succession of his dynasty, and peace and prosperity settled again over the country. As he grew older, Affonso matured into a capable and energetic ruler. He treated the last of his uncles with affection and respect, wishing perhaps to efface the grim and sordid events that had disfigured his early years. Henry seemed to watch the rise of the House of Bragança with indifference.

From 1450 onward there were so many voyages being made that many of them went unrecorded. Things that had been marvels twenty years ago were now accepted as commonplace. But the whole achievement still seemed little short of miraculous to visiting foreigners. One of these was a Venetian named Alvise Cadamosto.

Cadamosto was only twenty-two when he arrived in a galley, bound from Venice for the Netherlands, and anchored beneath the rock of Sagres. He had been to the Netherlands before as a merchant, and he was on his way there again, when a sudden Atlantic storm forced his galley to run for shelter. Prince

Henry was at Raposeira at the time, and the news that a foreign ship was anchored in Sagres roads was brought to him. The young Venetian was surprised to find himself visited by the Prince's secretary as well as by the Venetian consul. They brought with them sugar from Madeira, dragon's blood, and other produce of the newly discovered islands. Prince Henry, knowing the reputation of the Venetians as traders, thought that such things might be of interest to him. Cadamosto was more than interested. He had an audience with the Prince, and almost at once the whole course of his life was altered.

The stories Prince Henry told him of these new lands, the charts he showed him, and the whole conception of this vast ocean, which made the Mediterranean seem like a lake, inspired Cadamosto with a desire to see this new world. He at once asked the Prince on what terms it might be possible to make an expedition to Africa. Henry gave him two choices. Either Cadamosto could equip and freight a caravel at his own expense, and pay one-fourth of the profits to Prince Henry on return, or the Prince himself would provide the ship and freight, but in this case half of any profit would be his.

Cadamosto's galley sailed for Venice without him. He had made arrangements about the consignment of his goods and had suggested that he make a trading voyage for Prince Henry on a half-share basis. "The Prince," he wrote, "was very pleased that I stayed on at Cape St. Vincent." In the early days of exploration, the best men for African voyages had been like Nuño Tristão and Gil Eannes, knights and veterans of action, men who found their stimulus in danger. But already, by 1455, a new quality was called for in dealing with Africa—the ability to trade peacefully and to assess gold, spices, and the unfamiliar products of the continent.

A new caravel was fitted out, a Portuguese sailing captain appointed, and Alvise Cadamosto left on March 22, 1455, for

Africa. The ship followed what had by now become the standard route for all outward-bounders. From Lagos she made for Madeira, reaching Porto Santo after three days. The Venetian noted that the rabbits, which had been the curse of Perestrello, still abounded. But wheat and oats were growing, the coastal fishery thrived, and honey and dragon's blood were being exported. Thirty-seven years ago, this had been a wild, uninhabited island lost in the Atlantic.

From Porto Santo they sailed across to Madeira toward the strange cloud on the horizon that had so disturbed Zarco's sailors years before. Madeira was already a monument to Portuguese industry and to the visionary scope of the man who had sent young Cadamosto on his voyage. It was an Eden, green and fertile. Glowing under the sun, it was laced with shining rivers and artificial irrigation channels. They landed at Machico (where once, perhaps, the unfortunate Robert Machin and his mistress had met their end), but a Machico that was already unrecognizable. Sawmills spun under the driving currents of water, boats were building, and wood was being cut for export to Portugal. The cane that had been brought from Sicily produced so much sugar, and of such good quality, that the Venetian grew as ecstatic over the candied sweetmeats as he did over the fruit and wine.

"There is nothing more beautiful in all the world!" he cried, as he looked at the luxuriance of the terraced vines, over which the Atlantic wind passed like a wave. There were partridges, quail, and wild boar, peacocks, honey, and wheat in abundance. "The whole island is a garden!" Madiera was already a thriving colony, with nearly a thousand inhabitants divided among four main settlements. The climate was even better than that of Cyprus or Sicily. And all this, he reflected, had been achieved through the farsightedness of one man.

They unloaded the cargo they had brought from Portugal

and took aboard fresh meat, fruit, and fish. Then, having
topped up their water barricoes, they sailed south again for the
Canaries. Cadamosto, who was familiar with the Mediterranean and the northern route to Europe, now grew to know this
vast ocean, which seemed to be always heaving under the
impulse of some spent gale or far-off wind. Even the calms
were unlike those of the Mediterranean, for the rhythm of the
ocean was ceaseless. The mornings were crystal; brighter,
sharper, and cleaner than those of the inland sea. Soon the
caravel was driving before the northeasters in a steady hush of
foam.

The Canaries, though, he found disappointing after fertile
Madeira. If only the Prince had had control of these islands,
Cadamosto thought, they too might already be green with
cultivation and busy with ships and men.

He recognized the truth of this even more when he saw
Arguim Island. It was more barren than the most desolate of
the Canaries, yet it was already active with trade. Caravans
came bringing gold and Negroes from the interior. A thriving
fishing industry and fish-salting business were already established, and ships were coming and going as if this were a port
in Europe—and not just an inlet on what, until a few years ago,
had been a desolate coast.

Dropping Arguim Bay astern of him, Cadamosto sailed
down to Cape Blanco. From here he made an expedition inland
by camel to a trading post where the caravan routes converged.
He heard of the gold routes: how they met at Timbuktu, and
then separated, some going across the continent to Cairo, some
to Tunis in the north, and others to the Atlantic seaboard at Safi
and Tangier. White pepper from the interior was one of the
spices that were already reaching Portugal from here. Cadamosto the Venetian, although he was probably unaware of it,

was witnessing the opening of those new trade routes that would ultimately lead to the decline of his own proud republic.

He was an observant man, an observer of human beings as well as of commerce and communications, and he noted in his diary points of interest about the food and drink and customs of the Berbers and Arabs. They were Mohammedans, living mostly on dates, barley, and camels' milk. Their coinage was the cowrie shell, which, as Cadamosto knew, came to them via Venice, which imported them from the Levant. To his Latin eye, their criterion of female beauty was unattractive, for it was the length of the breast that made a woman seem desirable in this strange country. Young girls even tied cords round their breasts to break down the tissue and stretch them. A really beautiful woman was one whose breasts hung right down to her navel.

His mission completed, Cadamosto rejoined the caravel and went on to Cape Verde and the lands round the Senegal. Here the inhabitants lived mainly by pillage, and by carrying off their neighbors for sale to the Berbers and the Moors. They were very clean in their personal habits, washing three or four times a day, and spending long hours on their hairdressing. Their table manners, on the other hand, were barbarous in the extreme, and in all things he found them a strange mixture of opposites. They were great liars, yet at the same time so hospitable that even the poorest would freely give food and lodging to strangers. The King of the Senegal region had some thirty wives and spent most of his time traveling between one village and another, visiting them. The duty of entertaining him and his retinue fell entirely on the village concerned, and in this way the King and his followers were never obliged to work. Their only task was warfare. His children were very numerous, and as soon as one of his wives became pregnant, the King left her and moved on to another wife in another village.

Beyond the Senegal River, Cadamosto came into the territory of a chieftain called Budomel, who was known to be friendly to the Portuguese. Cadamosto gave him a present of seven horses, which were highly prized by the Africans, as well as linen and silk clothing. A hundred slaves were offered him in exchange for the horses, and as a small bonus for himself, a young Negro girl "to serve in his cabin."

He was the first European ever to make a prolonged stay in this area, and to make a record of the customs and habits of the Senegambia natives. It was November when he arrived, and he spent a whole month in the area, visiting Budomel and being entertained by him and his followers. He noted the primitive conditions under which even a powerful chieftain lived, but saw also that the respect accorded him would have been considered excessive by even the greatest sovereigns of Europe. Seven courtyards separated the entrance of Budomel's house from his private apartments, and his followers were distributed throughout the courts according to their rank. Petitioners from the people were allowed to approach the royal presence only under conditions of extreme humility. Stripped of all their garments except for a loincloth, they abased themselves by casting sand and earth over their heads, and "they feared him more than God himself."

On the subject of religion Cadamosto had some of his most interesting conversations, for the chief was a Mohammedan, and Arabic priests were present in his court. The Venetian was not afraid to tell Budomel, in front of his Mohammedan advisers, that their religion was a false one and that Christianity was the only true faith. The Negro chieftain, however, was a man of tolerance, and not without a sense of humor. He answered Cadamosto's arguments with irony. He was quite prepared to believe, he said, that the Christian faith was a good one, for the Europeans' prosperity and knowledge had already convinced him that they lived under divine favor. But still, he pointed out, there were things to be said for the Mohammedan faith, and if God was both good and just, then Budomel was not afraid for the Negro people in the future life. They stood a better chance of salvation, he thought, than the Christians. For the Christians were so rich in worldly goods and the black men so poor, that a just God must surely compensate for this by granting the Negroes salvation in the world to come.

Cadamosto tasted their local palm wine and found it as good and as intoxicating as the wine of Europe. The palm oil, with which they seasoned their food, he described as having "the color of saffron, the taste of olives, and the scent of violets." Everything in this strange land made a sharp impression on him: the snakes and the white ants, the lions, panthers, leopards, and wolves, and the brightly colored parrots. With a quick eye for business he managed to get hold of a number of parrots and took them back to Portugal where, he recorded with satisfaction, they sold "at half a ducat each."

It is not difficult to imagine how exotic a sight the caravels must have been when they finally made fast again alongside the quays of Lagos—laden with Negroes, sacks full of un-familiar tropical fruit, gold, parrots by the score in woven cages, scented with herbs and spices, and manned by tropical-tanned sailors who had seen all the wonders of Africa.

One of Cadamosto's most charming stories concerns the bagpipes he had brought with him, and with which he enter-tained the natives. At first they thought the instrument was some kind of animal that had been trained to sing. Later, when he handed over the pipes and explained through his interpreter how they worked, the Africans maintained that only a divine skill could have made such a work of art. Equally fascinated by the eyes painted on the bows of Cadamosto's caravel, they believed it was with these that the great bird saw its way over the sea.

The mention of interpreters is a further reminder of Prince Henry's foresight, for each caravel going to Africa now carried one or more of these. They were Negroes who had been trained in the Prince's court, taught Portuguese, and converted to Christianity. Some of them came to unhappy ends. After leaving Budomel, with a promise to return on his homeward voyage, Cadamosto went on south until he reached the mouth of another river (possibly the modern Djomboss). Here he sent his interpreter ashore to speak to some natives who had flocked to the beach, and to inquire who was the ruler of the country. The unfortunate interpreter was killed almost instantly by the natives. Cadamosto, deciding that men who treated a fellow Negro in such a way would hardly be friendly to Europeans, hastily sailed on down the coast.

By now two other caravels had joined up with him, and together they came to the River Gambia—to those vast tree-lined banks where no European had been since Nuño Tristão and his crew had been ambushed and killed. The smallest caravel, together with some rowing boats, was sent in over the bar, where at this time of the year there was only four feet of water. Sailing and rowing upstream, they surprised some natives, but bearing in mind the fate of Nuño Tristão and obeying Cadamosto's orders, they retreated at once. Next day Cadamosto waited for the tide to lift him over the bar and took his own caravel upstream. The other two ships followed him. They had not gone far before there was a repetition of the previous attack. This time, however, the Portuguese were prepared, and took cover behind shields and the boats' bulwarks from the flights of arrows. The discharge of their cannon and accurate fire from the crossbowmen demoralized the Africans and warded off the assault. The caravels then anchored together in the center of the river, lying alongside one another, and swinging to a single anchor in the steady flow of the current. They had weathered Atlantic gales and rounded many an uncharted headland. Now they proved that they could even sail up the unknown rivers of Africa.

Within a few days Cadamosto was able to talk with the natives through his interpreters, and to try to convince them that the Portuguese intended them no harm. He remembered the Prince's orders that, whenever possible, transactions with the natives should be conducted on a friendly basis. He found out that the reason for the hostility of these Gambia tribes was that they had been told by the Mohammedans that Christians were cannibals. Finding himself unable to convince them of his peaceful intentions, Cadamosto took advantage of a fair wind and got his three vessels safely out to sea. The Portuguese captains were prepared to have another attempt at sailing even farther up the river, in the hope of establishing contact with some natives that might be more friendly. A near mutiny among their crews prevented them.

Cadamosto's ship had now been away from Portugal for nearly a year, and she was due home for a clean and a refit. But the adventurous young man was determined to come back again the following year. He had been successful in his trading, and he had made many notes of geographical and human interest that were certain to please the Prince. He made one further discovery, which crowned his voyage. He had noticed, as they sailed farther and farther south toward the Gambia, that the night sky was changing. The captain had pointed out to him how low the Pole Star hung in the northern sky, and how to the south the sky seemed to be bringing up unknown constellations. One night, just before they turned north and began their long voyage back to Portugal, Cadamosto saw four stars grouped low on the horizon. They formed a diamond-shaped pattern, and their soft shine lay on the sea, due south of the caravel. He named them the "Southern Chariot." So to Prince Henry's protégé the Venetian Cadamosto fell the honor of being the first European ever to record the Southern Cross.

25

❋

The discovery of America by Christopher Columbus stemmed from the pioneer work of the Portuguese navigators. We know that during his residence in Porto Santo, Columbus was told by his mother-in-law, the widow of Bartolomew Perestrello, everything about her husband's voyages in the service of Prince Henry. She also gave her son-in-law all his old charts, instruments, and log books. The Spanish Bishop Las Casas, who knew Columbus's son Diego, tells us in his *History of the Indies* that the discoverer of America sailed several times with the Portuguese "as if he had been one of them," in order to learn their navigational methods. Ferdinand Columbus, the Admiral's other son and his biographer, also confirms the influence that the Portuguese voyages had on his father.

"... He learned from pilots who were experienced in the voyages to Madeira and the Azores facts and signs which convinced him that an unknown land lay to the west. Martim Vicente, a pilot of the King of Portugal, told him how he had taken from the water an artistically carved piece of wood, four hundred and fifty leagues from Cape St. Vincent. This wood had been driven across [the ocean] by the west wind—a fact which led the sailors to believe that there were certainly other islands in that direction which had not yet been discovered."

Further evidence of land lying to the west had been found both in Madeira and in the Azores. Large canes, pines of unknown species, and other pieces of carved wood had been picked up on the beaches of the westernmost islands. A branch of the Gulf Stream known as the Azores current flows steadily across the Atlantic from the Gulf of Mexico toward these islands. In Flores, the westernmost of the islands, the bodies of two men were washed up one day, and the colonists reported that their broad faces showed they were not Christians. It is just conceivable that these could have been two Indians who had been carried out to sea in a canoe and finally, after dying from starvation and exposure, been cast up on the shore.

Since Prince Henry required regular reports from the governors of his colonies, it is most likely that he heard these rumors of land existing farther to the west. We know, in fact, that he suspected there were further islands or land masses in the Atlantic from the chronicle of Diogo Gomes, a ship's captain who spent many of his years in Prince Henry's service, and who was with him when he died. "The Prince wished to know," he wrote, "about the western ocean, and whether there were islands or continents beyond those that Ptolemy described. [The Alexandrian astronomer's *Guide to Geography* was a standard reference book of the period.] So he sent caravels to search for lands."

But Henry's principal interest was always the search for a sea route round Africa, and consequently his voyages of exploration were directed to the south. Ferdinand Columbus confirms this: ". . . it was in Portugal that the admiral [Christopher Columbus] began to surmise that, if the Portuguese sailed so far to the south, it might equally be possible to sail westward and find lands in that direction."

Some of Prince Henry's ships did sail to the west. In fact, they narrowly missed discovering Newfoundland, nearly fifty years before John Cabot. (Cabot sailed from Bristol in 1497, landed at Bonavista, and claimed the land for Henry VII.) It is possible that Portuguese fishermen had been going to the Newfoundland banks from the Azores even in the lifetime of Henry the Navigator.

It was early in the 1450's, shortly before Cadamosto's voyage to Gambia, that Diogo de Teive, one of Prince Henry's squires, sailed into the Atlantic northwest from Corvo and Flores. Along this southern edge of the Azores current, where Sargasso weed drifts in the warm water, the winds often blow from a southwesterly direction, and this would have given Diogo de Teive an easy beam wind for his caravel. For day after day he kept on standing to the northwest. Then, to his surprise, he suddenly found that the warm humid air had turned cold. He seemed to have sailed into a different world. Strong westerly winds now prevailed, and there was a feeling of ice in the air. If we had no other record of his voyage than this, we could be sure that Diogo de Teive had sailed right across the Gulf Stream and come out where the cold Newfoundland current whirls down from the north. (Along the edge of the stream, where these two conflicting ocean currents meet, the division is so marked that it is possible for a large modern liner to have one side of the hull in the Newfoundland current and one in the Gulf Stream.)

Diogo de Teive and his men were not seamen and fishermen for nothing. They soon realized that they were sailing into shoal water. This was not the deep ocean, but the sea over a continental shelf. Unable to pursue his voyage any further, he returned to Portugal and recorded his view that there was land to the northwest. There are no other records of Portuguese voyages in this direction, but the rumor has persisted that Portuguese fishermen were lining for cod off the Newfoundland banks long before the official discovery of Newfoundland and North America. In view of the secretive nature of fishermen in regard to rich fishing grounds, these stories seem perfectly feasible.

Antilia, the mysterious island that appears in a number of old charts, always to the west of the Azores, has sometimes been claimed as a Portuguese discovery of the West Indies before Columbus. There is no evidence to support this theory, but it is just possible that Portuguese seamen, driving before the northeast trade winds, did manage to reach one of the Windward Islands of the West Indies. Again, there is a puzzling coastline shown on a chart made twelve years before Prince Henry's death, which seems to suggest that the chartmaker, an Italian who had worked at Lisbon, had heard of Brazil. Yet Brazil, according to known records, was not sighted until 1499. It is doubtful, however, if any land or islands west of the Azores were discovered during the lifetime of Prince Henry. What certainly seems to be true is that after the voyage of Diogo de Teive in the 1440's, it was known that there was land lying a long way to the northwest of Flores and Corvo.

It is not to disparage Columbus's achievement to say that he based his great Atlantic voyage on rumors that had long been current in the court of Sagres. Prince Henry's belief—that the route to the East lay round Africa—was, in fact, more accurate than that of Columbus. But neither he nor the great Genoese was aware that a whole continent lay between Europe and the Far East across the western ocean.

Whatever mysteries were still concealed by the Atlantic, every year results were pouring in from Africa. The belief that before very long the Portuguese would manage to round the continent was strengthened by a bull of Pope Nicholas V in 1454, in which he granted Prince Henry the monopoly of all exploration as far east as India. It was at about this time, between 1450 and 1456, that the Cape Verde Islands were discovered. It may have been Cadamosto on his second voyage to Africa, or a Genoese, Uso di Mare, who accompanied him in another caravel, or it may have been the Portuguese Diogo Gomes who first sighted them. Certainly, both Gomes and Cadamosto claim to have been the discoverer of these bleak volcanic islands, the outriders of Africa—and the nearest point to the American continent definitely discovered by Prince Henry's caravels.

Cadamosto's second voyage, which took place in 1456, started from Lagos. This time three caravels sailed in company and went direct to Cape Blanco, without putting in at Madeira or the Azores. Prince Henry, having found in the Venetian a man of Nuño Tristão's caliber and an astute merchant into the bargain, was eager for Cadamosto to go even farther south. Having sighted Cape Blanco, Cadamosto stood out from the land for three days. On the third day, a masthead lookout reported two islands off the starboard bow, and the caravels altered course toward them. They landed exploration parties and found that the islands were uninhabited. The first they came to they called Boa Vista, and the second São Tiago. São Tiago, St. James, was discovered on the feast day of St. James —the very day that, forty-one years before, Prince Henry, his father, and his brothers Edward and Peter had embarked for Ceuta.

The remainder of this archipelago of fourteen islands was gradually discovered over the next ten years. Unlike Madeira and the Azores, they did not invite colonization, for the climate was unsuitable for Europeans, and their volcanic nature made them unattractive. It was not until the close of the fifteenth century that the islands were properly colonized, mostly by Africans imported from the Cape Verde region. Their importance in the later phase of exploration lay in the fact that the Cape Verde Islands are in the track of the northeast trade winds. From November to May the trades are fairly constant, and once the Portuguese ships had dropped the Cape Verdes behind them, they had following winds to lift them across the South Atlantic to Brazil.

After his discovery of the first two islands, Cadamosto went on again to Gambia. Here he made friends with the local chieftain and traded manufactured goods for gold and slaves. Seeing that these were the same natives who the year before had attacked Cadamosto and his crews, and who had been responsible for the deaths of Nuño Tristão and his companions, this was a notable advance. It was now obvious to Prince Henry's captains that punitive raiding parties (which had been sufficient to quell the natives in areas like Arguim Bay) could no longer be employed against the inhabitants of this continent. Although the slave trade still continued, it was now carried on by an exchange of goods and merchandise. Prince Henry's policy of establishing friendly relations and "peace by agreement and not by force" was seen to be the better.

From the Gambia, Cadamosto also brought back some ivory for Prince Henry, and some elephant's flesh, which he described as "harsh and disagreeable." Fever aboard his ships compelled him to leave the river, but he was still not satisfied. He had been as far as the Gambia before, and he was determined not to return to Portugal without having extended his knowledge of the coastline.

He went south again, passing the mouths of great rivers until he reached one whose estuary seemed so wide that, at first, he thought it was a gulf and not a river at all. Closing the shore, he managed to make friendly contact with some of the natives. He named the river the Rio Grande, but did not stay long in the area, for his interpreters were unfamiliar with the language. On his way back to Portugal he also sighted the Bissagos Islands, which lie just off the coast—more new land, more islands to report to the Prince. The North Star, he noted, was even lower in the sky, and the "Southern Chariot" was clear above the horizon. The unknown shore still trended southward, but he saw that its general direction was now a little east of south. Was it possible that they were nearing the end of Africa?

That year Cadamosto reached a latitude of about 11 degrees north of the equator. The eastward trend of the coast, which the navigators noticed, was the point where Africa begins its slow curve into the great Bight of Benin. They had, in fact, passed the continent's westernmost point some years before at Cape Verde. From now on all the new voyages would be a little east of south.

At about the same time as Cadamosto's second voyage, Diogo Gomes not only came down to the Gambia River, but went several hundred miles upstream to drop anchor off the city of Cantor. Cantor was a center from which radiated caravan and trade routes to the Sahara and Morocco, inland to Timbuktu itself, and south to the Niger. Gomes did some good trade with cloth and jewelry in return for gold, and heard a great deal about the gold mines that lay beyond the mountains of Sierra Leone. He gathered information for the Prince about the cities and the trade of the continent.

Not all the news that he brought back to Sagres was unfamiliar to Prince Henry. It is an interesting proof of the efficiency of Henry's intelligence service that when Gomes told him about a great battle that had recently taken place in the interior, the Prince replied that he already knew about it. One of his agents, a merchant in the North African city of Oran,

had passed on this piece of information two months before
Gomes returned from his voyage. Thus, by the voyages of his
sea captains and by his informants along the African coast,
Henry was gradually piecing together a picture of the continent. When his ships left Sagres, the Prince was no less active
than his captains on the sea. At Raposeira, at Sagres, and at
Lagos a stream of information reached him. He was at the
center of a web whose perimeter stretched from the Levant to
the Gambia.

Gomes was finally forced to withdraw his caravels from the
Gambia because the heat, humidity, and fever were beginning
to take a toll of his crew. His had been a remarkable voyage,
nearly 500 miles upstream into the interior of Africa. It was
a triumph of seamanship, endurance, and tact as well, for
he had managed to keep his relations with the natives on a
friendly basis. So much was this so that during his stay at
Cantor, natives for miles around flocked to the town to see the
white men and to trade with them. Thus, with the success of
his policy of peaceful trading, Prince Henry was already
accomplishing one of his dreams. He was outflanking the
Moorish empire. He was bringing goods and gold to Europe
that would otherwise have had to come through Cairo, or one
of the Moroccan ports.

Gomes was also successful in making peace with a chief
called Nomi Mansa, who had previously been hostile to the
Portuguese. Gomes had already made friends with another
important Gambian chief, but his success with Nomi Mansa
was further enhanced when the chief embraced Christianity
and expelled his Moslem priests. Nomi Mansa also asked if
Prince Henry would send a priest out to the Gambia to teach
the Christian faith and to baptize him. In the letter he dictated
to Prince Henry, the African chieftain asked him for the gift
of a falcon trained for hunting, some sheep, geese, and pigs.

Nomi Mansa was clearly an astute man, for he also asked for two Portuguese workmen who knew how to build houses and plan a city.

On this same voyage Diogo Gomes attempted to chart new territory to the south. He passed beyond the Rio Grande but found that the currents were "so strong that no anchor could hold." The context in which this passage occurs suggests that it was the Portuguese habit, when coasting down an unknown shore, to drop anchor for the night—a sensible precaution when navigating in unchartered waters. In this delta land, where the mouths of so many rivers spill out into the Atlantic, and where the banks and shoals are constantly changing, it was not surprising that the caravels ran into some alarming currents. Curiously enough, this is one of the last occasions when we hear the revival of the old fears that the world came to an end off Africa. The captains of the two caravels who were in company with Gomes insisted that they put back because "they were at the limits of the ocean." In places off this coast, a little south of the Rio Grande, the south-going current sometimes runs at nearly four knots. In a fifty-ton caravel, with a maximum speed of about seven knots, such a current would certainly seem alarming.

Gomes achieved a further success on this voyage. He was on his way back to Portugal when he met two canoes just off Cape Verde. His interpreter warned him against these natives and told him that the chief of this area, Beseguiche, "an evil and treacherous man," was in one of the canoes. Gomes asked all the natives aboard his caravel and entertained them. He made them presents, and all the time pretended that he was unaware of the identity of his principal guest.

Just before the natives left, he asked, "Is this the country of Beseguiche?"

"Yes," the chief answered.

"Then why is he so hostile to Christians?" said Gomes. "Surely it would be better for him to trade with them in peace? If he did that, he would have horses and merchandise like the other African chiefs. Take back this message to him—that I have captured you at sea, but out of good will toward him I have let you go free."

He waited until all the natives had piled into their canoes to paddle back to the beach, and then he leaned over the caravel's side.

"Beseguiche! Beseguiche!" he shouted. "Do not imagine that I did not recognize you! I had you in my power and yet I behaved well toward you. See that you do the same to all Christians!"

In 1458 Prince Henry fulfilled the promise that had been made to Chief Nomi Mansa. He sent out an abbot to instruct him and his people in the faith, and the African chieftain was baptized. He took the Christian name of Henry, after the great Prince across the sea. Tact and treaties, friendship and trading posts, were the keys to the new world, as Henry had always maintained.

26

From the age of sixty until his death at sixty-six Henry's energy and ability were unflagging. Even his personal life now seems to have been happy. The unmarried man had found a son in Fernando, Affonso's younger brother. He found comfort in his grandchildren, Fernando's sons and daughters by Beatrice, the daughter of Prince John. To the young and to children he remained as indulgent as he had always been.

Perhaps it was the association of the name Fernando with his own brother, dead so long ago in Fez, that made him load presents on his adopted son. Certainly Henry never allowed the memory of his martyred brother to fade. When Father Alvares, a priest who had been one of Fernando's fellow prisoners in Tangier and Fez, was ransomed from the Moors, Henry ordered him to write the life and death of *The Blessed Prince Fernando* as a monument to his brother. He never allowed himself to forget that the price of his failure at Tangier, as well as the retention of Ceuta, had been paid by Fernando. If ever he felt proud of his achievements, he could soon humble himself by reading of his brother's captivity, courage, and death.

When Father Alvares returned to Portugal in 1451, he had brought with him a casket containing the heart of Fernando, which he and his fellow prisoners had preserved from the torn and mutilated body. Henry had met Father Alvares when he landed, and had followed the procession as it made its way to the great church of Batalha. There he had heard the Martyrs' Mass sung, and had knelt in silence beside the casket before it was buried.

Six years after Alfarrobeira, the body of Prince Peter was also brought home from the obscure church where it had lain since his death. Prince Henry organized the funeral of the last of his brothers. Peter was the one who had been nearest to him in his life, and he may well have felt some measure of responsibility for his death. Now, in the chapel that King John had prepared for himself, his wife, and his sons, there was only one place empty.

While the caravels were every year achieving new successes, Henry began to dream once more of a crusade into Morocco. Morocco had a particular claim on his attention at this moment. It was there that the only Christian success against the Moslems had been gained in nearly half a century. Everywhere else, the crescent was triumphant over the cross, and the situation in eastern Europe had become increasingly desperate with the fall of Constantinople in 1453. The capture of this great capital of Christendom by the Turks paralyzed Europe. The Sultan, Mohammed II (the Conqueror), had triumphantly reversed the Portuguese success at Ceuta, and it must have been with bitterness and anger that Prince Henry heard how the great cathedral of St. Sophia had been turned into a Moorish mosque. Already, in 1456, the year of Diogo Gomes's voyage to Gambia, Mohammed's armies had swept across Serbia and were at the gates of Belgrade. Now, if ever, was the time for an attack on the Mohammedans of Morocco.

The Pope, Calixtus III, appealed fruitlessly to the other kings and rulers of Europe for a crusade. Notorious for his nepotism, Calixtus was the uncle of Rodrigo Borgia (the future Pope Alexander VI), and not the man who could rally Christendom at such a moment. Only on the far flank of Moslem power was there a country and a man prepared to take up the challenge, and the Pope did not appeal in vain to Portugal and the grand master of the Order of Christ. King Affonso was as eager as Prince Henry to raise an army and sail for Morocco. He longed for another Ceuta to add glory to his reign.

He was even prepared, he said, to take a force of twelve thousand men into the Mediterranean and carry the war home against the Turks. But at this suggestion, even the most enthusiastic of his councilors demurred. Portugal was a small country, and could not afford to keep so large a force in the field several thousand miles away from home. In any case, what obligation did they have to do so, when the rulers of Italy were not prepared to do anything for the security of their own shores? If there was to be an overseas expedition at all, then Morocco was the only sensible field for a Portuguese crusade. They already had a fine base at Ceuta, troops who were familiar with the terrain, and as adviser to Affonso there was the veteran of Morocco, Prince Henry himself.

Absorbed though he was in his many affairs, Henry diverted his energy and enthusiasm into this new project. If the King and his cousins would assemble the fleets of Porto and Lisbon, then he would muster the men and the ships of the province of Algarve. This time he was determined there would be no repetition of Tangier.

On September 30, 1458, King Affonso sailed south to join his uncle at Sagres. The Portuguese objective had already been decided upon. It was the coastal town and trading port of Alcaçar, lying a little west of Ceuta, almost halfway between the Portuguese garrison and Tangier. At first Affonso had tried to revive the dream of a Portuguese Tangier, but even Prince Henry advised against any sea-borne attempt on that city. Alcaçar was an easier objective, and from Alcaçar their garrison forces would soon be able to harass Tangier's trade and caravan routes. Later the day might come when they could add the great seaport to the Portuguese crown, but Henry knew by bitter experience that it would not fall to a simple frontal assault. Alcaçar, slightly smaller than Ceuta, was another matter.

It was on October 3 that Henry looked down from his windows on Sagres and saw the King's fleet come sailing round the headland. The bulk of the Algarve fleet was lying off Lagos, but some of the ships were at anchor in Sagres Bay, and he must have felt a strange pride when he gazed out and saw the whole sea twisting with sails. The anchored caravels were reflected in the water below him, and the strong walls of his fortress were steaming under the sun. The combined fleet totaled 220 ships, and there were twenty-five thousand men embarked—about half the number that had been mustered for the attack on Ceuta, but more than double the force that had sailed for Tangier.

Henry could feel confident that he had an army capable of subduing Alcaçar and a fleet manned by seamen who were unlikely to find anything formidable in navigating the Strait of Gibraltar. Forty-three years had passed since King John's fleet had nearly come to grief in the strait, and since then a new generation of Portuguese sailors had come into being—the first men in Europe to be familiar with the Atlantic Ocean. He had turned a nation of peasants and coastal fishermen into a nation whose destiny lay on the sea.

King Affonso landed on the beach at Sagres, to be greeted by his uncle and entertained in the palace. His brother Fernando had often visited his adoptive father, but there is no record that Affonso had ever before seen the almost legendary home of the Navigator. Affonso, whose later exploits against the Moors earned him the title of "the African," must have found a stimulus to his ambition on the headland—in the bare rooms where so many enterprises had been planned, looking down on the bay where the first ships had anchored with their news of new-found islands in the Atlantic. Whatever discord may have existed between him and Prince Henry in the past was long since forgotten. Affonso had acknowledged the faults and hastiness of his youth on the day when he had accompanied the body of Prince Peter to its last resting place in Batalha. Even Prince Peter's eldest son, recalled from exile a few years before, was with him on this expedition.

It was the first time since Ceuta that the whole family was united in an enterprise, but of the older generation only Prince Henry remained. As he joined the King and the court aboard their ship, and looked back at the frowning cliff where he had made his home, he felt the weight of many memories. It had been a bare headland when he had first come here as a young man of twenty-two and gazed south over the sea to Africa. Sagres had harbored his ships and his men, his triumphs and his failures, for over forty years. Now, at the age of sixty-four, he was sailing again for the land where he had written his name forever.

The fleet crossed from Lagos to Tangier in the fair autumn weather. Once again Prince Henry saw those lofty walls that had mocked him so many years ago, and the long beaches down which the survivors had fought their way to safety, and the road back to town, which Prince Fernando had ridden to captivity and death. Inflamed by the memory of that Portuguese defeat, Affonso suggested to his council that they should attack Tangier rather than Alcaçar. He was at once dissuaded, and there is little doubt that his uncle was among those who advised against it. One step at a time—Henry had learned that lesson now. In war, as in exploration, it was method and steady persistence that led to success.

Two days later the landing parties streamed ashore on the beach opposite Alcaçar. The Moors, forewarned of the fleet's approach, put up a stiff resistance. But gradually the steady wave upon wave of men drove the defenders back toward the city. Always in the forefront of the invaders was a lean old man, almost as dark as a Moor, followed by a squire bearing a banner with the motto: *Talent de bien faire.*

Eager to shine under the eyes of Prince Henry, the young noblemen and soldiers beat down all resistance. Soon they were surging round the walls of the city, as the Moorish troops took cover inside and barred the gates against them. Artillery and siege implements had been ferried ashore on the second wave of the assault, and at midnight after the landing, Prince Henry supervised the bombardment of Alcaçar.

A heavy cannon was levered into place and bedded down, the Prince directing its positioning and its line of fire. Then, amid the flicker of torches, he gave the order for the bombardment to begin. Standing there in the smoke and roar of the cannon, after a day's hard fighting, he was alert and indomitable even in those small hours of the morning when the youngest and strongest begin to tire. Time and again the cannon hurled its solid shot against the section of masonry that Prince Henry had indicated. Soon the stones began to crumble and the dust to trickle down. It was not long before the great wall of Alcaçar started to spill slowly outward.

The Moors had fought well throughout the day, inflicting many more casualties on the Portuguese than at Ceuta, but now their spirit began to fail. A further shot from the Prince's battery burst through the wall and breached it. They ac-

knowledged defeat. Soon afterward an embassy came out under
a flag of truce and made its way toward the Portuguese lines.
The Moorish representatives were brought in front of King
Affonso and immediately asked for the terms of surrender.
Affonso, acknowledging his uncle as leader of the expedition,
left it to Prince Henry to decide on the conditions.

What memories of Tangier must have invaded him at that
moment! If he had been of a vindictive nature, he now had it
in his power to take revenge and impose harsh conditions. But
the ambassadors were treated kindly, and Henry told them
that no one wanted their money or possessions. The King of
Portugal, he said, had come to take their city in the name of
the true faith, but not to force any ransom from them.

"You may depart with your wives, your children, and all
your worldly goods. All I ask is that you leave behind any
Christians you may have in captivity."

He had not forgotten the treachery at Tangier, though, and
when they asked him for time to consider the terms, he insisted
that they accept them now.

"If you force me to take the town by the sword, I will show
no mercy."

The Moors looked at their conquerors, and at the old man.
Even if they had not known who he was, they would have
recognized that this was a man who did not bluff. Wisely, they
accepted. Under their flag of truce they withdrew to the city,
and began to make arrangements for the departure of the
inhabitants and the handing over of all Christian captives.

On that late November morning, with the dawn coming up
over the Mediterranean, Prince Henry knew that Tangier was
avenged. Around him stood the sons of his dead brothers and
his own adopted son, Fernando. The men were drinking hot
spiced wine and warming themselves over the flames of campfires. The cannon had ceased firing, and there was silence over

the conquered city. Behind him the long lines of soldiers were preparing for the new day, ferrying supplies ashore, landing water barricoes and ammunition, kindling fires, and boiling sun-dried cod for the morning meal.

The news of the Moorish capitulation began to spread through the assembled ranks, first in a steady buzz of voices, and then to the sound of cheering that swelled up from the pikemen and archers grouped behind the artillery. Gradually it spread to the beach and to the sailors on the ships. The light began to quicken in the east, burnishing the armor of the knights and gleaming dully on Henry's black chain mail. The dawn wind began to draw on shore, bringing with it the scent of the sea. The long lines of ships were tide-rode. They lay back against their taut anchor ropes, their pennants and ensigns lifting in the new-day breeze.

Constantinople might have fallen, but tomorrow the great mosque of Alcaçar would be consecrated to the Christian service. King Affonso had promised that he would not rest until Tangier had been taken. The conquest of Morocco had begun. Henry's work in North Africa was finished.

27

Henry left Africa for the last time in November, 1458. He sailed back to Lagos and stopped in the dockyard to watch his new ships building, and to talk with his captains and agents. He had plans for a number of voyages the following year, and there were ships lying in the port that had recently returned from Guinea, Madeira, and the Azores. All was well with his islands, and trade was flowing from Arguim Bay and from the Gambia. There were many Africans as well as sailors in the streets, and it was now, on his return from Alcaçar, that Henry arranged for the Abbot of Soto de Cassa to sail for Gambia to instruct Chief Nomi Mansa in the Christian faith. Success over the infidels, Christianity penetrating Africa, trade and peaceful commerce starting along all the coast south of Bojador—his was a rich harvest.

The winter had come. There was drizzle and gray mist over all the coastline from Cape St. Vincent to Lagos. Sometimes the southwesterlies blew off the Atlantic, driving the nimbus clouds over the headland of Sagres and lashing the spray against the cape. There were no ships at anchor in the bay. Only occasionally would a straggler back from Africa or

Madeira, or a merchantman bound out of the Mediterranean for the English Channel, take shelter under the lee of the headland. Here at Sagres, or in his villa at Raposeira, Henry continued his work.

One of his chief interests was the great map of the world that he had prevailed upon King Affonso to have made. The commission had been entrusted to one of the most famous cartographers of the day, a Venetian monk, Fra Mauro, and a draftsman, Andrea Bianco, also from Venice. All the information that Prince Henry had collected from his navigators over years was to be incorporated in the chart—the bays and headlands and the islands that he had dredged out of the ocean. The map was finished in the spring of 1459, and it is evidence of the information that Henry had collected from all over Africa that the Cape of Good Hope, called the "Cavo di Diab," is shown on this world map. Forty years before Vasco da Gama rounded the cape, either the Prince or his cartographers had heard of an Indian sailing vessel that in 1420 had rounded the cape from the east after a voyage of 2,000 miles. The "Cavo di Diab" was shown separated from the presumed outline of the continent by a narrow strait, as if it were part of an island—which they may well have believed it to be.

The Doge of Venice, Francesco Foscari, saw this world map when it was being made in Murano. Information obtained on Cadamosto's two African voyages was incorporated in it, and it is possible that the Doge met this great Venetian sailor. He wrote in a letter that he hoped "Prince Henry would find in the work of Fra Mauro further inducement to carry on with his explorations."

Henry had never needed any inducement, other than his own desire to know what lay beyond the horizon. It was true that Africa and the islands were showing some return for all the money he had spent, but he died heavily in debt. The exact amount that he owed may never be known, but one debt alone to the House of Bragança was for well over $280,000 in terms of modern currency. His estates were mortgaged, his revenues from the islands and from the African trading expeditions spent before they reached him, and his private fortune long since swallowed up. If ever a man bankrupted himself in the service of the future, it was Henry of Portugal. As the Englishman Samuel Purchas wrote of him in the seventeenth century, "He never gave up his endeavours of discoveries, till he discovered the Celestial Jerusalem. . . . His navigations explored only the coast from Bojador to Sierra Leone, one thousand one hundred and ten miles in nearly fifty years of continual cares and costs. So hard a thing it is to discover."

In the last two years of his life he was as preoccupied as ever with his many cares and responsibilities. The King of Fez had besieged Alcaçar, and it was only with the greatest difficulty that the garrison managed to hold out. After the withdrawal of the Moorish troops it was decided to build a mole running out from the beach in front of the city, to facilitate the loading and unloading of ships. Henry was still governor of Ceuta, so all matters regarding the defense and security of the Portuguese possessions in Morocco were ultimately brought to him. As grand master of the Order of Christ, he had to deal with all the problems that concerned the war against the infidel. As "protector of the studies of Portugal" (a title he had earned by establishing a chair of theology at the University of Lisbon), he was also involved in many details of the university's curriculum, and with the payment of the lecturers.

With so many calls and demands upon his time, it is extraordinary how much energy he still retained for planning new expeditions. The navigator Pedro de Cintra was being supplied with caravels and merchandise for another voyage—one which would lead him to the coastline of Sierra Leone. Diogo

Gomes, Cadamosto's rival claimant to the discovery of the Cape Verde Islands, was also organizing an expedition to Guinea.

The secret of Henry's amazing ability to concern himself with so many things at once was that he had largely solved one of the great problems that harass all human beings—the problem of time. The question that has often been raised—Why did Prince Henry never go on any of the voyages of exploration himself?—is easily answered. There is time, and there is space. If you travel in space, you use up time. By cutting himself off from the distractions of the world, and by remaining for over forty years of his life almost entirely at Sagres, he had "found time." Movement from one place to another involves an expenditure of time—something that his navigators did for him. Undistracted by domestic cares, with all his energies channeled to one end, he was able to concentrate exclusively on his great ambitions.

One of the things that must have pleased him most in these last two years of his life was the news that from Cape Verde onward, the coastline definitely started to trend eastward. Below the Bissagos Islands, as he knew from both Cadamosto and Diogo Gomes, this feature of the continent became marked. It is doubtful whether Prince Henry ever appreciated the vast extent of the continent to which he had devoted his life. Most probably he saw the eastward trend of the coastline as evidence that the end of Africa was almost in sight.

When he began his voyages of exploration, the farthest point known on the African coast was Cape Not, opposite the Canary Islands on approximately the latitude of 29 degrees north. In over forty years of steady navigation, his seamen had explored and charted a coastline stretching over 18 degrees of latitude —a little more than one thousand miles. In the four decades that followed, Africa would be rounded, and contact made by sea with India, the Far East, and the Americas. Distances like a thousand miles were to be constantly covered by ships, sailing entirely out of sight of land, within thirty years of his death. Henry initiated the great Age of Discovery; he did not live to see its full growth. But it is the first step in any new venture that is the most difficult, and Henry had to combat a whole climate of superstition and destroy a centuries-old conception of a limited world. He and his assistants had to evolve by trial and error the charts, the instruments, and the ships for long-distance seafaring. He had to train and educate a new type of man, making navigators out of courtiers, and deep-sea sailors out of coastal fishermen.

His achievement was unique—something that can never be repeated. For tens of thousands of years, the races of mankind had been living in separate continents and islands. Vast and complex civilizations in Europe and the East had risen and sunk into decay, without ever having communicated with each other. The wisdom, the technical knowledge, and the culture of one group of peoples were kept apart from those of others by the barriers of the ocean. Henry changed all that, and in doing so changed the course of world history. The Renaissance was a rebirth of the knowledge and skills of the classical world —a rediscovery, in fact. Prince Henry's achievement was the discovery of things that had never been known before.

It was curiosity and the spirit of inquiry—voiced in that one word "Farther!"—that drove the caravels into the Atlantic and down the coast of Africa. The years of apparent failure between 1418 and 1434 (when Gil Eannes finally rounded Cape Bojador) were perhaps the most significant in Henry's life. It was during this period that he, and he alone, persevered in the face of contumely, ridicule, and endless expense. It was the ability to go on and on, listening always with tact and patience to tales of failure, that distinguished this man. He set in motion not only the Age of Discovery but four hundred years of European colonization—a process that has been decried in our own time, but without which vast regions of the globe might still be in a state of barbarism.

After his return from the triumph of Alcaçar in November, 1458, Henry was busy setting his affairs in order. Aware perhaps that his death was not far off, he began to plan the extension of his life's work into the future by seeing that the foundations were well ordered. Businesslike and methodical, he was attending to the affairs of his islands, to the University of Lisbon, the chapel he had founded at Belém near the mouth of the Tagus, the hospital he had built at Tomar (the headquarters of the Order of Christ), and the erection of further buildings on Sagres. The sound of the sea was always in his ears—the ceaseless rumor of the Atlantic and the sigh of the wind over the headland.

In the summer of 1460 he formally transferred the islands of Terceira and Graciosa in the Azores to his adopted son, Fernando. He arranged for the Cape Verde group to be administered by the crown, and two of the Azores by the Order of Christ. The first discoveries of his life, Madeira and Porto Santo, were already under the spiritual jurisdiction of the Order, and Henry requested that in them, and in the other islands where churches had been founded, Masses should be said for his soul. Like a sailor securing his ship for sea, he made his last preparations.

Diogo Gomes was always with him in these months. It was Gomes, one of Henry's finest navigators and closest companions, who left us the short record of his master's death. "In the late autumn of 1460 Prince Henry fell ill in his town on Cape St. Vincent. . . ." The sailing season was over, and all the ships were home from Africa and the islands. Morocco was quiet. All was well at Ceuta, the garrison at Alcaçar had been reinforced, and the new mole had been completed. There was nothing to keep him any more. He had known "that lust for search which drives sails toward undiscovered lands" and now he could cry, "The shore has faded! The last fetter has fallen from me. . . ."

On Thursday, November 13, 1460, Prince Henry died in his palace on the rock of Sagres. He was sixty-six years old. That night they carried his body to the church of Santa Maria in Lagos, and "King Affonso and all the people of Portugal mourned the death of so great a prince."

Beneath the dark November sky, to the boom of Atlantic rollers on the cape, the procession made its way by torchlight to the Port of the Caravels. For over a month Diogo Gomes remained in Lagos near the body of the Prince. While the priests kept their vigils, and Masses were said for the repose of his soul, the faithful navigator watched over his master.

It was not until the end of December that the coffin was transferred to Batalha, where King Affonso and his brother Fernando awaited the last of their uncles. When Gomes looked at the body before its removal to Batalha, he found that Prince Henry, in death as in life, was wearing a hair shirt next to his skin. Without any great pomp or ceremony, he was laid to rest in the chapel, next to King John and Queen Philippa and his brothers. "I will have no mourning made for me," he had ordered in his will. "Only let me be commended to God decorously and simply."

Such was the end of one of the most outstanding men the world has ever known—Henry, Prince of Portugal, Grand Master of the Order of Christ, Governor of Ceuta and the Algarves, Duke of Viseu, and Lord of Covilham, Knight of the Garter—the Navigator. "Fortunate Prince . . . I think of the manner in which you welcomed all, how you gave ear to all, and how you passed most of your days and nights busy with so many cares and labours, in order that many people might profit thereby. I see, too, how the land and the seas are full of your name; for, by continual effort, you have united the East with the West. . . ."

On the frieze of his tomb is carved his motto: *Talent de bien faire.* The carved stone figure of the Prince tells us nothing. His monument is on the sea, where the ships of all nations pass the Sacred Headland along the ocean trade routes of the world.

Chronology

List of Sources

Notes

Index

CHRONOLOGY

1394, March 4   Birth of Prince Henry

1411   Peace with Castile

1412–15   Preparations for capture of Ceuta

1415, July 18   Death of Queen Philippa

1415, August 21   Capture of Ceuta

1416   Prince Henry made Governor of Ceuta

1418   Return to Ceuta with Prince John

1418 or 1419   Porto Santo discovered by Zarco and Teixeira

1420–23   Discovery of Madeira

1424–25   Colonization of Madeira begun

1431–32   Gonçalo Velho Cabral discovers Santa Maria, Azores

1433, August 14   Death of King John I

1434   Gil Eannes doubles Cape Bojador

1435   Eannes returns to Bojador with Baldaia

1436   Baldaia discovers the Rio de Ouro

1436, March 7 Prince Henry adopts his nephew Prince Fernando as his son and heir

1436–37 Preparations for expedition to Tangier

1437, September 20 Portuguese attack Tangier

1437, October 13 Portuguese capitulation

1437, October 16 Prince Fernando delivered as a hostage to Sala-ben-Sala

1438 Prince Henry returns to Portugal

1438, September 9 Death of King Edward

1438–41 Troubles of the regency

1441 Gonçalves and Nuño Tristão to Rio de Ouro. Discovery of Cape Blanco by Nuño Tristão

1442, October Death of Prince John

1443, October 22 Royal decree grants Prince Henry exclusive rights to send ships south of Cape Bojador

1443 Second voyage of Gonçalves to Rio de Ouro

1443 Voyage of Nuño Tristão to Arguim Bay

1443, July 5 Death of Prince Fernando at Fez

1444 Cape Verde discovered by Denis Dias

1444 Death of Gonçalo de Cintra

1444 Slave market at Lagos

1444 João Fernandes left on mainland of Africa near Cape Blanco

1445 Alvaro Fernandes sails to Senegal and the Cape of Masts

1445 Lançarote and others to Senegal and Cape Verde

1446 Death of Nuño Tristão
Return voyage of Aires Tinoco

1447   Voyage and death of Abelhart the Dane at Cape Verde

1447   Lease of Lançarote in Canaries by Maciot to Henry

1447   End of Prince Peter's regency

1448 onward   Fort erected at Arguim

1449, May 20   Alfarrobeira and death of Prince Peter

1450, January 8   Bull of Pope Nicholas V confirms Portuguese rights to all the newly discovered lands. Second bull grants Henry monopoly of exploration as far as India

1452   Voyage of Diogo de Teive to Newfoundland Banks

1453   Constantinople falls to the Turks

1455–56   Cadamosto to Gambia

1456   Diogo Gomes to Gambia

1456–60   Discovery of Cape Verde Islands

1456–58   Preparations for conquest of Alcaçar

1458, October 17   Capture of Alcaçar

1458, November   Prince Henry returns to Portugal

1460   Last Will and Testament

1460, November 13   Prince Henry dies at Sagres

LIST OF SOURCES

These are only the principal authorities I have consulted in preparing this biography. A detailed bibliography of writings about Prince Henry has been compiled by the Lisbon Geographical Society.

Azurara, Gomes Eannes de: *Cronica da Tomada de Ceuta.*
——: *Cronica do Descobrimento e Conquista da Guiné,* edited by Carreira and Santarem, 1841. English translation by R. Beazeley and E. Prestage, 1896–99. English translation edited by Virginia de Castro e Almeida, 1936.

Barbosa A.: *Historia de Ciencia Nautica Portuguesa da Epoca dos Discobrimentos,* 1948.

Beazeley, R.: *Prince Henry the Navigator,* 1895.

Bensaude, J.: *Historie de la Science Nautique des Découvertes Portugaises,* 1912.

Cortesão, A.: *Cartografia e Cartografos Portuguesas,* 1935.

Fonseca, Quirino da: *Os Navios de D. Henrique,* 1959.

Gomes, Diogo: *Relações do Descobrimento da Guiné e das Ilhas dos Açores, Madeira e Cabo Verde,* 1847.

Helps, Sir A.: *Christopher Columbus,* 1868.

Hitchins, H. L., and W. E. May: *From Lodestone to Gyro-Compass,* 1952.

Howe, S. E.: *In Quest of Spices,* 1946.

Livermore, H. V.: *History of Portugal,* 1947.

Major, R. H.: *The Life of Henry of Portugal,* 1868.

Martins, J. P. Oliveira: *The Golden Age of Prince Henry the Navigator.* English translation by J. J. Abraham and W. E. Reynolds, 1914, of *Os Filhos de D. João I.*

Mees, J.: *Histoire de la découverte des Iles Azores,* 1901.

Nowell, C. E.: *History of Portugal,* 1953.

Oldham, Y.: *Discovery of the Cape Verde Islands,* 1892.

Prestage, E.: *The Portuguese Voyages of Discovery,* 1939.

Renault, G.: *The Caravels of Christ,* 1959.

Sanceau, E.: *Henry the Navigator,* 1946.

Schefer, C.: *Relation des Voyages de Ca' da Mosto,* 1895.

Taylor, E. G. R.: *The Haven-Finding Art,* 1956.

Torr, C.: *Ancient Ships,* 1894.

Trend, J. B.: *Portugal,* 1957.

Veer, G. de: *Prinz Heinrich der Seefahrer,* 1863.

Villiers, A.: *The Western Ocean,* 1957.

Walker, W. F.: *The Azores,* 1886.

Wouwerman, E.: *Henri le Navigateur et l'Academie Portugaise de Sagres,* 1890.

Ocean Passages for the World, Admiralty, London, 1950.

NOTES

Throughout the book, none of the dialogue is invented. In some cases I may have paraphrased the conversation as recorded by Azurara. In no case have I altered or distorted his meaning.

Chapter One

The nature of the plague which broke out in Lisbon and Porto—and from which Queen Philippa died—can only be surmised. It may possibly have been typhus fever, which is known to have occurred in epidemic form for many centuries in all countries of Europe. Conveyed by lice, it is the inevitable companion of poverty and overcrowding. On the other hand, it may have been an outbreak of bubonic plague, which for centuries had its home in North Africa, whence it would have been easily conveyed by ships and traders to the Portuguese seaports.

Chapter Two

The description of the court of Portugal under the influence of Queen Philippa is based on the book by Prince Edward (Dom Duarte), called *The Loyal Counsellor* (*O Leal Conselheiro*). The analysis of the Queen's character is quoted from J. P. Oliveira Martins's *Os Filhos de D. João I* in the translation of J. J. Abraham and W. E. Reynolds (*The Golden Age of Prince Henry the Navigator*).

Chapter Three

The reason King John was unwilling to see any of his sons married to the widowed Queen of Sicily was that, on the death of her husband, Martino I, the kingdom of Sicily had been annexed to Aragon. The Queen had thus lost not only her husband, but also her kingdom. It was her hope that by marrying Prince Edward she might cause the intervention of Portugal in the affairs of Sicily.

King John's stratagem in formally declaring war on Count William of Holland served a double purpose. There had, in fact (as we learn from Azurara), been cause for complaint about the Dutch treatment of Portuguese merchantmen. After the visit of King John's ambassadors, these acts of piracy ceased. In this way, King John managed to "kill two birds with one stone."

Chapter Four

The description of the Portuguese fleet is based on the *Livro da Guerra de Ceuta* by Mateus Pisano, translated from the Latin into Portuguese by Roberto Pinto. A painting in the National Maritime Museum, at Greenwich, England, by Joachim Patinir (1485–1525) shows a collection of fifteenth-century Portuguese vessels. Among them is a typical galley of the period, with a lateen sail.

Chapter Five

For the details of the attack on Ceuta, I have relied on Azurara's *Cronica da Tomada de Ceuta* and, to a great extent, on the English translation by Bernard Miall of Virginia de Castro e Almeida's edition.

Chapter Six

King John's action in conferring the title "Duke" on his two sons Prince Peter and Prince Henry was a signal mark of his favor. Prior to this, the title had never been conferred in Portugal.

Chapter Seven

For the description of the Phoenician circumnavigation of Africa, I have used Henry Cary's translation of Herodotus (1891). My reason for considering at some length the exact order of the motives which prompted Prince Henry to his African expeditions is the fact that it has been often maintained that his aims were those of a medieval knight, or were solely guided by the desire for material gain. E. J. Payne, in the *Cambridge Modern History* (Volume I, 1934), and J. P. Oliveira Martins, in *Os Filhos de D. João I*, incline to these views, which in my opinion are not substantiated by the known facts.

Chapter Eight

I refer to the voyages to Porto Santo and Madeira as "a rediscovery." The Laurentian Portolano (1351) in Florence shows the Madeira group quite clearly. There is some reason to think that the Genoese had known of the islands even before this date. It is not an impossibility that the Phoenicians may have called there on their way to the tin mines of Cornwall, although as far as I know there is no archæological evidence to support this.

Some historians have been more than skeptical about the story of Robert Machin. R. H. Major, however, in *The Life of Prince Henry the Navigator* seems to have made a fair case for putting some trust in it. It is also dealt with in his *The Discoveries of Prince Henry the Navigator*.

Chapter Nine

The derivation of the place name "Machico" from Machin is highly disputable. As a place name and a surname, it had been known in Portugal long before the discovery of Madeira.

Chapter Ten

For much of the information on early navigational methods, I am indebted to *From Lodestone to Gyro-Compass*, by H. L. Hitchins and W. E. May.

Chapter Eleven

There are numerous theories as to the first discoverers of the Azores. The subject is dealt with at some length in W. F. Walker's *The Azores* and in J. Mees's *Histoire de la découverte des Iles Azores.*

Chapters Fourteen and Fifteen

The main source of information for the aftermath of the Tangier disaster is the *Cronica de D. Duarte* by the historian Ruy de Pina (1440–1521). Calderon's play *The Constant Prince* portrays Prince Henry in an unsympathetic light when contrasted with his brother Fernando—a fact that may have helped to bias some historians against the Navigator.

Chapter Seventeen

The last years of Prince Fernando are described in the chronicle of João Alvarez, who was Fernando's confessor and fellow prisoner. Alvarez wrote this chronicle at the instigation of Prince Henry, who desired it to be a permanent monument to his dead brother.

Chapter Eighteen

There is no mention in Azurara of the type of vessel in which Balthazar set sail from Lagos for Africa. I have assumed that it was a barinal, for the reason that Azurara specifically mentions Nuño Tristão's command as being a caravel. This suggests that, whatever Balthazar's vessel was, it was not of the new type. For the description of the barinal, I am indebted to Quirino da Fonseca's *Os Navios de D. Henrique.*

Chapter Twenty

Here, as elsewhere, my basis for assessing Prince Henry's character is the work of Azurara. Although the chronicler was undoubtedly concerned to eulogize the Prince, he was meticulous in his record of facts—facts which do not seem to contradict Azurara's character assessment.

Chapter Twenty-two

The downfall of Prince Peter presents a difficult problem. There are certainly some grounds for thinking that Prince Henry was not as active in his brother's support as he might have been. It is unlikely that the truth will ever be known. Azurara's chronicle stops at this point, and, as I have indicated, there is reason to think that Ruy de Pina's account is biased against Prince Henry.

Chapter Twenty-seven

The quotation "The shore has faded! The last fetter has fallen from me . . ." is taken from Friedrich Nietzsche's *Also Sprach Zarathustra*. I am not aware whether Nietzsche was familiar with the life and achievements of Henry the Navigator. If he was, he may well have seen in him many of the qualities which he was to ascribe to his *Ubermensch*.

INDEX

Abelhart the Dane (Vallarta), 216–217
Abyla, 17
Abyssinia, 69, 180
Adahu, 146, 150, 164, 167–168
Affonso, Fernando, 217
Affonso, João, 19
Affonso, Prince, 157; King, 198–199; troubles, 200–211; and Alfarrobeira, 212, 221; and Alcaçar, 243–248, 250, 255
Africa Pilot, 124
Agincourt, 12, 129, 205
Albergaria, Vasco Martins d', 48
Alcaçar, 87, 125, 243–248, 251, 254
Alentejo, 27
Alexandria, 114
Alfarrobeira, 210–212
Algarve, 51, 204, 214, 243–244
Algeciras, 25, 40–42, 44
Alhos Vedros, 9
Aljubarrota, 12, 18, 27, 32, 100
Almina Point, 23, 25, 46, 48
Alvares, Father, 241–242
Amalfi, 114
America, 63, 170, 176, 231, 252

Andeiro, Fernando, Count of Ourem, 12
Angra dos Ruivos, 122
Antilia, 234
Arabia, 93
Arabs, 17, 26, 91, 95, 146, 168, 180, 225
Aragon, 28, 30, 116
Arfet, Anne d', 80–81
Arguim Bay, 170, 173, 180, 183–184, 218, 224, 249
Arguim Island, 171, 184, 192, 224
Arzila, 125, 139, 142
Atlantis, 194
Atlas Mountains, 105
Aviz, 11–13, 53
Azores, 87, 97–99, 181, 192–193, 218, 232–235, 249, 254
Azores current, 232–233
Azurara, 31, 67–68, 101, 111, 137, 146, 169, 173, 175–177, 184, 196, 204, 216

Baldaia, Affonso Gonçalves, 121–124
Balearic Islands, 17

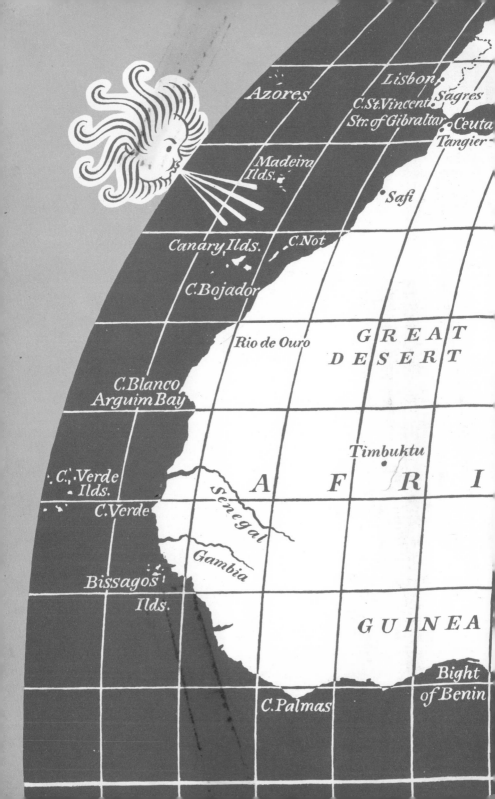